ALANA FAIRCHILD

CRYSTAL STARS
11.11

CRYSTALLINE ACTIVATIONS
WITH THE STELLAR LIGHT CODES

BLUE ANGEL®
PUBLISHING

CRYSTAL STARS 11.11
Crystalline Activations with the Stellar Light Codes

This printing 2021
Copyright © 2020 Alana Fairchild

Published by Blue Angel Publishing®
80 Glen Tower Drive, Glen Waverley,
Victoria, Australia 3150
E-mail: info@blueangelonline.com
Website: www.blueangelonline.com

Artwork by Jane Marin

Edited by Leela J. Williams

Blue Angel is a registered trademark of Blue Angel Gallery, Pty. Ltd.

ISBN: 978-1-925538-76-2

DEDICATION

For the star-dusted hearts
that help keep humanity
attuned to the light.

CONTENTS

INTRODUCTION

THERE IS A TYPE OF MEANING, healing and belonging that can only come from an experience of unity with the stars and the earth. Falling in love with the earth while honouring our connection to the stars can help us be completely ourselves—quirky, divine and human—and live with a deeper sense of higher purpose.

This book is for star seeds, old souls, lightworkers, healers, spiritual teachers, priestesses, mentors, guides and soul coaches. Even if you don't identify with one of those terms, if you are seeking to live from the higher consciousness of the heart, this book has been written for you. This book is for all of us presently growing love, light and peace on Earth.

Souls with the mission of bringing light to this world can attract the mystical and inspiring spiritual energies that support such a purpose, as well as encountering the dark and disturbed energies that they have incarnated in order to heal. By using the former to deal with the latter, we can make progress and find peace. Learning to utilise the darker experiences of our journey to increase our wisdom, compassion and spiritual fortitude helps us strengthen our commitment to being here on this planet. Only then do we have the substance to successfully bring the light of our inner world to the outer world where it is so needed. This creates joy and fulfilment. The stars may seem otherworldly and far away from the earth, but consciously working with their energies can transform the soul and open us to divine success for the greatest good.

In this book, we explore healing earth medicines such as grounding, nature's restorative beauty and the wisdom of our bodies. We learn about star blessings, divine missions, shifting multidimensional realities and high-frequency stellar transmissions. We look at how integrating star and earth energies can help us deal with the challenges of toxic energies, cult-like groups (or lower-level consciousness), disconnection, addiction and mental suffering. We discover special techniques for wholeness, wellbeing and how a sacred connection with the stars and the earth within can empower us to live our light and embrace the pleasure of being attuned to the goodness and grace of our Universe for the spiritual benefit of all beings, ourselves included.

TRUST WHERE YOUR SOUL IS LEADING YOU

Your soul is constantly guiding you to the message, teaching or frequency needed for your continued journey and healing. The soul is brilliant like that. It leads us from within and we usually have no idea what it is up to or why. And then, we somehow stumble upon exactly what we need to know or understand. We may not even realise how important that information is until a later moment of need. If you are wondering why you are attracted to this book, there's your answer. Your soul already knows and when the time is right for the rest of you to catch on, so will you.

You may recognise the information your soul is guiding you to and quickly shift out of a lower-frequency pattern that has kept you stuck in cycles of suffering, frustration or unwanted repetition of negative experiences. Your understanding may come together more like slow cooking as you soak in the energy of this book and allow it to move into your mind, body and energy field to lovingly heal you, little by little. As you read, pay attention to how you feel and what comes up for you. Either way, this book can be a caring friend and spiritual guide as you take the next steps on your path. *Crystal Stars 11.11* was inspired by higher guidance and written from the heart, so you can experience deep, inner-soul healing and connect more readily to your authentic life path.

The healing energy of this book is particularly relevant for shifting issues to do with abundance, prosperity, spiritual guidance, leadership, individuality, hope, healing and finding ways to belong that do not compromise your authenticity. There is a focus on the fulfilment of divine purpose through awakening and expressing spiritual abilities and soul talents. Another recurring theme is how to navigate negative energy by becoming more conscious of our potential for negativity and developing skilful means for dealing with the negativity in the world. We learn how to work with negativity to strengthen our peace, wisdom, light and compassion. We also look at how to summon our light for our own healing and for global healing, too.

ARE YOU A STAR SEED?

You have stardust in your being. I mean literally, not symbolically. Some scientists claim that everything in our created Universe, including our bodies, is made from the remnants of stars. The stars are relevant to all of us. They are our home, our cosmic birth mother and the material or matter (or *mater*, Latin for *mother*) we are created from. Although working with the stars can seem quite out there, it is actually about connecting to the sacred origins of our being, our lineage and our divine ancestry. In understanding where we come from, we can more easily connect with the luminous potential we have for this lifetime on Earth.

You may relate to the notion of being a star seed or feel a connection with one of the other soul types (lightworkers, priestesses, healers and so on) that resonate with a wisdom and spiritual light that is deeper than mainstream consciousness can recognise at this time. Perhaps a friend, child, family member, colleague, life partner or someone else you know, fits the description of a star seed? Even if you don't exactly feel like the star seed souls described in this book, you are still, in your own unique way, a type of star seed.

Star seeds are unique beings. There tends to be certain traits many of them have in common but depending on their individual path, some star seeds will never fit into a general description. That is part of their challenge and their specialness.

LIFE ON EARTH CAN BE HARD FOR STAR SEEDS (AT FIRST)

The more in touch we are with our inner being, the more profoundly we can experience a connection with the stars. This feeling of connection can be a spiritually enriching and pleasurable experience for many souls. It reminds us that we are vast spiritual beings that belong to the Universe as a whole, who are having our 'spiritual schooling' on Earth for a time.

For others, feeling connected to the stars gives rise to a deeply painful sense of yearning. For such souls, the experience of life on Earth can be so different to their soul memories of a peaceful and evolved star home that it can be difficult to bear. This may give rise to depression or more severe emotional and mental distress, at least for a while. It is important to know that such a phase *will* resolve and there is an enormous gift of joy and fulfilment awaiting such souls on their earthly path.

At first however, some souls can struggle to accept their human incarnation and find it hard to feel at home in their bodies and on Earth. They may think there is something wrong with them when they are just experiencing spiritual culture shock. It's entirely normal to go through that experience, as if one were travelling to a strange country for the first time and struggling to adjust to a different culture.

Earthly life can seem downright strange to star seeds. Human behaviour—especially the darker side of ego that is based in fear and anger and judges, hates, harms and takes pleasure in other's pain—can utterly confound star seeds. They are learning that these expressions stem from the unresolved pain of the soul in question.

I have been through this process. I know how confusing it can be when the purity in your heart is a witness to negative behaviours. It can make you wonder if you have somehow ended up on the wrong planet. It takes courage to believe the Universe doesn't make mistakes, that all things are working for good and, that as you accept the journey, you will eventually come to understand it and feel empowered to respond creatively.

However, that doesn't necessarily happen quickly. At least, it took me quite some time to accept. A star seed may wonder if it is possible for them to truly live their light on Earth. As they take their journey, they will eventually realise that they *can* and that the Earth will generously support them in doing so. They begin to recognise— and then more actively attract—the abundance of spiritual resources that are available especially to them.

WHEN STAR SEEDS COME INTO THEIR OWN ...

As soon as those beautiful souls, homesick for the stars, choose to trust in their human experience (no matter how weird or dark it may seem to be at times), their entire journey changes for the better. Instead of scarcity, fear and confusion, they can experience abundance, fulfilment and appreciation. Abandonment and disconnection are replaced with belonging and relating at a soul level. They fall in love with the earth and allow her to provide all they want and need to fulfil their inner journey. Instead of being a source of terror and darkness, this world becomes a creative playground for soul growth and the development of wisdom. Frustration and never being understood, gives way to enjoyment and celebration. They can share their uniqueness, claim their difference for the great treasure that it is and inspire others to become more courageous and authentic.

Star seeds have all the usual human emotions and experiences to grow through, but their journey can have a depth, power and spiritual beauty that others recognise subconsciously and find healing. They are motivated to serve a higher plan, so just being around them can help others relax and feel more peaceful and loved. Eventually, star seeds discover the extraordinary gifts of being in a human body — including the pleasure of creating reality according to the inner visions of the soul, actively transforming their own lives and the lives of those whom they love and serve in their own unique way.

WHAT ABOUT ALIENS?

I have never believed Earth was the only planet supporting intelligent life. In the movie *Contact* (based on the novel by Carl Sagan) there is a line that goes like this:

> "The *universe* is a *pretty big place. It's bigger* than anything anyone has ever dreamed of before. So, *if it's just us ... seems like* an *awful waste* of *space."*

And, I agree!

I often prefer to use the expression 'non-earthly beings' rather than 'alien' because of the emotional and psychological content that has been loaded onto that word over the years. In mainstream consciousness, there is considerable fear around aliens. The general response to the notion of alien life tends to be based in incredulity, ridicule or horror. The belief that beings from other worlds are intent on enslaving humanity in fear (as if that hasn't been happening through advertising for a long time already, I might add) doesn't help much either.

These fear-based ideas can shut the soul off from the goodness and love that our non-earthly and deeply wise, kind and helpful guides from other parts of this Universe want to share with us. Many of those beings are further along the evolutionary trajectory than we are. They can help us understand that if we don't want to be enslaved by anyone or anything, then we can choose to embrace our spiritual path and discover our innate freedom, just as they have done.

This is a vast Universe with many types of beings in it. Some are interested in love and others are interested in generating fear for what they can get out of it. This is true for humans and non-humans. I also know that human beings have free will. We get to choose what sort of energy we invite into our bodies, our minds, and our world. When it feels as if fear is taking us over, we may forget we have a choice. We can learn how to deal with that fear and eventually gain mastery over it (without judging how long that process may take). Or, we can claim we have no power and refuse to take responsibility for our psychological and emotional wellbeing. The choice is always ours.

When we are willing to recognise that we have the power to heal ourselves, we are less afraid. In opening to life, we know that painful experiences are inevitable and that we can manage them. When we have that confidence in ourselves, our natural curiosity opens us to the many divine beings that wish to help us heal our hearts from fear and experience freedom and truth. In this book, we will connect with some of those beautiful and powerful star guides who have a special connection to Earth. Far from needing to be afraid, we can embrace these loving wisdom beings as friends of the soul.

STAR ENERGIES SUPPORT LIGHT BEARERS ON EARTH

My natural tendency in the earthly realm is to seek out the people, situations and information that feel good for my soul and cast aside that which is without goodwill and aims to create confusion, fear or disconnection. I take this approach when I tune into other worlds, too. I am open to spiritual beings from many traditions, cultures and realms beyond this earthly world. I experience all those beings as loving, wise and of higher consciousness. In recognising their elevated awareness and expression of divine love, I know they can be helpful and constructive for my own work in the world. I wanted to make sure the stars beings included in this book know how to get to the desired destination of loving and peaceful realities and are willing and able to help us get there.

Have I encountered beings who do not hold loving and higher-level consciousness? Oh yes. I have never sought them out, but I have nonetheless encountered the presence of lower-level energies from time to time. I learned from personal experience how important it is to listen to my heart as it tells me which energies to invite into my realm and which ones to keep out. If unwanted negativities have somehow filtered through like an uninvited guest in my home, then I know to eject them promptly and firmly by reaffirming the true nature of love, compassion and wisdom within me.

Keeping a sense of humour helps prevent us from feeling victimised if negative energies seem to be following us around like an unpleasant smell. We can learn to recognise when it is our own thoughts that are causing us grief by providing a way for negativity to grow in our minds and hearts. Humour and wisdom can help us acknowledge suffering and gently turn it around, to a place of restfulness, gratitude and grace, preferably with a hefty dose of giggles. What makes you laugh most? Pictures of a loved one being a dork? Funny cat videos on YouTube? I never underestimate the value of a good belly laugh. It can lighten the heart and send negative energies scuttling away faster than you can say, "Snort laugh."

Every human has free will and gets to choose their own reality. For some that means embracing a miserly, self-involved and fearful way of being. I have compassion and respect for each person's freedom to choose, and we all have our wallowing moments. There can be courage in embracing the depth of our suffering. Certainly, we cannot heal without acknowledging our pain. However, keeping a connection to the light means we don't feel lost in the darkness of our struggles. Fortunately, when we work with the stars, we strengthen our inner light, which is of benefit to ourselves and to those who are attracted to our light and can gain benefit from it.

STARS ARE ALCHEMISTS THAT
MIRROR OUR SOUL JOURNEY

Stellar evolution is the process by which a star changes over the course of time. Their lifetime can range from a few million years to trillions of years. These are very ancient beings. Even before we get to the metaphysical, spiritual and healing properties of stars, what astrophysicists tell us about their physical existence is already astounding. For something that seems so delicate and ethereal to our earthly view, stars are incredibly powerful and dynamic beings. They have their own life cycles, some phases of which are so dramatic and transformative as to be alchemical. They change from one type of star to another. Like the butterfly who sheds her caterpillar nature, stars go through such profound change that they cannot go back to what they once were. Their consciousness can help us let go and embrace our own radical transformation of body, mind, soul and life.

Stars are born out of nebulae, cosmic clouds of hydrogen and dust referred to as stellar nurseries. Stars form due to gravity and compression. They generate their own light and heat through an internal process of nuclear fusion. There is a correspondence with the soul going through spiritual initiation in that deep challenge or crisis forces us to evolve, and as we heal the trauma, emerge transformed. It can feel like life is pulling and pushing and pressurising. Like the star, greater forces are acting to help birth our new reality. This process can feel so intensely difficult that we may wonder if something is very wrong! Star wisdom helps us remember that initiation and evolution is part of the natural workings of the Universe, and that something genuinely good will eventually come out of it, if we choose to work through the process.

Stars can be red giants, supergiants, red or white dwarfs, or yellow dwarf stars like our Sun, just to give some examples. When our Sun runs out of hydrogen fuel, it will expand to become a red giant, shed its outer layers, and then settle down as a compact white dwarf, slowly cooling down for trillions of years. Fair enough, it's done a lot of work, it deserves to have some time scheduled in its celestial plan to chill out. When massive stars explode in a supernova, they can form incredibly dense neutron stars, such as pulsars (a fast-spinning neutron star) or even a black hole. Stellar remnants can become a nebula from which new stars can form.

Many spiritual teachings ask us to consider death as a transition into a new cycle. Stars remind us of this. A star never really dies, but changes form and function to become something different and new. Understanding the powerful transitions a star goes through can help us realise that our own souls go through this process too, and sometimes, even in our earthly lives, we will feel these changes. There is the ebb and flow of creativity, times for release, times of high energy, times to be dynamic and powerful, and times when we need to rest and surrender into transition. The ending of a phase or identity may feel like a symbolic death from which a new self will eventually emerge. There is loss, the ending of something that may have defined us, and through that loss, there is freedom to birth a new expression.

Significant points in a star's life take place when it has achieved equilibrium or stability. Once this happens, the star begins to transform once more. So it is with the soul, in that we make progress, reach a plateau of mastery, and then the journey of evolution continues. I often say to clients that the soul doesn't want to keep repeating the same thing over and over, it needs change and growth to feel alive. Energy wants to move and evolve. When we trust that process, we can live in harmony and flow with the Universe. We can let go more gracefully and use our energy to progress in our life, rather than getting caught up in fear or trying to make things stay the same.

ASTROPHYSICS AND METAPHYSICS

As a child I contemplated the size of the Universe as a type of meditation. It was one of the only things that would quieten my restless mind. I would consider the enormity of our galaxy and beyond, and the only thing my mind could do in response was say, "Wow!"

Unlike planets, stars burn hydrogen in their cores. To achieve this nuclear process, an astronomical object must be at least 75 times the size of Jupiter, the largest planet in our solar system. To paint a picture of the size we are talking about, Earth could fit inside Jupiter more than 1300 times.

Astrophysicists have discovered that some stars are incredibly dense compared to their size. You could compare this to a boxer who punches above their weight or an ant who shows superman-level strength. When a large star dies by exploding in a supernova, a gravitational collapse can take place and result in a neutron star, where all the empty space is squished out of the atoms and the neutrons are jammed together. The result is a small star with a massive amount of power. One astrophysicist likened the density of a neutron star to a Boeing 747 airplane compressed into a small grain of sand.

Apart from being fascinating, this paints a picture of the nature of energy and change, and the truth of inner power versus the appearance of it. We can see that sometimes the smallest thing is the most powerful. We can draw wisdom from astrophysics to support spiritual teachings. Adjusting an attitude or moving from fear into gratitude can be powerful enough to cause a change in the physical world. Stars help us realise that there can be great power in unassuming practices such as prayer or setting a positive intention. Big, bold actions have their purpose and their place, but so do the seemingly insignificant or small actions and sometimes they can be the most powerful steps to take.

Stars are not close to one another. Most stars are out there with no-one around, so to speak, for huge distances in any direction. Sometimes star systems have so much space between each star that it takes a while for scientists to recognise the relationship between them. For those who sometimes feel like lone lights in the darkness or wonder if their soul tribe will ever appear, star therapy can help us feel a deeper connection with the sustaining love of the Universe, especially if we must go it alone until it is time to discover our soul tribe. If we are going through an experience of aloneness on the surface, we may even discover our soul tribe is already connected to us at a deeper level.

HOW TO WORK WITH STARS

All realised beings—including the wise and ancient star guides—are willing and able to assist those who ask for help. For a human being, the first step in this process is relaxing the heart and mind, so that when you ask for help you are open to receiving it. From that place, the healing processes and mandalas in this book can heighten your receptivity to beautiful transmissions. The sensitives amongst you may find that just reading about a star guide is enough to stir your heart, mind and soul, so that the connection becomes more conscious, and the energy begins to flow between your soul and the star teacher more freely.

A star guide will answer your human request for help with a transmission of stellar intelligence. This response will move through your energy field and into your cells. You may perceive it or not, but it happens, nonetheless. We register transmission in countless ways. We feel uplifted, clearer, inspired, or something that was bothering us will no longer seem like an issue. We may suddenly have the energy and drive to deal with a matter effectively rather than procrastinating in confusion or doubt.

One day when I was sitting down to write this book, those around me were going through some intense challenges. They were handling them with grace and courage but were also leaning on me for support. I didn't realise how much of a toll that was taking until I began to write. Then suddenly, I was bathed in the lightness and grace of these star energies as they came through to guide the writing process. I realised how uplifted and inspired I felt and that I hadn't felt that way for some weeks. I was surprised at just how rapid and radical the shift was in that moment. The healing took place in a matter of seconds.

I have always trusted the immediacy of spiritual response, instinctively understanding that it exists beyond time and space as well as within it. That's why we don't have to worry about light-years, distance and whether our prayers to the stars may take 85 light-years to reach them, and another 85 light-years to get back to us! Not the most practical timing for a human life form. Fortunately, when you understand the freedom that spiritual intelligence has to move and respond, you'll relax and trust in the process, allowing it to bring swift healing into your life.

ARE THE STARS INTERESTED IN US?

Spiritual traditions from India, Tibet, Egypt, Australia, Africa, the Americas and Greece all reference beings from the stars that are aware of humanity, have evolved beyond our consciousness and want to help us. Some star communities send avatars that incarnate in human form and others send transmissions of grace through light and sound to help humanity.

Human souls that have evolved some way along the spiritual path have a genuine and compelling need to help others on their life journey. Likewise, evolved star beings have a genuine ability and interest in encouraging our evolution, developing our consciousness and guiding us along the path they have already taken. From a place of goodwill, these evolved beings transmit their frequencies generously and specifically to civilisations—such as those on Earth—that they know they can assist.

These stars and the beings that dwell within their fields (e.g. Pleiadeans in the Pleiades), have walked the path ahead of us and, like an older, experienced sibling, have a lot of wisdom to offer us. They have figured out what works and what does not, and because of that, they have reached a position of mastery relative to human civilisation. In short, they can help us find our way.

They are particularly interested in helping humanity shift from seeking power for its own sake and the destructive end that evokes. Many humans have a soul memory and intuitive understanding of the dangers of being obsessed with power through the fall of Atlantis. We recognise that power can become an addiction that is devastating to the spiritual path of individuals and the survival of a planet. Star beings look for humans who have enough awareness to work with them consciously and reach out to bless, help and guide them to fulfil a higher purpose.

The stars appear so far removed from us that it seems unlikely they would be aware of what is happening on Earth or want to help. We may not be aware of it, but we broadcast our consciousness as an expression of who we are all the time. Sensitive human beings (like psychics and empaths) pick up on this so accurately that others often think they have magical powers! Most of the time they are simply reflecting what is being projected to them at a subtle level. You could think of it as a way of reading between the lines. The unspoken is communicated, just in a less overt way.

For non-earthly beings who are sensitive and interested enough to pay attention to us, it is not so difficult to pick up our broadcasts and gain an understanding of what is happening within humanity and on the earth. As a collective, the earth is a pretty noisy place. People typically have a lot to say through their beliefs, emotions, thoughts, words and actions. Even humans who are quieter and have more stillness are heard and responded to by loving higher beings who want to help.

There are many star beings who are interested in humanity for all the right reasons, and those are the ones we will be connecting with through this book.

WHAT IS 11.11?

The title of this book includes 11.11 because the content is tuned to this frequency. This energy harmonises with star consciousness and our own inner light. The 11.11 frequency is a feeling and a function. It is inspired, optimistic and a trigger for recalibration. That process often begins with a purification that destabilises the status quo, uproots patterns that are stifling your spiritual expansion and leads you into a new and enhanced experience of freedom, authenticity and grace. It is, in a healing and inspirational way, a total game changer.

Sometimes the Universe reminds us that we have this sacred frequency within us— like a built-in freedom fighter—and encourages us to let it open us to new ways of living. When you see 11.11 on the number plate in front of you, your bank account, the title of this book or on your clock or phone when you unconsciously check the time, and you feel something stirring inside of you, you've just received a transmission. The Universe is letting you know the way things have been is not the way they should continue to be. Sometimes we need a nudge to break our habits of thought and expectation. We need a spiritual reset, so we can get back on track. When we challenge our self-imposed limitations, we allow the Universe to dazzle us with its generosity, grace and creative opportunities. As you have picked up this book, you can be sure that the Universe is guiding you deeper into your own experience of the 11.11 vibration.

This powerful number pattern supports a quantum leap in consciousness to bring the message that something completely new is wanting to break through the old reality to transform it. It says that if you move boldly toward whatever the next level is for you, the Universe is going to be there waiting for you.

The 11.11 energy is about evolution. It marks a move into a higher frequency of being. Higher frequency reality means less fear and more love, less doubt and more peace, less holding back and more saying yes. It means less being trapped in past patterns and more creativity and spontaneity. Living in a higher frequency feels better. We still have our growth edges, but we move through them with more grace and effectiveness. We heal in places we doubted could ever heal. We open to life, feel more trust in ourselves and feel less tentative about living our destiny.

It's wise not to underestimate the pull of lower frequencies. Giving up attitudes and actions that promote pain in ourselves and our world really takes courage, patience and persistence. Even when we dream of a different life, the mind can convince us that the familiar is safer than the risk of the unknown. It takes strength to listen to the voice in our hearts that urges us to be open and willing to take a more inspired journey. And, even more strength to trust it. Every 11.11 is the Universe reassuring us that it will be okay to take the journey with trust.

When you upgrade a computer system, some older programs simply won't work anymore, but new and improved features will become available. The 11.11 frequency is like a computer upgrade for your energy field which relates to the nervous, emotional system and endocrine systems as well as your heart, gut, cellular activity and so on.

If you want to access a lighter and brighter reality, you are going to have to give up some of the old belief systems and social programming that you've been running through your body and mind. This can feel like an upheaval before you get the hang of the new way. Going through such a transition is not always easy. Sometimes an upgrade can feel like a system breakdown. At first, it might seem like everything is falling apart and you won't know how to handle situations because the old ways don't suit you anymore and the new ways are not yet completely available to you.

If we choose courage and growth, we *will* make the transition. There is a hilarious meme that I stumbled across on social media. It pictured a woman in deep reflection with the statement, "I miss my old, fear-based reality … *said no person, ever.*" It can be good to keep that in mind when we are confronting our fears and doubts. It is part of the transition into a more trusting and graceful way of living.

We have free will and the right to choose how we live. We also have a loving creative partner that wants to help us in all ways — the Universe and its stars! If we say to the Universe, "Look, I need this to be difficult because that is what I believe and sticking to my beliefs makes me feel comfortable psychologically, even if it creates emotional pain for me."

And, the Universe is going to say, "Okay, if that's what you choose, let's do it."

If you feel like you've had to struggle and fight your way through whatever has risen in your past, you may finally be ready for an opportunity to lay down your psychological weapons, open to and trusting of the divine presence in your life. You can then say to the Universe, "Okay, let's try something different. I don't want to believe that I must feel stressed, attacked, shamed or afraid. I want to feel peace in my heart and mind each day. I want to believe that everything happening in my life is an opportunity for me to live better. I want to trust, and I want that to become easy for me."

The Universe will say, "Sure! Let's do it."

Ever had a massage where the therapist finds that tight spot and presses on it? It takes intention and concentration to relax enough to allow your body to release the strain, rather than tensing up and resisting the temporary pain. You might need to remind yourself that this is part of your healing process. Once the pain releases, you will feel amazing. When the 11.11 frequency starts to activate within us, it can feel like a pressure-point massage from the Universe. This will nudge us toward emotional release and energy surges will follow. The stars also provide us with energetic hits of grace and light that help us see things differently and feel ready to upgrade our programming.

The challenges you have successfully moved through already have begun to reveal just how much courage you have within. You certainly have more than enough to deal with whatever arises in your life. You may not feel like you have handled everything perfectly, and that's fine. You don't need to be perfect. You just need to be open and willing to grow. If you are, you will find it easier to trust and when you trust, you will find it easier to relax. The more relaxed we are, the more the Universe can help us in ways we don't expect. Life seems so complicated at times. There are so many things to think about, consider and juggle, but it is possible for the most daunting situations to become simple. The Universe can help us in absolutely every detail of our lives with an unfathomable genius and generosity.

Here is a general invocation or prayer you can use to tune into the 11.11 frequency whenever you wish:

> *I am open to the unconditionally loving grace that wants to help me live my most beautiful, uplifting, inspired life. With mercy and compassion, please clear my path so that I may see, know and be empowered to grow with trust, courage and joy. Thank you for the blessings and guidance you gift to me with such abundance. The 11.11 frequency flows through stars and into my entire being, bringing grace, protection and divine alignment with the highest wisdom for the greatest good. So be it.*

HOW TO WORK WITH THE CRYSTALS

The crystals in this book are not always easy to find, but with the beautiful mandalas and prayers, you'll be able to work with them energetically and benefit from their healing power without having to access a physical specimen. However, I am sure many of you will want to obtain a physical piece to work with and this is something I completely understand. Here is some guidance for cleansing your crystals.

It's good to cleanse your crystals before using them for the first time or whenever you sense they need it — such as after working with them in a healing session. The energy of your crystal will feel vibrant when it is clean. When it is dirty, it will feel like sunlight trying to get through a dirty window. You will know there is good energy there, but it will be a bit hard to feel it. This means your crystal has been working hard, clearing energy and absorbing it too. It needs clearing so that it can continue to do its wonderful work. Trust your intuition on when cleansing needs to happen. You can never cleanse too much nor clear away the power of a crystal — even if you leave it out in the sun and its colour fades somewhat.

Cleansing removes that which isn't pure in the crystal, a bit like giving it a spiritual shower. It is safe and will not harm you or the stone. Just do some research before you expose your crystals to water or to too much sunlight as for some, this can cause fading. And, in the case of salts like beautiful halite, it can dissolve the crystal right before your eyes! This won't often be an issue as crystals have survived powerful earth radiation for a very long time, and typically, can handle whatever a human being sends their way.

You can cleanse all crystals by visualising a vibrant violet light flecked with white. Imagine it sparkling and crackling above the crown of your head, flowing down through your head and into your mouth. Gently blow the violet energy out of your mouth, straight into and through the crystal with the intent of cleansing it of all negativity. Do this until the crystal feels clean or for at least seven breaths. With practice and focus, you will be able to clear a crystal with one short sharp breath, but it may take time to feel confident with it.

If you are unsure about the breath technique, you can hold your crystal in one hand, raise the other above it and quite simply say (aloud or silently in your mind), "I call upon beings of unconditional love who can assist with cleansing my crystal and transforming negative energy into unconditional love. Through my own free will, so be it!"

You can also play beautiful music (I have created several sacred music albums featuring powerful prayers and mantras) and burn incense to clear the space and your crystals all at once. You can also recharge your crystals in nature. Placing them in moonlight, sunshine or a nice shady spot with fresh air, will do the trick for most crystals. Keep in mind that certain pieces need extra care. Mica can flake off when you dust it and others such as fluorite can be bleached in sunlight. They will still work beautifully, of course. If you are unsure, do a little research or stick to simple techniques for clearing and charging your stones.

CRYSTAL ANGELS

Every crystal has its own angel. There are angels in each individual piece and there is an oversoul or crystal angel that is the guardian for each type of crystal. So, if you held a piece of phenacite, and called on the Crystal Angel of Phenacite, you would be working with the energy of that individual crystal, as well as the consciousness of all the phenacite everywhere … in Madagascar, Russia, South America, the United States and Zimbabwe, discovered or yet to be discovered! Every piece of phenacite is energetically linked through the consciousness of the Crystal Angel of Phenacite.

We tap into divine, holographic unity through our intention. Although your individual crystal will have a unique energy, according to its source, shape and size, the greater consciousness of phenacite will be emanating through that individual stone like an oversoul. Therefore, even a small crystal can be immensely powerful. Through holographic intelligence, even the smallest part holds the power and wisdom of the whole.

By calling on a crystal angel, we can work with a crystal, even if we don't have physical access to it. Crystal angels help you tap into the greater healing properties and energetic intelligence of the crystal. I have worked with this technique for years. If someone is struggling and a crystal intuitively comes to mind, I simply call upon the crystal angel and ask for its consciousness to channel into the body and soul of my client through unconditional love. It works! And, the client's healing or meditation experience isn't interrupted by me rummaging around in the crystal cupboard for the exact stone that holds the vibration they need.

Working with physical crystals is fun, beautiful and it can make the experience feel more tangible as we are learning to sense energy. Yet, it is good to know that is not the only way to tap into their healing intelligence, especially if we are very drawn to a crystal and know it can help us, but just don't have it on hand at that precise moment. At those times, we can close our eyes and say:

> *Through unconditional love, I call upon the Crystal Angel for Phenacite* (or whatever crystal it is you need) *and I ask for you to bring your healing power to my body, mind and soul with compassionate grace. Through my own free will, so be it.*

Breathe in and out slowly, with your awareness in your heart, and an intention to receive. Done!

HOW TO WORK WITH THE MANDALAS

In this book, we work with mandalas as energetic replacements (or additional companions) for the physical stone as we did in the other books in this series, *Crystal Angels 444, Crystal Masters 333* and *Crystal Goddesses 888*. You can use the mandala images in the healing processes as you would regular stones. Place them in your healing room, under your pillow at night, gaze at them in meditation … whatever speaks to your heart.

HOW TO READ THE HEALING PROCESS AND DO THEM

The healing processes go deep, and you can either read them as you go or record them beforehand. You'll find my recordings of the healing process from the first three books of this series (don't worry if you are reading this one first, all the books are complete on their own and do not need to be read in any particular order). The healing processes for *Crystal Angels 444, Crystal Masters 333* and *Crystal Goddesses 888* are currently available on *CD Baby* and *iTunes*. Feel free to check out my website *www.alanafairchild.com* to sign up for a newsletter and stay on top of new releases such as the healing process recordings for titles in this series.

A NOTE ON HEALTHCARE PRACTITIONERS AND MENTAL ILLNESS

Please consult your mental healthcare practitioner if you have any predisposition to mental illness, depression, suicidal thoughts and so forth. You are so precious, worthy of love and meant to be here. This work will help you fulfil your purpose and receive all that you deserve (which is a great abundance of peace and love). Make sure you are supported while you do your inner work.

Please do mention to your doctor or therapist that you are doing energy work, especially if you are on a mental health program or medication. Whether your healthcare provider believes in energy work or not, they need to know how to work with you and keeping them informed is one way to ensure as good a working relationship as possible.

If their response isn't supportive when you inform them of your spiritual work, you may want to consider changing to a healthcare provider who is more interested in you doing whatever works for you rather than having you agree with their belief system. One of my Reiki teachers used to drum this advice into all her students, "Energy changes consciousness." So, your medication may need to be altered as you heal, or it may need to remain as is — only you, taking your own perfectly unique journey, can reveal that to you. If this information is relevant, you may find it best to be in consultation with an open-minded healthcare provider as you do this work. You deserve such care.

CHAPTER ONE

SPIRITUAL DIRECTION FOR OLD SOULS

STAR GUIDE: CANOPUS

CANOPUS IS THE SECOND-BRIGHTEST STAR in the night sky, after Sirius, and likewise found in the sign of Cancer which resonates with creativity and the Divine Mother. Canopus is the brightest star in the Cancerian constellation of Argo Navis which translates as *the great ship* and is also referred to as *the ship of the desert*, a term desert nomads used to describe their precious camels.

Canopus can help us learn how to conserve our emotional waters, so that we can nurture ourselves from within, especially during the dry spells when outer circumstances may not feel particularly inspirational. The energy of this star teacher delivers powerful nurturing onto our soul path and encourages us to stay true to the spiritual light that guides our way. Although, at first, it may seem to be asking us to go through challenging circumstances, even ones we believe would take a soul far greater than ours to overcome.

When you feel a soul connection to this star teacher, you can be sure it is a message from higher guidance that you have what it takes. Your inner resources are more than you may consciously realise, and you will be able to navigate your way through challenges where others may have failed. You have the soul power to take a big journey in this lifetime, so embrace it. Trust that you will find your way.

Canopus has strong associations with voyages and journeys. When this guide appears, there is deep and loving spiritual support for an inner and an outer journey. You could imagine it like the Divine Mother waving you off, knowing in her heart that you'll return home a hero, having achieved all that you set out to do.

Canopus is also associated with wealth, glory and fame. When it makes a connection with your soul, there is often some kind of learning to be experienced around these matters. Sometimes it is necessary to 'wear off some of the sheen' before it is safe for the soul to experience worldly success. If they would distract or seduce a soul from its real mission and higher purpose, those things may be withheld or postponed. Conversely, the soul may be granted many worldly successes until it realises that all that glitters is not gold. A soul may need to learn that no matter how much material gain may come from certain choices, the price of going against the integrity and wisdom of the soul will always be too high. The soul may need to learn that its value is not measured by external factors such as wealth or fame, and that those who have such circumstances in life are no better or worse as people.

Canopus can help us learn that financial or other circumstances do not in any way imply that someone has greater or lesser worth nor are they a sign of spiritual advancement. A soul can have a positive karmic inheritance and belief system around attracting money and still be working on becoming an abundant, rather than self-serving and fearful, individual. We cannot guess the inner state of one's soul from the outer state of their life circumstances. Every path serves the needs of the soul in unique and sometimes unexpected ways.

For those souls doing inner work to be open to abundance and worldly success without fear of becoming spiritually distracted, or with the intention of channelling one's abundance into helping others, then Canopus shows the way from poverty consciousness to a more generous experience of material abundance.

Once we overcome the possibility of being seduced and deluded by fame and fortune, the soul no longer blocks its ability to receive. Instead of projecting issues of self-worth out to the Universe, the soul is ready to accept worldly success to further its spiritual work. When Canopus makes a connection with the soul, it can be a sign this is unfolding at a deeper level. If you or a loved one is having issues with finances, with career success or making your mark on the world, this star brings a message of healing.

Considered fortunate and benevolent, Canopus holds the qualities of stabilising Saturn and abundant, generous and optimistic Jupiter. Saturn's presence offers endurance, long-term affluence, success and tends to set healthy limits. Jupiter tends to make things bigger. Canopus brings balance, so we can be open to advances in wealth and success, but not in a *here today, gone tomorrow* sort of way.

In the zodiac sign of Cancer, Canopus' blessings bring things to life, and relate to anything to do with creativity, nurturing and manifestation. As Cancer is a birthing sign, it holds strong associations with mothering on all levels whether it be a child, a soul purpose or a business. When we work with Canopus, we want to be certain that what we wish for aligns with our true heart's desires because there is a lot of cosmic support to bring it to life.

In Chinese astronomy, Canopus is known as the star of Shou, the star of the south pole, and is associated with life span and divine timing. The wise being known as Shou was said to have been carried in his mother's womb for ten years and was born as an old man when finally delivered. He is recognisable by his high, domed forehead. He often carries a peach of immortality or a gourd filled with the elixir of life. He is friendly, helpful and said to confer blessings for long life and endurance.

Shou is the quintessential old soul who has wisdom and knowledge that belies their years, and often appears in childhood. Feeling drawn to Canopus can be a reminder that we are old souls and have a deep well of inner wisdom that we can trust.

There may also be a need to focus on regeneration and replenishment. Some old souls will have times when they need to focus on taking care of themselves for a change. Giving back to their bodies and minds, will enable them to restore and repair the compassion fatigue that can come with wearing themselves out in service to others. Shou comes to us as a reminder that while the Universe is generous with healing energy, it is up to us to remember to be receptive to it. Canopus encourages us to nurture our vital energies. Even the hardiest camel needs time to drink now and then! And, the oldest souls need to receive to give.

In Vedic literature, Canopus is associated with the sage Agastya, one of the ancient rishis. Agastya is the reputed cleanser of waters. The rising of Canopus coincides with the calming of the Indian Ocean. The significance of this for the old soul is important. We can accumulate a lot of emotional imprints when we've been around the block a few times. Fatigue and world weariness can creep in when a soul has seen the same mistakes and cruelties again and again. This can be tiring and disheartening for sensitive souls. Reconnecting to joy, happiness, kindness, generosity, goodwill and good-natured humour will cleanse their emotional bodies of the distress and suffering they have so gallantly taken on through their journey. Tapping into the happiness and tranquillity that comes when our emotional waters are cleansed can put a youthful spring back into the serene gait of the old soul.

Canopus is associated with the ability to transform negativity into positive energy. If an old soul can learn to use their experiences of suffering—either their own or those they compassionately bear witness to in the world—as a way of demanding more help from Spirit, they can open their hearts without feeling emotionally overwhelmed or losing faith in humanity and the future of Mother Earth. They can then become channels for spiritual grace, empowering their own journey and the journey of the human collective, through the challenges of earth school. Their beautiful hearts can be moved by compassion and still have plenty of laughter to share.

No star closer to the earth, is more luminous than Canopus. It has been the brightest star in Earth's sky during three different epochs over the past four million years. Sirius eventually moved closer to us and in that process became brighter, and it will remain so for another couple of hundred thousand years or so. In due course, Canopus will resume its position of primary luminary. This reminds us that there are times to step up and shine, and times to turn within and do our inner work. We can allow others to take the lead, trusting that our time to shine will come again.

THE CRYSTAL ANGEL OF SHUNGITE

This stone is shrouded in mystery and there is debate surrounding its creation story. It could be part of a meteorite or remnants from a collapsed planet. However, it is agreed that shungite is a black-coloured stone sourced from a lake bed in northern Russia and is around two billion years of age.

Shungite is a stone of ancient earth medicine—and quite possibly extra-terrestrial healing technology—that clears negativity and increases psychic protection by deflecting harmful energies and purifying any pollutants that have managed to break through your protective auric layers.

Shungite has astonishing properties. It can purify highly polluted water, conduct geothermal and electromagnetic energy and shield against harmful electromagnetic emissions. It absorbs negative energy, promotes vitality and supports the immune system (psychically and physically). With antioxidant and anti-inflammatory properties, this protective healing stone has multiple uses.

When I first held a piece of shungite, and aware of its reputation, I was struck by how low key it felt. It goes about its tasks quietly and effectively. It might seem like a strange observation to make, but some crystals have very loud personalities. For all its power, shungite is unobtrusive and for those that wish to go about their business without attracting undue attention, this is a powerful companion stone. For some souls, being visible helps them carry out their life's work, but others feel it is more helpful to remain relatively unseen, flying under the radar so to speak. When that feels authentic for the soul, it is important to trust it. The yogi meditating in the cave does a lot for balancing light and peace on this planet, even if no-one sees him for thirty years or more and no-one is posting about it on social media!

If you are sensitive to EMFs (electromagnetic frequencies) and work around radiation—in environments with computers or medical equipment for example—this stone can be an ally for your wellbeing. However, it does need regular cleansing (with clean, fresh water as salty water will damage the stone) and recharging in sunlight.

SPIRITUAL GUIDANCE: EARTH SCHOOL

Life is a school of spiritual growth for the soul. It opens us to such beautiful blessings and yet we will also experience upheaval, change, frustration and uncertainty as we allow ourselves to be divinely worked upon by higher loving energies. Eventually, challenging situations transform into sources of peace, strength, empowerment and happiness. This is the sacred alchemy of life, working its transformational wisdom in our lives each day.

For the wounded part of us, growth can be frightening. It may need us to divest from familiar ways that give a sense of safety, but if left unchecked, also prevent us from making spiritual progress. Ultimately, we may agree that this will make us happier, healthier, more fulfilled and freer. That doesn't mean letting go and trusting things will all work out is going to be the easiest thing to do!

Sometimes, the direction we feel we need to take, to confront and release what we have held on to, may seem like a fast track to misery. Yet, I can honestly say, my most difficult journeys have ended up being the experiences I have the most gratitude for as they brought me the most benefit. It's like the Universe trying to take the snack out of our hand because there is a magnificent feast prepared for us. If our issues around lack or the fear that we will never have what we want are triggered, then we can resist, throw a tantrum and feel that nothing will ever work out for us … even though what is taking place is evidence the Universe wants to give us something positive and heal all those issues for us.

When I was in law school, I discovered books on psychology and the chakras. I certainly never found law quite so interesting. I had enrolled in law school because, at that stage, I didn't know what else to do. It was not the greatest reason to choose a career, but it was the best I could do at the time.

As impractical as my passionate interest in the New Age might have seemed, I couldn't get enough of it. I was even caught reading a book on chakras and aromatherapy (another of my passions) during a litigation exam. I passed my exam with ease, much to the annoyance of my tutor who enthusiastically expressed great offence at my indifferent attitude and lack of respect — which was a fair call. I hadn't yet connected my passion with my purpose. I knew I didn't want to practice law, but never considered an obsession with New Age topics could become a supportive career. My heart was leading me to a place my mind couldn't conceive of. It seemed I was headed toward *nothing*. As it turned out, I was being guided toward a definite destination, but my belief systems hadn't stretched enough for me to see it. I was on a soul voyage that my mind was yet to understand.

As I indulged in spiritual explorations of the chakras and psychology, I realised there were places in my energetic anatomy where I felt more at home than others. I was naturally drawn toward the higher centres of the third eye chakra, crown chakra and throat chakra. My love of dancing—the more drums, didgeridoo and instinctive tribal rhythms the better—kept me connected to my lower chakras, but I felt much more comfortable floating about in the world of ideas, light and spirit.

At a deeper level, I didn't want to get grounded and go into my body and feel the pain stored there from childhood, and from past lives, too. I was far more interested in flying high than grounding and connecting with the reality of my own body. I held a kind of arrogance about this for a time, as though the higher world were better worlds. It was a mistaken view, but it was part of what protected me from venturing into a journey of embodiment before I was able to handle it.

I couldn't face my emotional pain without a strong feeling of connection to the higher worlds of spirit. I needed to feel unconditionally loved, accepted, special in the eyes of the Divine, seen, loved *and* treasured, before I could confront the pain lodged in my lower chakras of not being acceptable, important or worthy of time and attention. I needed healing knowledge of the glorious higher worlds. I needed to feel they were real enough to depend on for the love I needed to face those feelings of unworthiness without being plunged into despair. And, real enough to help me with the down-to-earth matters of career, health, relationships and where I was living, all of which felt out of alignment and were leading me on a fast-track to depression.

The experiences that came through my somewhat obsessive pursuit of spiritual heights were a chance to let my soul breathe, to momentarily rise out of the ocean of suffering that I sometimes felt I was drowning in. It was a chance to be the real me, to learn who I was, and what I wanted and needed. To do that, I needed to be so in love with all things spiritual, that I was lifted out of my life for long enough to realise another way could open for me if I was willing to allow it. Once I had enough trust in this other reality, I found the courage to deal with whatever was in the way of me living that new and beautiful life for myself. I decided to process and clear however much pain was within me, so I could find a way into the happiness I glimpsed in myself whenever I read New Age books — even though I was not yet able to see that spiritual beauty reflected in my physical world.

The world I dreamed of and the life I was living were poles apart. It was clear that before I could lay claim to my happiness, I was going to have to do some work on feeling, naming, expressing and releasing a lot of sadness, fear, anger, shame, guilt and grief, along with the secondary symptoms of these repressed emotions, including anxiety, panic, depression and other health issues. I was intimidated but determined to break free from where my life was heading.

Before experiencing the solar plexus as a source of personal empowerment and self-possession, I tended to associate it with fear-based power issues and I didn't like that energy at all. I noticed power games and control where there should have been love, and this hurt me to acknowledge. I had to learn to respect my own value, to set boundaries and stand up for myself. This took me into health issues with my digestive system and brought up a lot of emotional pain from childhood.

Before I knew the sacral chakra to be a vast ocean of playfulness and intimate connection, I experienced it as a deluge of emotional suffering which I found difficult to accept and bear witness to without feeling overwhelmed. I had to learn how to be open without taking on other people's pain, how to care without feeling responsible for rescuing others from their choices, how to have compassion for others as well as myself, and how to feel all my emotions, including joy and vivacity, even when others chose to feel unhappy or victimised. This was a challenge as I am deeply moved by the suffering of others. Healing these issues took me deep into the pain of being a woman and a sensitive person. Eventually I could experience the power of being a woman and a sensitive, but I had to honour the pain first.

Before I experienced the base chakra as a safe, secure and loving connection to my own body and the Earth Mother, it felt like it was clogged with survival fears. I had to learn that the earth was a safe place to be, even if there were challenges to contend with. I had to learn to trust that if I had faith I was valued by the Universe, then my needs would be met, and things would work out on a practical level. I learned this bit by bit, practicing and trusting more, especially during crises that were outside my control. The belief systems I had inherited about survival, accomplishment and money that lacked any emphasis on personal fulfilment and true joy, had starved my heart of the trust and happiness it needed. It took some time to turn those belief systems around, to let them go and begin to generate more peace within me.

I discovered new ways of thinking and believing at spiritual events and bookstores. The way I felt at workshops and seminars provided an antidote to the torturous belief systems of mass culture that I had experienced earlier in life. I felt my energy lower when I returned to my life as it was then. I wanted to feel the same aliveness I felt in workshops and seminars in my daily life. I wanted that sense of light and freedom, where my soul felt inspired and optimistic.

As I went through the arduous process of acknowledging, feeling, naming and expressing my emotional baggage, and releasing it with forgiveness, the potential and blessings of the lower chakras slowly opened for me. This was when my passionate obsession with all things spiritual began to flow into my life, rather than just being in my head. Without that process, I would have been stuck in a type of spiritual obsession that could have become dangerous. If I had tried to keep going that way, it would have diverted, distracted and disconnected me from emotional healing. Instead, it gave me courage to ground myself and do the work to explore, heal and grow.

Dwelling in the spiritual, to dodge the pain it is meant to help us process and avoid the life it is meant to help us live, can be a form of escapism. In the long term, is not healthy. Some of us need this 'bubble' for a while, to gain confidence that a more beautiful way of being is possible. Others may want to dwell there permanently, content to live in their heads but losing the chance for spiritual progress that can only come from committing to being here, being human. Something like 'spiritual anorexia' can take place if the passion for Spirit goes too far. This is when the yearning for Spirit becomes so strong that one begins to deny love to the earthly and doesn't want to be human anymore. I see a similar disconnect from Earth and obsessive pursuit of disembodied perfection in anorexics. The desire to connect with Spirit (or bliss, or perfection, or light, for example) becomes confused with a desire to disconnect from the pain and hurt (and in doing so, also the sensuality, vitality, vibrance and joy) of the earthly world.

This happened to a sensitive and lovely man. He read some books describing spiritual worlds of higher guidance, and became overwhelmed by their kindness, attention and love. These three qualities were so missing in his family life where his emotional needs were ignored or ridiculed, and he was scapegoated and judged for being sensitive. He unconsciously responded to the constant barrage of criticism and meanness by getting sick often and feeling paranoid that people hated him. Given that he received hate rather than love from the family that should have been caring for him as a child, his projected paranoia and weak immune system was completely understandable. Eventually, the book learning began to shift from his headspace into a fuller recognition of his value. By tapping into his excellent intuition and beginning to stand up to bullies in his life, he was able to realise he was worthy of respect and kindness, just like any other being.

However, before that happened, this client was so engrossed in his books on higher worlds, and so miserable in his own life, that it triggered suicidal feelings. He wanted to leave his body so that he could return to spirit altogether. He eventually understood that this is not what would happen if he ended his life. He would still need to deal with the situations at hand and there were gentler, kinder and more loving ways for him to be able to do that in this lifetime. Fortunately, he was able to recognise his feelings were just feelings, and he could learn from them, rather than blindly acting on them. He sought support through counselling and worked through those feelings. Some are not lucky enough to have the support and inner strength needed to stand committed to life nor to transform these feelings into fuel for a passion for life. May any being plagued by such anguish receive blessings, protection and divine nurturance to overcome the pain through their life journey.

The moment our concept of Spirit tugs so hard on our heart strings that we lose our sense of belonging, here in the physical, we need to reach for someone who is grounded in spirit *and* on the earth to help us. Someone who knows spirit, loves the earth and experiences both as connected (which they are), can be a reassuring and powerful healing ally. Knowing such a person can be one of the most helpful experiences we can have when healing the painful experience of separation of spirit and life. This disconnection can happen when our spirit is not completely accepted, welcomed and protected in childhood. No matter how much our parents loved us, if they didn't have the necessary skills for nurturing and welcoming our spirit, we will likely struggle with such matters until we reach out for help and learn from someone who has developed those spiritual tools. Such a person can say "welcome to Earth — you belong with us and I'm glad you're here," and we really feel it at a deep level. It settles us. It helps us plug in and realise that there's a home here for our spirit. We relax into the prospect of taking our unique life journey.

The Universe doesn't want a painful sense of separation between heaven and earth for us. It understands that the light we love needs to shine through the 'lamp' of our bodies, so it can be present in the world. When we connect our souls with our bodies, the lamp is plugged in and the light of our spirit can shine. Then we feel at home, present, real, alive — spirit *and* human.

One of the turning points in transforming a pain-driven spiritual obsession into a life-affirming spiritual passion, is the ability to experience pleasure in the physical world. There are times when we don't need more exploration of the spiritual to grow spiritually or have a healing breakthrough. Sometimes, we just need enjoyable human downtime. We may struggle to recognise this, but there's no point having amazing frequencies pouring in through our spirit if we are not connected enough to our body to receive them.

Painful forms of spiritual homesickness can be transformed into a powerful sense of belonging to the earth. This intimacy between heaven and earth can culminate in a wild love affair in your soul. It requires a willingness to connect with the body, a sense of humour and compassion around the process. For the few amongst us who have not had any issue accepting and embracing pleasure—something which for whatever reason (I suspect a past life as a priestess of the dancing festival goddess, Bastet) has never been an issue for me—it is easy to include joy in our daily lives. This can be as simple as enjoying delicious and healthy food, taking an aromatherapy bath, rediscovering your inner teen as you passionately embrace your beloved, going for a solitary walk in nature, having a massage or grounding yoga session, stopping to breathe deeply when there is a beautiful scent on the breeze, and enjoying the feeling of that breeze as it playfully messes up your hair, and so on.

For those who have been shamed or ridiculed when they sought pleasure, or who feel awkward in the body and uncertain about relaxing into joy, allowing the body to experience delight can be confronting. There may be a fear that taking a single bite of chocolate cake will lead to overindulging on junk food for the rest of your life. Or, that one night out on the town will be the end of your respectable job and you will never work another day in your life. If you experienced violations through any kind of physical abuse, part of your journey may be to learn that your body is an amazing gift and can be treasured and trusted to be honest, and to heal over time through the love that you give to yourself.

If you have been repressing your natural desire for pleasure or binding yourself in disciplines that are too harsh, you might be over the top when you start to unwind. However, once you give yourself permission to listen to your desires, you can act in a way that balances discipline and delight. You don't have to binge like a person who will soon be starving again (literally or symbolically). You can nourish yourself in a consistent and loving way. When something is no longer taboo, denied or rejected, it can be integrated into our lives in a healthy way. It loses its dark power and simply becomes available to us, as needed. That process takes time and trust. A good sense of humour also helps one stay the course to integration.

For a star child, earthly delight is an important way of falling in love with the earth and really wanting to be here. If that means going on nature rambles, watching the Discovery Channel, hunting for the perfect crystal or searching for the most delicious meal ever, then so be it. One thing I universally encourage for anyone on the path of spiritual embodiment wanting to bring their most beautiful hopes and aspirations into reality, is some form of moving meditation. Yoga and dance are two of my favourites but playing a musical instrument and taking mindful nature walks are other examples. If this process is difficult for you, perhaps because mental or physical abuse has you believing your pleasure is something shameful or undeserved, support from a healing professional can be helpful.

Our healing journey brings peace, but the path often takes grit and determination. We need the fire of the solar plexus to transform fear into boldness and radiance so that we are willing to express our soul in the world. It lights the way for us to see what steps to take. I worked on issues and projects for years at a time without seeing any positive change, so I know we need faith, and that sometimes, it is all we have to keep us going. The fire in our solar plexus helps us find our way when we are yet to see outer results of our inner work. It can bless us with a sacred stubbornness that refuses to give up until we have our healing breakthrough.

Without the physical connection the lower chakras provide, there are beautiful dreams, fantasies, visions and possibilities, but no actual birthing into the world so that we can *live* those energies and share them with others. That can be frustrating and deeply disheartening for a soul who knows they are here to create beauty but cannot seem to accomplish it. In these instances, resolving a childhood issue lodged somewhere in the lower chakras almost always frees up that energy so it can flow into physical manifestation unimpeded.

Eventually the distance between the life I dreamed and my actual life experience, began to lessen. As I took simple steps away from what made me unhappy and toward what brought me joy, I didn't need to chase the spiritual high in the same way. I didn't need that intensity as spiritual joy was more and more available for me in daily life. I began to integrate my passion for spirituality into my every day experience. Of course, I still wanted the transcendent experience of bliss and joy, but I could hold my centre and feel spiritually connected within, even while I ventured into my psychological pain about belonging, survival and acceptance.

As I worked through my issues, slowly but surely, the spiritual light entered my lower chakras and reprogrammed the quality of consciousness operating through them. Those old issues claimed less space. It took time, persistence, several healing techniques and quality therapy to become more conscious of my childhood patterning and gently but persistently reframe it. The relief this process gave me made all the patience and courage so worthwhile.

During my ongoing healing journey, I have learned that we are much loved by the Universe. We are known intimately and guided continuously. We are meant to be here on Earth. We are meant to be who we are and to be having the exact journey we are having. There is something deeply meaningful each one of us can do with our lives, as team mates of the stars, to help manifest the divine plan of love upon this earth, and that task will look different for every person. Each one of us will fulfil this destiny through our uniqueness and the Universe has unending resources that it is willing to share with us to that end. It is usually our job to clear the pain of the past that prevents us from relaxing, opening, receiving, and trusting ourselves enough to act on our intuitive inner wisdom. The Universe takes care of everything else.

HEALING PROCESS

You can do this exercise seated, however, it is recommended that you stand comfortably—barefoot in nature if possible.

Place your hands at your heart centre. Feel the weight of your body pushing through your feet on the ground. Imagine, sense, feel or intend that there is a connection between your body and the magnetic energy of the earth. This connection creates a bond that is very real on physical, emotional, psychological and energetic levels. It feels good to connect with this magnetic field. It is grounding, drawing out negative energy and circulating positive energy back into all levels of your being.

Bring your awareness to the space just above the top of your head. This space opens out like a fan, a receiving dish, as though the arms of your soul were reaching out above you, inviting pure loving energy. Receive these blessings from the stars fully and openly, with complete trust. If you wish, you can open your arms up to the skies, as though you are reaching up and out to spiritual light and divine love.

Lower your arms comfortably and say aloud:

> *I open to pure divine light, unconditional love and blessings of merciful grace and compassionate wisdom. I ask for the luminous star teacher Canopus to help me in my journey and for the Crystal Angel of Shungite to gently purify and protect all levels of my being. I trust that there is a loving divine journey meant for me. I trust in the clearing process to transform past pain into helpful wisdom. I trust in my ability to tap into the liberating power of forgiveness. I open my trusting heart to the generosity and grace of the Universe that supports me with unlimited resources. May all beings know peace in their hearts. According to the highest wisdom, for the greatest good, so be it.*

Complete your healing process by placing your hands at your heart and bowing your head in reverence. You may like to feel, visualise, imagine or intend that a weight of stress is dissolving right off you, as you become vitalised and renewed by universal energies.

CHAPTER TWO

RECALIBRATION INTO PRIMORDIAL SOUND

STAR GUIDE: VEGA

FOUND IN THE ZODIAC SIGN OF CAPRICORN, Vega unites the spiritual and the physical. It has associations with good fortune and is said to facilitate artistic talent and increase luck, abundance and practicality. In esoteric astrology, Capricorn is the sign of spiritual initiation and manifestation. Vega helps bring our spiritual journey down to earth with joy, creativity and playfulness. It has a knack for helping us heal through creative self-expression and anything to do with music or sound.

Vega is associated with Venus and Mercury. Both planets relate to the higher mind and the ability to channel energies that are inspirational and high-frequency. When Vega is at play in our energy field, it brings a light that shines out as something special. We could say the light of Spirit has switched on within our being. Vega attunes us to higher wisdom, beauty, grace, loving expression and the subtle realms of divine healing.

The energies of Vega can be deeply healing for the ears, nose and throat. It helps cleanse and purify the soul when negativity or cruelty has disturbed us. Vega realigns us with the soothing qualities of divine beauty, which we can lose connection with when we get caught up in the ugliness of ego wounding.

The fifth-brightest star in the night sky, Vega is relatively close, at only 25 light-years from the sun. Over twelve thousand years ago, Vega was the North Star, and in another twelve thousand years or so, it will be so once again. This speaks of its interest in and ability to guide humanity. Vega has a continued presence even when other stars step forward to oversee human evolution. A little like divine vitamins for the human soul, certain frequencies are needed for wellbeing and healing at various times and for different purposes. The stars work in harmony with the great divine healing intelligence. Understanding that Vega has been a primary guiding light for humanity and will be again in due course is enough to increase our wonder and trust in the perfect love and healing intelligence that the Universe expresses.

Vega is in the constellation of Lyra (the lyre or harp) and is positioned at the top of the harp's handle. The harp represents the healing power of music and the spiritual significance of sound. All creation, all healing, emanates from the original divine sound. In Christianity, and in the Vedic scriptures of the East that predate the Western religion by thousands of years, the origin of the Universe receives the same esoteric explanation — all began with a sound.

Vega's association with music, talent, and luck (a general ease around manifestation), hints at its deeper spiritual blessings. It can help us consciously cultivate the healing power of sound or vibration. From the words we speak and the thoughts we focus on, to the circumstances, people and objects in our lives, or the colours we use in our home, we are choosing to cultivate certain vibrations in our lives in every moment.

Entire and distinct realities can be held within a certain frequency of sound. This is the basis of healing with sacred sounds such as in prayers and mantras. In Vajrayana Buddhist and Hindu teachings, there are seed syllables or bija. These are single syllable mantras—like the syllable *Tam* (sounds like TUM) for the goddess Tara—that can be repeated over and over again to evoke the reality of love and wisdom that is the divine feminine, for example. Repetition of the sound evokes the reality. Vega teaches us how to wisely use sound and frequency to alter our reality for the better. Everything in this Universe is singing its note, communicating its reality. To hear it, we need to listen with the deeper awareness of the soul. Just as a dog can hear sounds that humans cannot, the sound is real, but it is beyond the scope of the human ear. When we develop our ability for 'spiritual hearing' we can hear much more of the song of the Universe.

Vega is about taking hold of the handle of the harp — something that must happen before we can play the instrument. This star inspires us to take responsibility for the sounds in our life—for the physical reality we are living in—and to decide for ourselves how we want to play it. Through Vega we realise we have this choice, to create or release what we want, in accord with our inner sense of harmony. When a soul feels a connection with Vega it may be awakening to the power of sound as a healing frequency. These souls may have a talent for working with mantras and other sacred sounds for healing and transformation.

To me, everything in creation is constantly singing and dancing because everything—including your soul and mine—is vibrating with its own sound. Becoming more aligned with your own song or frequency, blossoms from trusting who, what and where feels right for you. Take note of how different notes or frequencies may enhance or disrupt your own. No judgement is needed, but adjustments may be required before you can co-create your path in honour of all you have come to do and be in this lifetime.

Typically, this means going through a process of de-layering and de-conditioning our ego minds, and building our strength and purpose, so we can deflect projections. Thus, when a wounded ego tries to tell us who we are, we can put their view to one side. The journey of self-discovery means being willing to bear the pain and the joy of figuring out who we are for ourselves. Vega is an advocate for this process and wants you to own your true soul vibration, so you can sound it with freedom and purity.

If we don't go through the process of discerning the energies that belong to us from those that belong to others, we can find it difficult to connect with ourselves. This can result in not knowing what you think, feel or what matters to you. It is like trying to sing with a group when the other voices are so loud that they drown out the memory of the notes you were to sing. You can intend to sing your line but end up going along with the overriding melody of the rest of the group! When you can hear the key melody while keeping a powerful sense of your unique harmony, you can sing your truth in connection with others. Vega strengthens your inner connection to your soul sound, so you can recognise and stay connected to your own frequency. You can then share it and listen to others, without losing yourself in the process. A connection with Vega often brings a spiritual message about staying true to yourself. Create or express yourself from your heart, no matter whether you think other people will understand it at the time.

The more unique your soul note, the more it is going to resonate along a different melodic line to what most people are manifesting through their souls, and the more essential the Vega principle is for you. For those souls who have the task of bringing in innovative ideas, higher consciousness and healing energies to correct imbalances and absences in the human collective, the soul note is going to be quite different to what the mainstream soul choir is currently belting out. The ability to consistently recalibrate and adjust our choices and expressions, keeps us attuned to our soul frequency. When we are resonating with our authentic vibration, it feels like everything in and around us is somehow in place. It really does feel like we are in harmony with ourselves and the world around us.

Conversely, when we've lost our connection to our true soul sound, our inner and outer lives feel out of alignment. Something feels off, dissonant. When I have this experience, it feels like the beautiful piece of music I was enjoying is suddenly discordant, with strange jarring notes disrupting my previously serene mood. I need to retune. When you move a piano, it is more likely to get out of tune. And, so it is with the soul. When we are connecting deeply with others, sensitive to energies or adventuring in consciousness, we need to tune up more regularly. Fortunately, Vega is there for us.

Old souls are big souls, so they are naturally vast in mind and open to energetic inflow. They need regular inner adjustments to stay in harmony with themselves. This can be quite simple and become a way of life. We can retune by adjusting a negative thought into a compassionate one; firmly and lovingly stepping back from relationships with energy we do not wish to cultivate; setting a boundary; saying a prayer; meditating; or letting something go.

Vega is a practical and inspirational being. This star teaches us the most joyful ways to recalibrate ourselves, to sense the connection with our soul note, and to balance solitude and connection, openness and inner reflection, so we can remain in tune with our souls.

THE CRYSTAL ANGEL OF PREHNITE WITH EPIDOTE

Prehnite is a pale-green, translucent stone with a soft and loving energy. It has great healing power for the heart. It emanates unconditional love and facilitates a strong and enduring gateway to the higher self and non-earthly beings that resonate with that same quality of unconditional love. Unconditional love is a rebalancing, realigning, reorganising frequency. It allows us to step into authentic expression, cast aside false idols and reprioritise as we evaluate our meaning and purpose. We can work with prehnite to heal belief systems based in distrust or unresolved experiences of betrayal and disappointment. It may also alleviate the compulsive drive to pursue goals that aren't reflective of our true selves but are another's dream for us. Prehnite breaks down our resistance to accepting who we are and reminds us that there is a place in the world meant for us.

Prehnite builds our trust in the abundant, generous Universe, the resourcefulness of our spirit and our ability to attract what we need and let go of what is no longer necessary. In this more open and relaxed state, we can begin to walk a path of increasing grace, connected to our inner purpose and allowing it to guide our outer journey. Bumps and bruises will still happen from time to time, but there will also be an increasing spiritual overshadowing where we feel protected, soothed, cared for and guided to fulfil our divine potential.

Prehnite is a gift for the big-hearted healer as it opens them to experience healing and restoration for themselves. As we learned with Vega, the role of the old soul does not have to be one of sacrifice. They are not here to martyr themselves for the wellbeing of others, but to learn how to cultivate spiritual fulfilment in themselves so they can more skilfully and generously support the soul growth of all beings.

When prehnite has epidote inclusions, it becomes an amplifier of the true soul note. On its own, epidote is an amplifier and is often recommended with caution, because it increases whatever vibration we are putting out to the Universe! Holding it when you are in a bad mood and feeling that everything is against you ... well, that could make life more difficult than it needs to be. However, hold prehnite with epidote when you are willing to come into your heart, and it can feel like you are melting into the most loving and embracing vibration. It is utterly beautiful.

From that place, we understand the reputation of this crystal combo for remedying relationship issues, increasing abundance, bringing clarity and healing, and imbuing us with the courage to let go of past pain and open ourselves to spiritual blessings.

Funnily enough, the first time I encountered this combination crystal was when I was writing this book. It happens of course. I feel like the crystals that want to be included introduce themselves to me — and I was drawn to this one. When I held the stone at my heart, it felt so good and I couldn't put it down! When that happens, I know my body wants the frequency of the stone, so yes, I did purchase it. I'm gazing at it as I write. It is resting on a stack of books on my coffee table. But, let me tell you the rest of the story ... The woman running the crystal stand was staring at me intently. "I see you," she said suddenly. She stared at me for a few more moments and then said, "You have unusual talents." I then realised the stone was amplifying my soul and the woman could see me more easily. That crystal was letting me know that it wanted to be included here for all the reasons mentioned above, and also for empowering those who want to feel safe *and* are ready to be seen at a soul level.

SPIRITUAL GUIDANCE: SENSITIVE SOULS, PEACEFULNESS AND EXPERIENCES OF VIOLENCE

I have always loved nature. As a child, I felt Mother Nature was my refuge and my friend. I trusted and relied on her to love me without judgement. However, I also found the natural instincts of some animals to hunt and kill confronting. Seeing a fly in a spider web would evoke sorrow in my heart, even though I understood the spider was just being a spider. I wondered how Mother Nature could allow this, but it never prevented me from loving her and seeing her as a mother.

I never stopped being deeply moved by the suffering of others. When I hear a tree coming down or see an animal in distress, sorrow can rise in me suddenly. Fortunately, in her infinite generosity and compassion, the Divine Mother taught me a couple of things, so I didn't collapse into a constantly broken-hearted puddle of sadness and despair!

Firstly, I learned I could grow my compassion so that it was greater than the suffering I was witnessing. It sometimes felt like my heart was stretching, but eventually I could hold the suffering and be present and compassionate without becoming emotionally distressed. The experience was one of gentleness and kindness rather than anguish or anxiety. If there were times when I couldn't quite get there, I took comfort in knowing I would be able to handle things more skilfully as I evolved.

Secondly, I learned about dependent arising, a Buddhist teaching where the existence of one thing is based on the existence of the other. In a leaf, there is sunshine, rain and earth. In the prey, there is the hunter, and in the hunter, there is the prey. Where there is life, there is death. Where there is suffering, there is comfort. These things cannot be separated from each other. They belong to each other and are one with each other. I began to recognise the deeper spiritual reality and order beyond the appearance of things. It was sometimes hard to accept this, but in the quieter moments of contemplation, it helped me trust that behind the things my mind struggled to accept, there was a divine creativity and loving wisdom at play, always.

The need to comfort my inner child drove me to learn and grow spiritually. I learned that I needed compassion for the hunted, but also for the hunter. A shark must be a shark, that is the nature of its being and it plays a role in balancing the ecosystem of the ocean. It is part of the ocean, part of nature, part of life. My inner child may have taken temporary delight in the fantastical notion that sharks could be transformed into daisies, but the long-term repercussions of that quirky substitution would be an imbalance in nature. My sadness would no doubt return at the resultant destruction. Genius can be hiding behind the things we don't understand. Through compassion I learned to trust in that, and to be kind to my childlike heart, even when it was difficult to do so.

Vietnamese monk, Zen master and peace activist, Thich Nhat Hanh, teaches that extending compassion to other beings and not including yourself is not true compassion. I agree with this teaching completely. You, like me, may need to practise extending compassion to include the pure child's heart within that wishes suffering was not necessary for any being. To be honest, I still feel that way, but I take that childlike desire and use my talents to do something constructive with it. I offer what I can through creativity, commitment and consciousness, to help those who are suffering to heal and grow wise through the process. If I didn't feel deep sorrow in my heart in face of suffering, would I be as motivated to do something about it? I think about the time, energy and discipline that I pour into what I do. Without a profound inner motivation and sense of care, I have no doubt all that energy would be directed elsewhere. Given the blessings this work has brought me and many others, how could I begrudge the pain that gives it life? Is this part of the Divine Mother's genius? We cannot understand divine mysteries—they are mysteries—but we can occasionally glimpse the truth that somehow the Universe is taking care of all beings.

For every brave soul seeking to consciously feel and perceive subtle energies of Spirit or healing, there are those that already feel a lot, and struggle with it. I encourage you not to be put off by the challenges of increased sensitivity. It has been my experience that the blessings far outweigh the trials that increased sensitivity can bring into our lives. Sensitivity is the key to sensing subtle worlds. There is breathtaking beauty to behold and ways to be moved and inspired that less sensitive and aware souls may miss out on altogether.

With any inner work—be it dream work, dance, psychotherapy, meditation, hypnotherapy and so on—much of the healing happens beneath the surface of everyday awareness. Often, it is only our highly developed sensitivity that registers *something* is happening, and we are rarely sure of the details. Inner work can be so deep and subtle that our conscious minds wonder if it is foolish to continue the process or question whether our sensitive awareness is nothing more than ego trickery and wishful thinking.

I have had such crisis-of-faith moments. There was a prolonged period when I felt as though all the forms I had built up over several years—social, financial, professional and personal—had suddenly washed away and I was left with a great spaciousness and emptiness in my life. At the time, the only thing that felt productive and constructive was journaling about my dreams.

I tried to 'fix' the situation in my life by acting in ways I felt were practical and down-to-earth, but nothing seemed to work. I had enough life experience to be able to recognise my reactionary desire to step up and get things moving even when it was time to allow the delays and pauses to work their healing magic in my life. So, rather than panicking about not being able to find my way out of circumstances beyond my control, I decided to embrace the wisdom I had relied upon previously — do what you can, and hand what you cannot do over to the Universe.

I embraced the inner healing process and discovered that I loved working with dreams. I learned about the extraordinary, strange and incisive language of the unconscious and how it was always moving us toward wholeness, fulfilment and healing. Even with my understanding of its value, the process was not easy. My nightly dreams led me into my deepest fears, pain and wounds, but in that confrontation there was a possibility for my soul to break through, and for me to learn how to operate in a less head-driven, more heart-guided way. That is what eventually happened, but it took a lot to get me to that place.

During that inner processing, I felt like I was in a holding pattern. If I wanted to push forwards and make things happen, I would fail spectacularly. Either nothing would come of it or more problems were created! It was like trying to fly with no air beneath my wings. My actions were out of harmony with the phase I was in. Nonetheless, the practical side of me struggled with just how much I was being asked to trust. I felt like my life was going nowhere. I was already a big believer in the power of inner work, but as months turned into years, I felt deeply challenged.

Every time I neglected to trust myself and the process I was in, a war rose within me. My sensitivity registered something was happening, but I had never been in such an intense and long-lasting phase of inner work before. After nine or so years, it finally shifted, and I felt a type of rebirth and aliveness that had been eluding me. I often joke that it took me so long because I was stubborn and fought the process, and perhaps that is true, but I also believe there is a greater good in all things, even the delays. Most people will not need such a prolonged initiation experience, but I wanted to share this, so you know that trusting your subtle perceptions is not always easy. This is especially true when there is no firm evidence to support what we feel is happening at a deeper level.

Whether seeing a therapist, a healer or both, doing meditations and healing processes such as those of this book, or otherwise working on growth and evolution, when we stick with the process, our sensitivity will increase. Eventually we will move through whatever healing process our soul knows it needs. The reason for the healing journey may make sense to us later.

Going through such a journey can be much more difficult for those who don't have the sensitivity to feel, let alone trust, that there is something real and meaningful happening beneath the surface. To be honest, I doubt they would be able to go through it at all. It would seem like an utter insanity to avoid at any cost. They may need a crisis, such as an illness or other divine disruption, to force them inwards for soul healing. Even then, they may resist. Sensitivity is a passport into the realm of soul. We need it to navigate beyond the physical world. It allows us to find our way when our logical self is out of its depth.

But what about those who feel their sensitivity is overwhelming or too much to handle? Some feel so crammed with psychic noise from their minds, from others and from the world, that sensing their soul's subtle inner process is like listening for a soft bell at a rock concert or seeking the proverbial needle in a haystack. Yet there is hope for such souls! I know because I am one of them.

I tend to learn through a psychic osmosis. When I spend time studying with someone, I absorb what they are teaching in terms of content, as well as their ways of thinking and being. This learning then needs to be filtered, integrated or cast aside, according to how it resonates with me. Sometimes this can be wonderful. When I studied with an astrology teacher for a time, some of my fellow students, who attended the same classes and read the same books, wondered how I was able to progress so rapidly. I knew it was because of this osmosis process.

Sensitives tend to have an ability for psychic, emotional and psychological synthesis. Most people can learn this way, to some degree or other, as we internalise the teacher and how they might respond in certain circumstances occurs to us as internal guidance, long after we may cease to be their students. Here, the student is distilling the essence of the teacher, finding what is true for them, and expressing it in their own way.

However, psychic absorption can also be painful and challenging. I often struggled with sensitivity and how much I was affected—often for the worse—by the people around me. They were not bad people, but they did have a different consciousness to mine. Rather than being uplifted by the joy of those around me, I often felt dragged into fear and depression. It could feel like being in an ocean of negative consciousness over which I had little control. Much of it didn't feel like it belonged to me, but I felt powerless to get myself out of it and stop it continuing. Any sensitive who has walked into a shopping centre and suddenly had to get out to avoid being emotionally overwhelmed, will know exactly what I am talking about.

Over the years, I learned how to own my power around this sort of unconscious psychic absorption. I learned to rest in my own being and claim my right to protect my internal space. I learned to allow for others' free will to choose consciousness be it fearful, loving or whatever else they wished. I could have compassion for people without feeling obligated to take any responsibility for how they felt. I could make an offering of higher consciousness without assuming a burden for another person's choice.

It was a difficult adjustment for me to make. I had to unlearn some of the habits and beliefs that I had adopted during childhood about being responsible for the quality of other people's lives. I had to confront my internalised judgements about being selfish or ungrateful if I took care of my own needs for peace and happiness instead of putting the emotional needs of others ahead of my own. I had to learn how to respect myself and that what I need and how I live does matter. I had to learn how to give to myself.

This had nothing to do with becoming less sensitive or 'toughening up' as conventional 'wisdom' would often have it. I didn't reduce my sensitivity or caring, I just learned to express it in a healthier way that included myself. I learned to love myself enough to value my happiness and wellbeing and to make choices accordingly. That gave me enough space in my aura, my mind and my psychic channels, so that I could witness the subtle happenings around me, without constantly feeling overtaken by energies that were not my own.

One of the teachings Spirit gave me about having a highly receptive nature is that it could torment or enrapture me, depending on what I allowed to flow into my field of consciousness. So, when I turned my face to the Divine to allow the receiving dish of my being to absorb higher energies, the results were profoundly healing, soothing and remarkably fast acting. Issues could be worked through swiftly and gently, even when intense emotion was arising. If I turned my face to absorb the darker light of negativity, fear, pain or despair, I came down like a proverbial ton of bricks! The sword of sensitivity can cut both ways. So, choosing how I saw a situation and what I focused upon really helped my sensitivity become the tremendous spiritual asset that it was meant to be.

If you are already a sensitive, working with the star energies can help you apply the spiritual teaching that was given to me. Through this book, you can turn your face to the light that nourishes and soothes you. It doesn't mean ignoring the struggles. It does mean learning to give to yourself so that you can respond to challenges from a more peaceful and fulfilled place. You'll have so much more energy, creativity and determination to draw upon if you take this approach. You'll also feel happier and more at peace overall.

The work with the stars will also support you if you are learning how to be more sensitive and aware, perhaps because you want to feel and work with divine beings or healing energy more consciously. I encourage you in that quest but ask you to remember that Spirit will work through a willing heart whether you are aware of it or not. It's so lovely to consciously sense the movement of spiritual grace, like watching the greatest healing artist at work, so I also encourage your desire to grow your sensitivity. Trust that through inner work, such as the healing processes or mindfulness practice like yoga and meditation, it *will* increase over time.

Star energies resonate at high frequencies and hold a powerful and pure spiritual sound. Like a vibration that makes iron fillings move, they can shift the content of our bodies, minds and souls. Stars can help us cut through lower consciousness and become stronger even as we become increasingly sensitive.

I studied for a time with a Chi Gung teacher who was an exceptionally powerful man with many extraordinary skills — some of which could be used to end life or to support it, depending on intention. Fortunately, by the time I met him, he was using them strictly for healing purposes! If needed, he could radiate such intense joy that if someone was intending to attack him, by the time they got close enough to do him any harm, he could manipulate their energy so that they became filled with joy and would double over with fits of gleeful laughter.

From his martial arts background, he developed a very macho appearance and a lot of physical power. From his unfolding spiritual journey, he chose to channel his abilities into helping others in the best ways that he could. With all that energetic power and ability to consciously control it in very particular ways, you may be surprised to know that his sensitivity was extreme. If he wasn't careful, he could be physically burned by negative energy that was directed toward him. Sometimes he would have so much psychic information coming in to his head from people's thoughts around him—even several blocks away from his home—that he would struggle to block it out.

Now this is an unusual situation, and this man works with extreme abilities and enjoys pushing the limits of what the body is capable of in terms of working with energy. That is his path and it won't be relevant for many people. What *is* relevant here is that our sensitivity is not a sign of weakness. It is not something to feel ashamed of or to feel badly about. It is just something that we need to work with by learning how to manage our feelings and set boundaries.

Sometimes feelings and boundary setting seem much harder for sensitive spiritual types who feel much more than most people. In such cases, I find it helpful to remember that if a lot is being asked of us, it is because we have great ability, although we may not realise it. I find that the Universe (unlike some people!) has very realistic expectations of us. It doesn't ask us for more than is possible for our souls. So, when a situation makes us quake in our boots, it is our expectations of our abilities and potential that need to change, not what life has placed in our path. I also believe that when a lot is asked of us—such as dealing with painful childhood issues—then even more will be given to us in return. When our path is challenging, we are not doing something wrong, but are learning a lot — and there may be more homework to do if we are to master our studies.

The Universe is very generous. We need to go through challenges, but the Universe provides us with everything we need to triumph, and the rewards are ample. For every issue I have dared to face, I have been given joy, knowledge, energy and greater power to create and hold my centre. This helps me do my work so that others can find their way. This brings me such a deep sense of soul healing, satisfaction and peace.

So, I don't mind when I cannot get away with things that others can or when I must hold a higher standard of discipline or personal integrity and self-care than what some consider necessary. That's okay. I've got my flaws and issues to deal with, but I know I get plenty of help with this because the Universe loves me. I can help others more effectively as I heal myself. I also have more freedom and joy in my life than many people experience, so there are obvious blessings that come from doing this work. It's not only challenge. A lot of the time it's grace.

This is not just about me. This is about you. It is about everyone who is far enough along on the spiritual path to want to help others in some way. It might be as a healer or it might be that you would like to be a source of positive energy and light in this world. It might be that you want to experience Spirit more tangibly. These are healing impulses within the soul and the fulfilment of them benefits all beings — sometimes directly, sometimes indirectly, but the benefit is absolutely real and important.

This process of accepting my sensitive nature and life in all its darkness and light, culminated in me getting my first tattoo. I was celebrating my 40th birthday with some friends in Byron Bay, and planned to mark the occasion by getting a tattoo when I was there. I had wanted a tattoo since I was sixteen but had never been able to settle on a design I felt would remain meaningful to me for my entire life. When I eventually found the design—a beautiful Tibetan script that says, "precious human existence"—I burst into tears. It resonated as so completely courageous and beautiful and loving that I knew it was the right tattoo for me. I wanted it on the back of my neck, a place I feel is inherently vulnerable and yet also filled with dignity and nobility.

The friend who came with me brought along her huge crystal singing bowl (as one does). As we entered the tattoo shop, we were greeted by blaring heavy metal music and friendly tattooed men who were curious and keen for us to have the bowl playing during my tattooing. When it was time, I settled in my chair. On my right, a man getting his leg tattooed was beating his fingers to the heavy metal music. To my left, my friend was playing the pure-white crystal singing bowl. I surrendered into the pain of the tattooing process and drifted into a meditative state.

Toward the end of the tattooing process, I had a powerful feeling Archangel Michael was standing behind me, with the forces of night or darkness pouring in on one side of my soul and the forces of day or light on the other. This was neither good nor bad, they were just the basic energies of life itself. I felt completely committed to being in this human body and meeting whatever was meant for me to experience with dignity, trust and courage.

As the tattoo artist completed the design, I brought myself back from meditation into the moment, and looked up to find that the shop had become filled with very curious passers-by. I don't know if you are familiar with Byron Bay's reputation, but to do something weirdly alternative enough to capture attention in the land of hippies and fringe festivals is really quite something! The tattoo artist and his team said they had not experienced anything quite like that before. It was new for me too, on a number of levels. I had made peace with being human in a deeper way than ever before. As we left the store my friend said that she had seen and felt Archangel Michael standing behind me. I then told her about my experience, which was about so much more than a tattoo. It was about accepting being a wild star child in a human body, committed to whatever it was the Universe had in store for me this lifetime. May all beings find peace on their path, as they fulfil their spiritual destiny.

HEALING PROCESS

Place your hands on the crystal mandala for Vega and prehnite and epidote. Allow the energy of the mandala to flow into your palms, along your arms, into the heart, and gently out through the back of your heart in a soft, loving flow of energy. Close your eyes and rest in this process for as long as you wish. It can feel like your heart is gently being washed in healing green light.

When you are ready, say the following aloud:

> *I call upon the unconditionally loving star teacher Vega, and the Crystal Angel of Prehnite and Epidote. I give thanks for the healing love of the Universe that touches, opens and gently cleanses my heart of fear, confusion and deception. I gratefully receive the protection, healing and blessings that will mercifully and compassionately recalibrate me into authenticity. I choose to love and express my true soul sound in my life, according to the highest wisdom, for the greatest good. So be it.*

You may choose to play at making some sounds — singing, toning, or just speaking aloud to the Universe, from your heart. Allow yourself to express some truths, maybe some you have not even acknowledged for yourself prior to this moment. Let your truth just be. In its expression you give it the chance to heal and to manifest in a new and improved way.

To complete your healing process, simply rest for as long as you wish, as though you are bathing in the truthful frequencies you have been exploring.

CHAPTER THREE

TRUSTING YOUR SOUL PASSIONS AND HIGHER PURPOSE

STAR GUIDE: ALDEBARAN

ALDEBARAN HAS A REDDISH GLOW, is extremely bright and is incredibly large. It is the fiery eye of the cosmic bull in the constellation of Taurus. Taurus is a powerful sign of endurance, practicality and, as it is ruled by Venus, it also heralds the ability to create true beauty in this world as children, ideas, businesses, artworks or through a flair for fashion. In esoteric astrology, the eye of the cosmic bull is said to be the eye of the Buddha or the clear-seeing divine eye. Sometimes referred to as the Eye of Revelation or the Eye of God, Aldebaran relates to our inner or third eye and the possibility of pure vision and insight beyond the appearance of things.

When the soul connects with Aldebaran it has some significance around vision. It could be confirmation of a clairvoyant awakening or be directing one to pay close attention to a vision or dream. It could also be a message that looking deeper beneath the surface of things, in a more compassionate and detached way, will bring clarity. When we get caught up in our judgement of situations, other people or ourselves, we are not seeing clearly. Aldebaran helps us see with our third eye or inner spiritual vision, so we don't become confused or afraid of what our ego-mind may be seeing. When your perception of a situation is making you feel victimised, afraid, confused or doubtful of your value in any way, then you are not seeing with your inner eye. Aldebaran can help you be free of that painful and limited perspective, and more open to a higher, more helpful and empowering view.

Throughout the ages, Aldebaran has been associated with holding a higher vision. This can include the inner vision of our unique soul blueprint. For those that feel they are here to offer a meaningful contribution, that there is a mission they are here to complete or a destiny they are meant to fulfil, Aldebaran can help bring clarity and detail to that vision.

The energy of Taurus can transform our desires and passions so that instead of serving a need for immediate ego gratification, they become fuel for our soul fire. An example of this could be a soul that develops a passionate obsession with someone and wants a relationship, but the person is not emotionally available to them because of addiction, involvement in another relationship or otherwise. Aldebaran would help evolve that desire from being painful to the ego into something more constructive and fulfilling.

In the example of romantic obsession or unrequited love, the soul in question may realise that what they are truly looking for is a great and powerful experience of love. They could then explore ways of bringing love into their life that are beyond their obsession with an unavailable person. They might become attracted to prayer or meditation, change their line of work so it resonates with their heart, or actively seek ways to give love more generously and freely to others, without thinking of what they could gain in return. They could start to live as a love-struck soul in a broader way by opening their heart to love and not allowing their mind to limit how that love should manifest in their life. From that open and loving place, they become the great and powerful love that they were seeking and through doing so, experience something even more fulfilling and healing than what they would have had if their ego got what it wanted earlier on. Aldebaran helps us sense our potential and realise it in the world, taking the small, self-serving and unimaginative vision of ego, and opening it up to the more expansive and fulfilling creative expression of the soul.

The higher soul vision that Aldebaran evokes is so helpful for all forms of leadership on this planet, from governments and business groups, to activists, spiritual leaders and other free thinkers who are helping move humanity forward. The Taurean energy is very earth-oriented, and so the vision that comes through Aldebaran includes practical steps for fulfilling our divine life purpose. It bestows the vision, and the way to best manifest it. Transmissions from this star teacher help us understand that where there's a divine will, there's always a way.

As one of the four Royal Stars honoured by the ancient Persians, Aldebaran is the *Watcher of the East* and was relied upon for navigation. It has a history of helping human beings find their way. Numerous civilisations have associated the star with fertility and new life. Some five thousand years ago, the rising of Aldebaran marked the vernal equinox and the beginning of the Babylonian year. In some ceremonial magick practices, east is the direction of beginnings and corresponds with opening sacred space and gateways into other worlds. When we connect with this star, it is a sign something new is on the horizon, that a doorway is opening, and a new soul chapter is beginning. Just like the rising sun in the east, it is a sign of new life and a new light that will chase away the darkness of night in our lives. This can bring great hope for those going through a lengthy period of challenge, anguish, confusion or frustration about their life path and higher purpose. Aldebaran brings blessings of guidance and protection for all aspects of our authentic life path.

If this luminous, massive and ancient star teacher was situated in our solar system, it would take up so much space, and emit so much light, that life on Earth would not be possible. This helps us realise the need to balance our passion for the light with care for the physical needs of our bodies. Like sunlight and vitamins, the right amount of spiritual focus will promote health in the body. Too little or too much can become harmful rather than healing. The nervous system will let us know when spiritual energy is flowing in enough potency to help us grow. When there is enough, we will feel enlivened, more peaceful, trusting and non-judgemental. If there is too little, we will feel as though inspiration, trust, serenity and a clear sense of higher purpose are missing in our lives. If there is too much, we can feel overwrought, overstimulated and overemotional. I talk about this in more detail elsewhere in this book because it's a topic not often discussed or understood. For now, it is enough to recognise that when the soul is connecting with this potent star teacher, it has access to powerful spiritual energies and will need to learn how to channel those energies in a balanced way. Some days opening to spiritual grace will feel effortless. On other days, we need time and space to ground ourselves in practical, day-to-day matters, switch off and let things settle.

Aldebaran reminds us that there are always more blessings, grace, spiritual light, wisdom, resources and answers available to us than we can use in an any given moment. It is okay to pace ourselves. There is no need to try to figure everything out at once. When we respect our physical, mental, emotional and spiritual limits, there is no need to become frustrated when it is time to pause, to ground and discharge everything that we've been taking in.

Aldebaran is one of the archangel stars known to be ensouled by various divine beings whom we may recognise by other names. The archangel associated with Aldebaran is the loving, wise and powerful Archangel Michael. When you feel a soul connection to Aldebaran, you can be sure Archangel Michael is close, offering guidance, protection and help to recognise the loving workings of divine will in your life.

THE CRYSTAL ANGEL OF PETALITE

Petalite is partially opaque, usually soft white in colour and tabular in formation. This stone exudes a pure healing vibration that combines gentleness, voluptuous feminine energy and pure angelic frequencies. I find 'resting' with the crystal best allows it to share its qualities with us as it does so in waves, like an unfolding of petals or an unveiling of layers. Slowing down and becoming receptive is often the best way to experience feminine energy.

Petalite helps us let go of our temporary identities and connect to the enduring universal light within. I find it to be strengthening, protective and calming for the heart. When you feel depleted or heart weary, because of personal challenge or caring for others through their difficult times, petalite can be a soothing and comforting friend. It can help us more deeply connect with a pure source of loving wisdom, so we can find our way through times of spiritual testing. Petalite is a stone for initiates as it helps us grow compassion and higher understanding through even the darkest night of the soul. If you want to learn more about initiates and how you may be one, a book in this series called *Crystal Masters 333* may be of interest to you.

I have only ever found small pieces of petalite. From a holographic perspective and a crystal angel perspective, size doesn't matter. Even the smallest specimen would be enough for a powerful experience of its raw but soft energy. However, I understand the mind can enjoy the beauty of larger pieces.

In the auric field, petalite works beneath our conscious awareness for healing on a cellular level, of ancestral soul lineages in this and other lifetimes. When we understand where we come from and process any forgiveness that needs to take place, we are free to access the benefits and blessings of our ancestral legacies. Unresolved pain from past generations often has more influence in our lives than we realise. Petalite gently brings that to consciousness so it can be cleared with compassion. Without the karmic wounds of our ancestors we have more freedom to be ourselves.

We may not be able to do the work for another person on a spiritual level, for each being has its own divine destiny to live with dignity and courage, but we can certainly help break the cycle of pain from continuing in our lives and in the lives of our descendants. With petalite, we can deal with our karmic inheritance in a more empowered way. Instead of feeling like we are carrying the pain of our ancestors as an extra weight upon our shoulders, petalite helps us clean up our legacy at the spiritual level, simultaneously growing in wisdom and clearing the path for future generations to be able to manifest their divine destiny.

Petalite functions well in the human realm and in other spiritual worlds, too. It has a multidimensional reach that makes it so useful for those of us who really do feel as though we are part human and part earth angel, goddess, mermaid, star child, dragon or faery spirit! Petalite helps soften any sense of fragmentation, using the frequency of unconditional love to gently weave our various aspects into a coherent whole. In this sense it is a cosmic tantric stone, capable of uniting realities or qualities that may appear dissonant. As a stone of loving integration, petalite can help those suffering from post-traumatic stress, recovering from abuse or feeling like they are being pulled in too many directions at once. It is a powerful stone for healers who work with soul retrieval processes as it helps bring all parts of us back into connection with the heart.

Petalite can help us translate spiritual experience into practical guidance through the same unity consciousness that Aldebaran promotes. Connect with petalite to blend inspiration and real-life action for healing change in our lives and the world. Both petalite and Aldebaran help us realise that the spiritual worlds and the material world are not actually separate. They are meant to be experienced together, as one. We can know this intellectually while still holding the painful belief that Spirit is unwilling or unable to help us in our physical lives. Petalite reminds us that Spirit is very much with us in the here and now. This can bring emotional reassurance and comfort to the human heart that can sometimes feel trapped in frightening imaginings of loneliness, helplessness or worthlessness.

Petalite is a therapeutic support for those with the courage to be present in the darker realms of experience, and a desire to bring the loving light and wisdom of Spirit into that darkness for healing. It is recommended for those working with addictions and any form of emotional or psychological traumas in themselves or others. Working with this stone is particularly helpful for calling on a high and unconditionally loving source of spiritual guidance to assist in any healing process.

SPIRITUAL GUIDANCE: WHEN YOUR INNER WOLF WANTS TO HIJACK YOUR SPIRITUAL PRACTICE

In Buddhist psychology there is a personality type referred to as the Padma or lotus type. We all have traits of the Padma personality within us, though in varying degrees of intensity and development. Driven by love, connection and affection, Padma personalities experience deep feelings of desire and yearning. This passionate yearning can drive the motivation to create, share and give in ways that heal and inspire others. In its purest form, the Padma personality is the Bodhisattva or Star Child. They are the ones with a spiritual longing to help others find freedom, love and peace, even if doing so creates personal challenges to work through.

When the Padma part of us is wounded, it cannot support our spiritual fulfilment or help us create happiness, even though that is still its ultimate function. We may feel this wounding as a yearning that doesn't translate into motivation and inspiration but is a repetitive cycle of pain. It can cut deeply into the soul to create a hunger that cannot be satisfied, and so we feel as though our deeper self is starving. In such cases, the part of us that wants to create and share and connect can become more like a hungry wolf — always devouring, consuming, demanding and needing more. What could be constructive and radiant can become destructive and dark.

How does Padma nature become so wounded? When we have unresolved abandonment or neglect, whether emotional, psychological and/or physical, we tend to develop beliefs to help us make sense of that experience. Those beliefs are founded on experiences of lack, deprivation and absence. An intense inner hunger arises as part of that belief system. The more severe the neglect and abandonment experience was for the soul, the more intense the hunger that arises as an expression of that inner pain. Those most likely to crave for more are those expecting imminent starvation.

This craving underlies any form of excessive consumption, obsession or addiction that involves taking something in, in an attempt to feed the inner hunger. Amassing personal possessions such as money, technological toys, various collectables or even toilet paper (I once met a lovely woman who would not feel at peace unless she had an entire floor-to-ceiling cupboard in her apartment crammed to the brim with toilet rolls) is a symptom of Padma wounding. In relationships, this wound can show up as a neediness that feels overwhelming and is impossible for another person to satisfy, no matter how much they love you.

When inner hunger becomes compulsion, there will be emotional and psychological meaning unconsciously attached to the subject of desire. Food, alcohol, books, odd little collectables like salt and pepper shakers, or a massive collection of shoes, could be stand-ins for security, safety, feeling valuable or knowing you are worthy of time and attention. We may not be conscious of the ascribed meaning of the object, but it will somehow relate to the original wounding. It is part of an attempt to resolve it.

For example, new shoes can be more than shoes. They can also be proof that you are special and worthy of attention. Feeling good about your new shoes is not a sign of a deep soul disturbance. It is a matter of degree. If going without the shoes would send you into a spiral of pain and trigger other avoidance behaviours (or secondary addictions), you may need to address a deeper issue, so you can feel peace and happiness irrespective of your shoe collection. If shoes are dominating your living space (and I've worked with people who physically struggled to move from one room to the next due to the stockpiles of hoarded objects) then you know the wounded Padma aspect of your being is crying out for help.

The problem is, no matter how much of an emotional reaction you may have to them at first, shoes are shoes and cannot satisfy your deeper needs. They cannot do the job you need them to do. As the saying goes, "Painted cakes cannot satisfy hunger." In the same way your body needs physical nutrition rather than painted cakes, the Padma soul needs to experience unconditional love, not substitutes in various forms.

We can understand this intellectually but until we get to the deeper cause and resolve the pain, the voracious desire to quell the hunger will not go away. We cannot simply decide to stop yearning for the love-substitute. The desire for a fantasy relationship with an emotionally unavailable person, every brand-new gadget on the market or a stash of fabulous new stilettos will remain. It is not a question of willpower, weakness, a lack of awareness, or any other judgemental interpretation. It is an issue of trying to heal the pain by attacking the symptoms. We need to go to the cause.

Hunger may seem to be a symptom of wounding, but the passionate hunger of Padma can do great good in the world. For this magnetic and creative aspect of us to grow into spiritual passion we must figure out *what we are truly hungry for*. Only then can we contemplate how to feed that hunger in a genuinely nourishing way. The distorted Padma quality doesn't know what it is really hungry for because when the original hunger arose (for love, acceptance, physical affection, safety, protection, peace, or more often than not, permission to be, and be unconditionally loved for being, one's self) and was not met, those completely appropriate human needs were driven deep into the unconscious.

To heal the Padma part of us, the part that holds the energy for passionate purpose, we must first figure out what our true needs are and how to meet them. I have met many beautiful souls who want to realise their purpose and yearn for a sense of mission, but do not know what they are supposed to be doing with their lives. They want to know what career or job they should be doing, as they want to know how to be happy. They think that if they just do this or that, then happiness will come, but until they know and accept who they are, they will not experience genuine fulfilment.

The authentic self tells us who we are and what we are meant to do in the same way a bird needs to fly, a fish to swim, a flower to bloom, a writer to write, a dancer to dance and so on. There is an innate relationship between authentic being and authentic living, which includes every facet of life from health and finances to work and relationships, and of course, our inner sense of meaning and purpose.

That authentic self is always inside us, beautiful, unique and vital, but it can become so coated in unresolved pain that the conscious mind cannot access it and when we reach for that inner guide, we hit walls of hurt instead. It can be hard to keep turning within if you keep meeting depression, anxiety, anger, fear, doubt, guilt or shame rather than clarity and direction! However, with some wisdom and some help (which the Universe always provides by presenting opportunity after opportunity for healing) we may realise there is something beneath those painful layers that is real and enduring.

When the soul has enough 'grip' on the personality, steps will be taken toward healing the pain. We will suddenly find ourselves making progress on our path. We will somehow be more receptive, willing and ready for life. We might feel drawn to dream work, journaling, dancing, meditation, yoga, chanting, crystals, colour therapy, singing, sound healing, psychotherapy, inner-child work, aromatherapy, flower essences, massage or other body work. These are all beautiful supportive practices for strengthening the connection of body, mind and soul. Eventually, a sense of true self will emerge from whatever healing journey was initiated by the soul. This often includes the discovery and development of various talents. It also comes with an understanding of the ways of being that suit that unique self which can be quite different to the ways of living mandated by mainstream society.

As the old ways of shame and judgement begin to crack and break away from the authentic self, and the legitimate need for love, recognition, time, attention, nourishment, affection, freedom and respect are honoured, a deep rebirth takes place. Outward life begins to align with inner truth. It can feel like a completely different life, experienced as a completely different person, and yet, one is more genuinely and fully 'yourself' than you were before. Through this process, there comes an understanding that *you are the path*. By being our true selves, the path opens for us. It is not something external that we can find and just do, but something that manifests organically as we become willing to uncover, reclaim and be our true selves.

At this point, our hunger is no longer caught up in that which cannot feed our souls. We can begin to trust it to guide us to what can really sustain and nourish us. Our passion will drive us toward meaningful purpose and we feel capable of living our inspiration. We go after what we want without fear. We attract what we need more easily. Instead of worrying that we may take bold steps forward only to have the rug pulled out from underneath us, we feel supported from within and by the Universe. This gives us serenity and the confidence that we will be able to make progress, even if the challenges before us seem great. We trust our hunger and we trust we will be fed.

When I met my first in-the-flesh spiritual teacher this lifetime, I fell head over heels in love — with her lifestyle! I was doing a double degree at university, studying subjects which failed to inspire me. I had done part-time work in corporate legal positions and felt utterly depressed at the prospect of continuing in the same vein. When I met this teacher and took her meditation and psychic development classes, I felt relief and excitement. Her line of work—and her non-corporate, non-office, non-power suited, bohemian, creative, time-in-nature lifestyle—awakened fantasies and an inner resonance that was new to me. For the first time as a young adult, I had a model for the way I wanted to live my life. I realised my passionate fascination with all things New Age, spiritual and metaphysical could be seeding my vocation and life purpose. I felt so much joy at this prospect.

For the next two years, taking those classes became an obsessive pursuit for me. I felt like they were a way out of a life I found bleak and deeply unsatisfying. They were a doorway into a life that sparkled with soul and the promise of inner fulfilment, along with sunlight and wellbeing, rather than artificial lighting and depression! It was a beautiful beginning.

Then one day, after bingeing on more classes and workshops, I realised having too much of a good thing could become a problem. My mind was desperately clinging to the inspirational fantasies I had found because I was still so uncertain about whether my life could really change. If I wanted to change my life, rather than just dreaming of it being different, I needed to let go. And, I had trouble doing so.

Rather than constantly cooking up plans or always needing to know why, when, who, how or what, I eventually learned that change needed space, surrender, trust and patience. Before a new lifestyle could begin to unfold for me, I needed to embrace uncertainty and let things happen. I paid attention to any fear that Spirit wouldn't support me if I gave up trying to make things happen, and instead learned to trust life to bring results. I took a leap of faith and learned a new way to be which involved dropping my support systems and trusting the Universe. Of course, for me to do that, I needed to deal with the issues from earlier in my life that had made it so difficult to trust that my needs would be met.

Going into the pain of childhood to unravel the negative effects it was having in my life was not easy. I suspect it's not easy for anyone — one reason why so few people who could benefit from such deep inner work actually do it. The relief and healing change this brought me made the struggles so worthwhile. It allowed me to slowly release layers of anxiety and distrust and make choices from a place of trust. The Universe could begin to make its move, when I finally let go, created space, was prepared to be patient and allowed myself to be guided.

Unexpectedly, I began to enjoy the experience of trusting and allowing life to unfold. No longer quite so overly self-reliant and hyper-independent, I enjoyed having the Universe as a trusted friend who was helping me find my way. When I felt overwhelmed, overburdened or overcommitted, I calmed myself by emptying my mind of plans and questions, and focused on the moment. I learned to enjoy more spaciousness within myself and my life. I understood that when we create space, we are inviting the Universe to bring something new into that space. This is what I wanted to happen, but I had to get used to a different way of living, and not fill every space with thoughts, plans or ideas. For me that was quite a challenge.

I realised I needed to give ideas and new directions time to reveal their value and purpose, so I could choose what resonated most with me. This became much easier as more and more opportunities rolled in. It might seem to be the opposite, but once I realised I could have so many things, I also realised I needed to stop and figure out what I was hungry for at a soul level. Trusting the Universe would provide meant I didn't feel the need to gobble up anything and everything that came along in case it was all that was ever showing up for me. It was a mental shift from lack to abundance.

The space that we take for ourselves is where the raw ingredients in our soul stew get a chance to simmer. We put the lid on the pot and stop adding more things. The ingredients can meld together, and the flavours mature and become delicious. The stuff of transformation occurs in the space where our minds usually tell us nothing is happening, and we start to worry instead of trusting the process and sitting with what is happening. Typically, this is when we want to rush out to fill the space with plans from a reactive, distrustful, controlling place. It's like taking the lid off the pot and making the cooking process take longer or adding more ingredients before their time and throwing off the delicacy and balance of the meal.

I remember a sensitive and responsive student's experience with a spiritual healing template from my online healer training. It had a powerful effect that uplifted and inspired her into an entirely new viewpoint. Spiritually speaking, it really rocked her world. Instead of allowing that ecstatic experience to settle into her being and help her change her behaviour and lifestyle choices over the weeks or months ahead, she craved a repeat of the spiritual high. She did several extra templates again and again in quick succession.

What do you think happened? The influx of taking in so much energy, too soon, wore her out and triggered an emotional rollercoaster for her. Like trying to watch four movies and eat four meals all at once, it was too much to assimilate. Secondly, she lost the gift of the first template because she didn't give it time to solidify from the spiritual realm into her life. She filled the space instead of holding it gently and letting it be open. The opportunity for birthing something in the long term was not realised for her at that time. The Universe is generous and will grace her, and all of us, with other opportunities. When they come, we want to make the most of them in the here and now. Instead of rushing or chasing or grasping the spiritual high, which is what a distorted Padma energy can do, creating space allows the gap between our inner spiritual life and our outer physical life to close.

In a way, there are times on the spiritual path where doing less will accomplish more. This doesn't mean sitting on the lounge waiting for the Universe to manifest our fantasies as we overindulge in Netflix. It does mean choosing the right sort of action, that comes from a passionate energy grounded in trust and patience, rather than scrambling to do as much as we can from a place of fear and desperation. I know from personal experience that getting to that place of trust can take some work, especially if we have trust issues to resolve first! But that is okay. In my experience, the areas we must work hardest to heal are where we eventually become the most masterful.

An example of right action based in trust could start with meditation and once we have clarity, we can take helpful steps in the physical world that feel natural. It can be a matter of pausing to sense the flow of universal energy and guidance, and then respond. We are active, but our activity flows from a receptive inner state. This inspiration then perspiration approach to the world means taking the practical steps needed, without feeling like a lone wolf. The Padma aspect of us needs connection. When we act this way, in trust, we feel that connection with the Universe, with our inner self, with our spiritual team and with life itself as all facets of existence work together to birth the soul light in the world in various beautiful forms.

By contrast, if distrust is underpinning our actions, even if they seem logical, correct or socially mandated, they will not create peace of mind for us. Nor will they help us climb the right mountain. When we strive, push and try to force the Universe to deliver according to our mind's view of when and how things should happen, we may end up climbing the wrong mountain. This is something I have done many times, and believe me, there's little joy in the experience.

Imagine you are a surfer on your surfboard out in the water. The ocean is flat, but you want waves. You meditate and visualise the perfect waves. You say affirmations, "There is an abundance of waves available for me to surf now." You stand on your board and do a wave-building ritual dance. You scream out to the Universe, "How can you deny me waves? You don't even care that I am in the ocean wanting to surf!"

You become emotionally drained by feelings of abandonment and neglect. Rather than bowing down to the ultimate flow of life, trusting it will serve you and recognising that you are your soul, not your ego, you became caught up trying to dominate life. It got you nowhere except tired and triggered! This experience may have reinforced your painful old view that you cannot trust in the abundance of life. You feel alone, rejected and disappointed.

Compare that to sitting on your board, taking sensual delight in your feet dangling in the water and feeling at one with the ocean as your board bobs gently up and down. Imagine anchoring your awareness into your feet and feeling for the shifting currents of the water. You notice the undercurrent tugging lightly at your toes. You sense the ocean moving in a new way, building up energy, and so you begin to paddle, gently at first. You feel the energy of the sea coming faster and stronger. Before you see the rise, you feel a slight lift underneath your board as the swell builds and the perfect wave begins to form. You know you need to put all your energy into paddling fast and so you go for it! Then, you are lifted. You have caught the wave and the wave is taking you for a ride! You fearlessly jump up on your board, grounded in your belly and feet to balance yourself and are in joy, freedom and connection with that great power of the ocean as it moves you.

The beauty of the more receptive and trusting approach is that it supports our inner energy to regenerate. We have more downtime and when we are acting, we work productively rather than being busy for the sake of it. Sometimes I think being busy is modern society's version of being important. Whilst I believe we are meant to engage in the fulfilment of our purpose, and that it may take a lot of work, I also feel we need to be aware of the motivation behind our actions. When we work in harmony with the Universe, there will be times when we burn a bit too hot, like a midsummer's day. There will be times to cool down, too. Being constantly switched on is not natural for the body or the soul. Nature's feminine wisdom shows us that we need time to integrate, rebalance and empty out. How can we live our purpose and act on our intuition when we are too tired? We run ourselves ragged, when we say yes to everything and no to our own needs in the process.

The Universe knew how to provide me with what I desired, and the desires were coming from an authentic place. I was far more suited to a bohemian lifestyle where I could focus on my spiritual path and create. However, the more I tried to force it to happen, the more I pursued rather than allowed, the more I pushed away the very thing I desired. I was fighting and striving because that is what I had learned to do in the world of ego. It helped me get through law school and gain coveted legal job offers. The problem was that was the wrong mountain for me.

I eventually realised that I didn't need to give up on my fantasy, so much as let it go so it could go through the process of becoming my reality. That wasn't easy. The transition from fantasy to reality has its disappointing moments. You might fantasise about a perfect beach holiday. If you book the holiday, you will soon find yourself on your hammock with the lovely smell of coconut oil on your sun-kissed skin. It is only when you hear the buzzing that you recall every outdoors vacation inevitably comes with flies and mosquitos! Bringing fantasy down-to-earth as reality is a bit like dealing with flies in the summer. Some aspects will not be as perfectly airbrushed and fly free as your fantasy promised. On the positive, you do get to live your dream! Even if you do need insect repellent sometimes …

HEALING PROCESS

Start by saying the following aloud:

> *I call upon the unconditional love of Archangel Michael and star teacher Aldebaran. I call upon the healing energy of the Crystal Angel of Petalite. I open my heart, my body, my mind and my soul to the genuine nourishment of the Universe, surrendering any memory or belief system based on starvation or neglect, from this or any lifetime, into your healing grace.*

Pause for as long as you wish here. Imagine, feel, intend or visualise that you are 'emptying out' from your inner being. Your mind can empty out, your heart can empty out, your body can empty out, and your soul can empty out. It is a relief to experience this letting go. You could visualise old energy pouring out into a massive black vortex of divine consciousness that just absorbs it all. That vortex is so vast and powerful that it can liberate that energy and return it to Source.

When you are ready, then say aloud:

> *I ask to experience the fullness of divine love, so that I may allow space in my life, where my divine destiny can manifest with grace, generosity, joy and abundance. Through the highest wisdom for the greatest good, so be it.*

When you are ready, visualise, imagine or intend that there is a beautiful, soft, white energy pouring from the heart of the Universe into your soul. It fills up the soul, then gently overflows into the world, until you are empty again, feeling free and relaxed.

Then another transmission of soft, white light flows toward you from the Universe, filling your soul until it flows over with joy and light. It naturally flows out of you, into the world and you feel peace and emptiness again.

This process can continue as many times as you wish — filling and emptying, filling and emptying. You can choose to relax and trust in the natural rhythm of this cycle.

When you are ready, place one hand over the crystal angel mandala for this chapter and allow yourself to feel nourished by it on all levels. Feel its goodness enter your soul, the cells of your body, and the deepest recesses of your mind. This happens easily and generously, with a simple intention to be open and receive. Relax into this process for a few moments to complete your healing process.

You can finish the process by bowing your head to your hands in prayer at your heart.

CHAPTER FOUR

GALACTIC CONSCIOUSNESS AND THE COSMIC CREATRIX

STAR GUIDE: THE GALACTIC CENTRE

OUR GALACTIC HOME, THE MILKY WAY, holds an extraordinarily loving, creative and nurturing consciousness. To me, the Milky Way is the body of a great galactic being, a mother goddess who is always birthing spiritual blessings and divine light. I believe this is why gazing at images of the Milky Way can evoke such emotion. We may think we are looking at a picture of stars, but what we are seeing at a deeper level is the body of a benevolent divine being. When I look at a picture of our galaxy, my soul recognises our beloved mother and that can be profoundly heart opening. I invite you to be open to having a heart connection with the galactic mother in the same way. You may feel something stir within as you connect with this star guide.

An internet search for images of the Milky Way can yield surprising and spontaneous spiritual healing that facilitate breakthroughs and bring through supportive energy for your healing journey. This is especially the case for issues to do with mothering such as acceptance, unconditional love, belonging, and feeling like you matter and have a right to exist, claim space, be touched, listened to and mirrored with loving attention.

The Milky Way is a cosmic creatrix, the life-giver, the galactic goddess of divine blessing. She bears mother's milk for the soul — she is our soul mother, the one who generates life, who nurtures the soul so that it can attain spiritual maturity. Just like mother's milk is a naturally nourishing food for infants, the spiritual mother's milk of the galactic goddess is naturally nourishing for all of life birthed through her, which includes you and me. We take our path of soul evolution through the portal of her galactic grace. If we lean into her, there is great healing and divine mothering that we can experience in her spiritual embrace.

The age of our ancient mother galaxy is estimated to be 13 to 15 billion years and she's still going strong. Her longevity, sheer size and complexity are testimony to her tremendous reserves of creative energy. The Milky Way is made up of a hundred billion stars and has a diameter of around one hundred thousand light-years. That's a complex cosmic system in an extraordinarily vast divine being transmitting high levels of spiritual consciousness, light and power. Connection with the Milky Way as a star teacher can help us re-establish vitality and refresh our energy reserves to provide even the oldest, world-weary soul with a youthful spring in their step.

For our work here, we are going to zone in to a particularly powerful and active aspect of the Milky Way known as the Galactic Centre. The Galactic Centre is a vast black hole at the centre of the galaxy. It is the size of a huge star, but with an incredible intensity of energy, estimated to have the mass of four trillion suns! One of the spiritual empowerments of the galactic mother is that we discover our innate and divine capacity to punch above our weight. We could compare this to the wisdom teachings of ant medicine. By accessing incredible strength, Ant can sometimes lift around fifty times its body weight.

The message that comes through the Galactic Centre is that we have more strength than we may have once believed was possible — on all levels, mind, body and spirit. We may have to grow into that strength and develop it with practice and by trusting our process and capacity for evolution and progress. We are asked to nurture and tend to our minds, so they do not override our potential by becoming negative or self-limiting. Putting this guidance into practice in our lives takes courage and from that courage, we build confidence. If you feel a prominent soul connection to this star teacher, then there is special guidance for you personally: you have enough courage to gain confidence in your abilities. You may be surprised by what you are capable of accomplishing, even in areas you may not have considered to be your forte. Be open to growth, to developing your strengths and know that you have more ability than you realise.

As the source of most of the gravitational energy in our galaxy, the Galactic Centre infuses our souls with magnetic pulling power for manifestation. The black hole draws a staggering amount of material into itself. If you trust in it, with an attitude of relaxation and optimism, you'll be better able to use your natural ability to kick the law of attraction into action in a way that works well for you.

Connection with the Galactic Centre guides you to realise the magnetic spiritual energy you have at your core. This energy constantly attracts what you want and need, although sometimes we are too full of energetic content to be able to receive, readily and freely. One of the best ways to be more receptive is to create some energetic space. I often recognise when a blessing or new cycle is imminent, because I am overcome with a sudden urge to clean out my wardrobe! At a deeper level, this is about creating energetic space by letting go of attachments, ideas, emotional content and memories associated with various possessions. Creating space on a physical level supports the creation of emotional and energetic space.

During such phases I also want to meditate, rest, declutter, finish projects and cross everything off my various to-do lists. I experience a kind of divine restlessness that shifts into peace once there is a sense of completion and a space has been cleared. Divine gifts and new energies can then flow into that spaciousness. Whenever you feel the urge to spring clean, I encourage you to act. It makes it easier for universal energies to flow through you — and ultimately, this benefits all beings.

The Galactic Centre provides us with the energy and magnetism to manifest and pull toward our higher authentic purpose. This includes opportunities, objects, relationships, connections, life direction and more. Once we rest into this, our experiences of manifestation can be great fun. When used for a greater purpose and higher good, it can result in heart-melting joy, spiritual empowerment and tremendous progress. There is also a heightened sense of the inner compass that guides us from within, so confusion and procrastination can no longer get a grip on us. Decisions that are right for us at a deeper level seem to make themselves. The Galactic Centre helps us find certainty as we are increasingly attracted to and connected with our true nature — eventually we recognise we are one with it.

Located around 26 degrees of Sagittarius, the Galactic Centre transmits the astrological medicine of that zodiac sign. The galactic goddess is always nourishing us, but there are times when we are ready for deeper spiritual intimacy through closer alignment with her vibration. When this happens, certain Sagittarian themes tend to arise in our lives. These will vary depending on our soul journey, but can include challenges to our beliefs, so that they can shift to reflect our relationship with the cosmos more authentically.

Sagittarius encourages tolerance, open-mindedness and higher understanding, particularly in areas of spirituality, religion, culture and social conditioning. When the soul connects to the Galactic Centre, shifts in these areas may come through a crisis of consciousness or a gentler recognition of the legitimacy of differing opinions without feeling your beliefs are under threat. This can create greater peace in yourself and in the world — one of the higher purposes of Sagittarius. When you connect to the Galactic Centre at a soul level, your awareness opens to the cosmic support for increased peacefulness in yourself and your world.

You may be at a point where your beliefs need to change quite dramatically to accommodate your spiritual journey. Wounded or limiting beliefs can create mental resistance to what your soul wants to attract to your world. A connection to the Galactic Centre stimulates and supports the release of old beliefs, with a recognition that they served you for a certain time on your journey, and now it is time for a more expansive spiritual viewpoint. The galactic mother amplifies the Sagittarian influence, so our souls can express an increased interest in higher worlds and broadening our horizons through travel in the physical world and explorations of the spiritual realms.

A deepening alignment with the Galactic Centre often accompanies an increased sense of interconnectedness with other worlds and beings from places beyond the earth. It is when we are in deep connection with Her that awareness of our star-seed nature often arises. Following this, you may sense you have an important life mission and experience a temporary but powerful urgency to complete it. This is a real 11.11 wake-up call. Our loving earth goddess then provides us with the resources, opportunities, relationships and more to manifest the divine plan our soul has sensed.

All realised beings work for the same outcome and are expressions of the one divine essence, so there is no competition between our Galactic and Earth Mothers. They love, nurture and encourage us, giving us energy and life in their own unique ways, to foster the growth of our souls and provide us with what we need to complete our spiritual mission. We are so blessed.

THE CRYSTAL ANGEL OF ZEBRA ROCK

There can be confusion over zebra stone and zebra rock. I have heard them described as two different stones and by others as one stone manifesting in assorted colours depending on the source location. Zebra stone features black and white whorls and bands, like the patterning on a zebra. The zebra rock we are working with here is an earthier red and pinkish-brown stone sourced from Western Australian. To me, they carry such distinct energies that I consider them as individual crystals with their own healing properties.

Zebra rock is over 600 million years old. It is incredibly dense and heavy for its size and is profoundly grounding. It is cool to touch and can help heal inflammation. It slows us down, in a good way, by helping us switch over to the parasympathetic nervous system, a relaxed state essential for healing, regeneration and repair. For such purposes, having the stone in contact with the skin in some way can be best.

Zebra rock gives us the reassurance needed for deep rest. Sometimes, especially when we are overly stressed or running on adrenaline for an extended period, it is hard to rest even though that is what we need most. When the body and nervous system are in such a state they can be compared to a spinning top. They need to run out of steam before they can slow down. As the body loses momentum, it will wobble and eventually fall over with a thump!

When we have been pushing ourselves to keep going, slowing down is just what we need, but it can feel awkward — like a wobble and inelegant collapse. It is what the body needs, but when the mind's fantasy of invincibility has disconnected us from the body's natural need for limits, rest and regeneration, it can be a shock.

A fearful mind may try to resist dealing with the problems a too-busy lifestyle creates. Becoming busy again and avoiding rest can only distract us from the reality of our physical needs for a limited time and make the situation worse in the long term. Zebra rock supports us through the sometimes-challenging shift from constant overdrive to acknowledging the bone-deep weariness and exhaustion it has created. It helps us give ourselves the time, space and rest we needs to heal and repair. It takes courage to recognise that it is safe to let this process happen and to find wise people who will support your decision to heal rather than presenting you with fear-based nonsense such as "it is all mind over matter, just push through it."

This stone is great for building energy levels, grounding excess mental energy and learning how to relax. It supports those wanting to take pleasure in the moment by balancing a dedication to a higher purpose with contentment and happiness in the present. Once we make that healing connection to our bodies, we can learn how to take delight in our divine downtime. When we pay regular attention to our wellbeing, we have more to offer the world and enjoy our lives and love our bodies in the process.

SPIRITUAL GUIDANCE: CHANNELLING DIVINE ELECTRICITY WITHOUT NEEDING TO EAT AN ENTIRE PIZZA

After experiencing higher frequency energies and the genuine love, bliss, freedom and insight that comes with it, we may feel that little, if anything, could compare to it. Although we are not instantly enlightened and will still have stuff to work through, we are spiritually ignited and an evolution in consciousness is inevitable. The hungers of the ego are fickle and insatiable, but our craving for spiritual experience can result in authentic nourishment. We want to come back to it again and again, and it is good for us to do so.

When we feed our spiritual hunger by reading spiritual texts, praying, consulting oracle cards, chanting mantras, engaging in sacred ritual, meditating, channelling healing energies, doing the healing processes in this book or otherwise, we generate divine electricity in our system. We can benefit from those many practices for positive life change and develop our awareness of warning signs, too. Warning signs are our body's way of telling us we need to step it down a few levels to let things balance out before proceeding further.

Why would we need to do that? The spiritual practices that have emerged out of the New Age movement can be quite beautiful and one of the qualities which resonates for me is the utter freedom of choice. You can do as little or as much as your heart desires. You can work with advanced practices or beginner practices. You can work with many teachers and multiple modalities, free to distil what you learn. You can keep what resonates and cast aside that which does not, to discover your own unique spiritual practice. In some ways this freedom brings significant benefits. It is a pathway where people can develop a love of Spirit and experiment with spiritual practice until they find what works for them. If the New Age environment was overly structured or highly organised, many people would not feel willing or able to try out any spiritual practices at all.

However, a freedom-based, structureless approach to the spiritual journey can have its challenges. When given a choice, humans tend to overlook the more unexciting or difficult fundamentals for the pursuit of pleasure and fun. So, we may eschew basic purification, considered extremely important in organised spiritual practice, to focus on opening our higher faculties to psychic ability, clairvoyance, channelled healing, and so forth. Without a teacher to wisely guide us through the foundations before we approach higher levels, we will hit problems soon enough.

The good news is those problems are all fodder for our spiritual growth. Obstacles or pain can be opportunities to go deeper into our purification practices. Some people do not like the idea of purification. They sometimes feel it suggests we are dirty, sinful or unacceptable to Spirit unless we are 'cleansed'. I don't see it like that at all. Purification is about preparation. It is a way of helping our minds and bodies receive spiritual energy more fully and without struggling.

Consider an animal that was treated meanly early on in life. That animal learned to associate human contact, a hand reaching out, as a sign of imminent pain. Due to the abuse that precious animal suffered, it learned to retract from human contact, to be fierce, to growl, to bite or defend itself from any reaching hand. Imagine that animal has now been adopted by a loving family. They want to love, pat, care for and nurture it. They are aware of its abusive history and will be gentle and patient and understanding. They want to reach out to the animal, but know it needs time to learn it is safe and loved, that the past is over, and it is free from that nightmare. Until that happens, the animal cannot receive all the love the caring family wants to share with it. The family may help the animal move beyond its fear in skilful and kind ways. At first it won't be easy, but with a consistent and careful process, it is only a matter of time before an entirely new reality of loving connection opens for that sweet creature and its adoptive family.

Purification helps us clear away that past conditioning that makes it difficult to accept gifts of love from spirit. Those gifts could be higher understanding, deep insight, psychic revelation, healing abilities, and other things we might 'chase' via workshops or other means. As we open to our true nature, we discover those gifts are there within us. Other gifts might include clarity and vision of our life path and higher purpose, and wisdom teachings that allow us to grow and teach others.

As we focus on doing our inner work, the basis of purification practice in the New Age movement, we clear ourselves of the conditioning that would have us shut down in pain rather than open in trust. Most of this conditioning comes from childhood experience, but past life issues can surface from time to time. By becoming aware of our issues, we can learn how to compassionately witness them, and make new choices about how to respond to life situations.

Typically, it takes time and the consistent support from a skilful and well-trained therapist or healer for us to work through our issues effectively. We need someone skilled in conscious mirroring, who can help us identify our issues, hold an integrated wisdom and show us how else we might respond. If you have ever recognised an issue but not been able to shift it, you'll know that awareness is not usually enough on its own. We need help to remodel our inner structure and this is what quality mentoring and therapy can do for us. Ideally, a therapist is a soul friend who helps us recognise how we see the world and any beliefs that relate to core wounds. They can then suggest alternative, non-distorted views. By gently and firmly reinforcing this learning for us, we can internalise their conscious, loving and wise voice and replace the wounded ego voices that once held us captive in suffering.

Purification practices allow us to handle the frequency-raising qualities of spiritual energy without excessive resistance from the body. It might be enough to ask the body and mind to be more trusting, up to a point. We may feel at ease meditating on our love life, but not on our mortgage or job security. We might be able to forgive everyone, except that one person we think should be expunged from the face of the earth! Those places in ourselves where we do not experience higher frequencies such as peace, forgiveness, love and compassion are where we need purification. They are not bad, or anything to be ashamed of. They are just part of how we grow and are certainly something to work on.

Our resistance to higher frequencies is not always emotional or psychological. Sometimes it is just a physical reaction to the energy. We might do a lot of meditation or three days of workshops in a row, only to eat an entire pizza or drink the better part of a bottle of wine afterwards. I giggled when I heard of the experiences of the great mystic Therese of Avila (we will meet her in another book in this series). She startled the nuns in her spiritual community because after her mystical ecstasies (such as levitating so high in prayer that the nuns would have to tackle her to keep her grounded — now that's quite a visual) she would greedily devour an entire partridge. The nuns couldn't account for such behaviour that flaunted the vow of renunciation and poverty. To me, it seems that she was trying to ground her body after extraordinary spiritual highs. Genuine spiritual energy effects the physical body and we need to recognise and learn how to manage it.

Start by recognising when the flow of spiritual electricity is right for you. In such states you will feel unconditionally loving, open, accepting, peaceful, generous and kind. You will feel grounded and vitalised. Your insight and sense of wisdom will be keener and more expansive. You will feel spacious, softer and more receptive. You will be optimistic, ready to tackle your challenges which seem more surmountable and less daunting than when you were not 'topped up' spiritually. You may appear more bold, confident and focused, but are just living from a state not driven by ego. In the realm of non-ego, you can recognise that you are not the fearful workings of the mind. You are freer to be your authentic self without the distortions of endless thoughts, past obsession or future anxiety. You are present.

This spiritually-infused state may be fleeting or last for a longer time. I believe it is the divine destiny of all beings to exist in that state permanently, when they are ready to do so, because it is our authentic state. Actively seeking spiritual experience can have a good and true outcome, but if our pursuit of the Divine is unchecked, the toll on our bodies can undermine rather than enhance our progress.

A build-up of spiritual electricity in the body can have symptoms which are manageable, amusing or mildly inconvenient. This is the stuff you can talk about with like-minded friends. They will share similar experiences and you can all laugh about it. Your energy field might be interfering with electrical equipment or setting off alarms at the grocery store. I once recorded a client's reading and when she went to listen to it again later, instead of my voice, all she had was an hour of gleeful dolphin-like sounds!

At other times the effects can be more problematic. At one time, when I was teaching a lot of workshops in a row and was very full of energy, I reached to pull a plug out of the socket with what I felt was a normal amount of force but ended up ripping it in half. In normal circumstances, I couldn't have done that if I tried. The woman organising the workshops for me just looked at the torn plug in my hand, absolutely astonished.

A more severe example happened when I was teaching some years ago. It was one of those exceptionally powerful experiences where it felt like energy was pouring through with great intensity. Some of the participants had such strong experiences that negative patterning that had plagued them through years of conscious inner work suddenly and permanently shifted. It was as if the inner darkness could not withstand the presence of that much light. On one level, it was beautiful.

However, at the end of the day, one of the participants asked me how I felt. Without thinking, I replied, "Like I've been plugged into an electrical socket and been burned." He replied with a laugh, thinking I was joking. I thought I was joking, too. It wasn't until later that night when I was doubled over in physical pain, feeling as though I had burned a hole in my stomach, that I realised my unconscious response to the participant's question was expressing a deeper truth. I had burned out my solar plexus chakra and it was absolute agony for my physical body.

I booked in to see a doctor. She did tests and prescribed medication for a stomach ulcer saying I would need to take them on and off for the rest of my life. I knew however that what I was experiencing was in my energy field, and not my physical body. I had glimpsed what could become a concrete disease if I didn't change my ways, though. I was advised to take the medication for at least three weeks but in two days the pattern was out of my system and I no longer needed it — and have not needed it in the many years since.

Now, please understand that this was not Spirit blasting me and causing me harm. It was my own wilful action pulling through more and more energy. I was exercising my free will, ignorant to the impact it was having on my body. I was labouring under the illusion that more would always be better and therefore couldn't recognise the signals to slow down and proceed more gently. In the enthusiasm of the moment, I could forget to put on the brakes. I had to learn to balance my willpower with mercy. I had to soften the driven quality of my mind into a gentler approach. Given that I like to throw myself into my endeavours with great passion and total abandon, this was not always easy for me to accomplish.

Until that experience, I didn't understand just how much impact such work could have on my body. Afterwards, I began to understand the connection between some health issues I'd had and how much energy work I was doing. At one stage I was doing many hours of readings — sometimes seeing eight or ten clients in a day. I was experiencing health issues and looking back, it was no wonder! I began to see where health issues were affecting other healers and psychics, and realised this issue was relevant on a broader scale. Yet no-one had ever talked about this with me. In the many years since then, the people I've met who understand spiritual energy as spiritual electricity—and are therefore able to create light but also burn—I could count on one hand. It makes sense of course. It is like sunlight — we need it and being scared of it and avoiding it causes health problems, but too much too soon can cause problems. The benefits can flow abundantly when we take a more balanced approach.

There is a belief that when you are truly connected with Spirit, no harm can happen. That's not only untrue, but dangerous and misleading. There are many examples of experienced spiritual masters that outright tell us energy is real. It creates pressure and heat in the body, and although it can be used for marvellous things, it is powerful, and we need to be careful with it. Fire can burn, but we wouldn't have got far as human beings without it and it is the same with divine fire.

I don't want to create fear here, because there is no need for that. Spiritual energy is love, wisdom, peace and light. Our spirit is not tempered by the laws of nature, but our bodies are and that is why our spirit can bring through more energy than our bodies can handle. The spirit is always 'on' and that is natural, as it should be. The body needs time to switch off. That is also natural, and as it should be. The aim of the game, so to speak, is to find the most loving relationship between body and spirit so as to spark evolution and encourage growth. When we have a talent for channelling, we especially need to take care to proceed gradually and not overdo it by trying to shift everything all in one sitting.

We may like the idea of a summer that never ends, but it would burn the earth to a crisp and life would die off. The bright sun of divine presence gives life but can also overwhelm and dry it out. Just think of those beautiful moments on a hot day when we step into the shade. Such relief! Or the cool days when we get a warming blast of sun and it is utter bliss. It's all about balance, not one thing or the other being more valuable. The shady recesses of the body need light, but also time to retreat into darkness to replenish. The spirit can fly fast and free from many physical restraints and the body has a wisdom that brings the spirit to life. Spirit cannot live without the body. They need each other. Learning to respect these aspects of our being is a way to make the relationship we have with ourselves one that is positive and healing.

As we learn to heal our hearts and minds, and love ourselves, we will naturally and instinctively take care of our body and find the natural flow for our spirit that works best. A loving relationship will develop between all parts of us and we won't want to overdo it quite so much, as tempting as it may be at times! When I learned to take better care of myself, the relationship between my spirit and my body was much more respectful, and my work became both gentler and more powerful.

When we work with the stars, meditate or pray, even though it seems soft and ethereal, we listen to our bodies, carefully. Spiritual energy is subtle but also powerful, so we can go from feeling barely anything to feeling overloaded very quickly. As the Chinese proverb puts it, "When journeying into the mountains often, one will eventually encounter a tiger." We want to learn to recognise when we have had enough and minimise potential issues.

Trying to blast an unprepared body or mind with spiritual light doesn't get us to the goal faster. We move bit by bit, purifying, doing our inner work, two steps forward, one back, developing the body's ability to handle more energy over time. We give the body a chance to switch off and integrate what it takes in, so it can adjust to the new vibration and settle into a new 'spiritual metabolic rate'. Soon enough, the body will easily be able to handle what was previously challenging. Over a period of years, the growth becomes even more noticeable. Slow and steady wins the race, as the expression goes.

There will be signs when it is time to slow down, and you learn these by paying attention and experimenting with what works for you. You may feel extremely high — the sort of high where you know you are going to crash afterwards. By bringing that feeling down, and grounding the energy a little, you can avoid the opposite extreme of experiencing a low over the next few days. The rising heat of spiritual energy may cause your head to feel hot, or you might feel agitated, overly sensitive or triggered. When this happens, it is time to ground, to withdraw inwards, and give all that has been stimulated a chance to settle. A simple thing, like speaking overly quickly, can be a sign that a pause and a deep breath is needed.

Some signals are instinctive attempts to slow us down, ground and lower our vibration a little so that the body can balance out excess spiritual light. A sudden and intense craving for heavy food or alcohol, a shopping binge, an upsurge of rage or an intense desire for any kind of emotional or physical release are a few ways the body might express an unconscious need to lower the vibration and discharge excess energy. It is the body's attempt to do what it does so brilliantly — come back to balance.

Those examples are not the only ways to restore balance. In fact, they often aren't particularly good ways because they tend to come with negative repercussions of their own (health issues, bank balance issues and so on). It can be better to listen to those urges and consider whether there are better ways to meet them. By experimenting with supportive and non-damaging ways of bringing our vibration back to a more comfortable realm for the body, we develop practical tools for when we overshoot the mark, spiritually speaking.

You might try yoga, watching a favourite film, comfort reading a beloved novel or eating heavy but nourishing foods. Taking time away from spiritual pursuits can be helpful. Some people try to meditate their way through, but to discharge the energy, exercise and movement is often more effective. A healthy grounding meal and silly antics that will wear you out in a good way can help you have a good night's rest — which also helps the body regulate energy. With these practices, the body can continue to adjust to spiritual energy and higher frequencies at a more manageable, comfortable pace. We gradually embody an increasing spiritual light, wisdom and healing energy in a way that nourishes our path.

I take care of those I am teaching by taking breaks and creating space. So, we'll go deep into dance, meditation, channelling or whatever we are working with, but I leave space for integration, especially on retreats. Many participants find this surprising. They are amazed I don't want them to work for ten hours a day on spiritual materials or that my workshops only run for five hours with breaks. But I know when a group is 'full' and cannot take any more in. I see it in my workshops all the time. I'll talk for a while and then it's like nothing else is going to go in. It would be like pouring more water into a full cup. Better to drink the water and empty the cup before adding more! So, we dance, we do ritual, we talk, or we have a lunch break. We honour the intelligence of the body and the power of the spirit. Group energy is an effective receiving dish for spirit. So, we open to the generous flow of spiritual energy required to support change whilst aiming to do so with wisdom.

HEALING PROCESS

Find a place to relax where you can sit or lie down. If you can be in connection with the flooring or ground, it is helpful but not essential. Become aware of the gentle flow of your breath. If you are breathing shallowly, into the upper chest, take time to allow your breathing to become deeper and more restful. Take as long as you need. Gently bring your awareness back to the flow of breath, again and again.

Then, simply rest. Feel the weight of your body in connection to the earth beneath you. If you are not making physical contact with the earth, or even if you are, you can visualise, intend or feel the energies of the earth as they support you. Allow your awareness to drop deeper and deeper, like a feather floating slowly down, down toward the deeper energetic layers of the earth. As your awareness descends, the energy becomes slower, more restful, deep and restorative. Allow your awareness to settle beneath the surface layers and as deep as you wish into the energies of the earth. Here you can become still and rest for as long as you wish.

When you are ready, say aloud:

> I call upon the Crystal Angel of Zebra Rock and the star
> teacher known as the Galactic Centre. I open to your endless
> blessings, to heal, balance and awaken my true nature in

harmony with the higher loving plan of the Universe. May
I surrender unnecessary action and settle into a place of
connection with you, with myself and with the wise and
sustaining rhythm of the Universe. May all beings be gifted
this grace. Through the highest wisdom for the greatest good,
so be it.

Visualise, feel, imagine or intend that your connection to the earth allows any excess energy to discharge into her magnetic field. The earth easily draws excess energy out of your body with her greater magnetic pull and circulates it through her system. What may seem overwhelming for you, is comparatively minuscule for her great being. It is safe to allow her to do this. She returns healing energy to rebalance you, just the right amount, up through the soles of your feet. Relax and allow this healing cycle to take place for as long as you wish, to complete your healing process.

CHAPTER FIVE

AUTHENTICITY EXPANDS YOUR SPIRITUAL HORIZON

STAR GUIDE: ANDROMEDA GALAXY

THE ANDROMEDA GALAXY is our celestial neighbour. She is next to the Milky Way, over 2 million light-years away. As the closest spiral galaxy to our own, it was thought Andromeda and the Milky Way were twin galaxies of comparable size. It has since been realised that Andromeda is the largest local galaxy, home to many minor galaxies and over a trillion stars, spanning over 200 thousand light-years and weighing in at more than twice the size of the Milky Way.

When a soul makes a meaningful connection with Andromeda it suggests there is a greater capacity for spiritual growth than one may initially expect. Such souls can help many people in unique ways. When you connect to Andromeda at a soul level, you will be learning not to allow fear to make you play small. Andromeda helps us embrace our greatness. This is not the nonsense of the ego believing it is superior, but the greatness of courage, open-heartedness and surrender into a course steered by the guiding hand of divine wisdom. It is a willingness to grow into our potential, even when that challenges our views about life or ourselves. Andromeda helps us grow bold, big and bright at a soul level, whilst keeping the ego in check so we don't fall into the distorted view of psychological inflation that would have us erroneously believe that we matter more than anyone else.

Andromeda is one of the brightest deep-space objects viewable from Earth with the eye alone, even in less-than-ideal viewing conditions. Estimated at around 10 billion years of age, scientists believe Andromeda's star formation is slowing down. Galaxies, like stars and human souls, evolve through stages of maturation. Andromeda can teach us how to honour the ageing process in such a way that we do not switch off and opt out of life as we grow older, but instead allow our point of empowerment to shift. If we do not feel as physically dynamic as we were, we can acknowledge that and recognise that the energies once utilised in physical pursuits can be channelled into spiritual practice. Our physical power may shift as we age, but our spiritual wisdom can exponentially increase. Irrespective of age, if you were conditioned to value yourself according to what you can do, Andromeda can help you transition into a deeper sense of self-worth that focuses on your way of being as a truly valuable contribution to the planet.

For someone who feels they are no longer relevant or at the top of their game, because they are facing retirement, redundancy or some other transition from the youthful sense of power, Andromeda Galaxy reinforces the value of all phases of life and being. She also teaches that spiritual power and influence increase with the maturity of the soul. Reduced physical vitality does not mean one's spiritual and healing presence in the world needs to decline. On the contrary, Andromeda is about an increased ability to become a 'spiritual home' for others by offering comfort and reassurance.

Andromeda is considered to be in the 'green valley' — a stage of transition when a galaxy stops forming new stars and planets. During the green phase, a galaxy holds a mix of old and new stars. For the soul, this provides supportive grace and higher wisdom to handle transitions effectively. It helps us live in a way that honours and sustains what already exists, while being open to new creations. This wisdom can relate to moving from one phase of life, career, lifestyle, identity or other transitions. Andromeda understands how to balance the old and the new and supports the soul in gaining that skill in human life.

Scientists predict a collision will occur around 4 billion years from now, where Andromeda and the Milky Way are likely to merge and become one massive galaxy. What will happen to our solar system in that process is not clear, but one possibility is that it will become part of the Andromeda Galaxy. In this sense, Andromeda is an embracing and receiving entity, capable of absorbing foreign elements into herself, growing rather than being overcome. This mirrors the soul's ability to grow through exposure to other elements, cultures and worlds. It can take in those qualities, integrate them and expand. We do not have to protect ourselves from being affected by our life experiences. If we embrace change, even those that seem dramatic, we can integrate them and become more 'soul full' in the process.

A soul who connects with Andromeda is in a significant phase of maturation. The natural and necessary self-orientation of youth that helps us discover ourselves, begins to give way to a broader sense of collective consciousness and the ways one can make a meaningful contribution to the planet. Andromeda souls understand the spiritual teachings of interrelatedness, not as a choice but as a reality. Andromeda is a macrocosmic expression of spiritually and physically evolving relationship. Tribal wisdom bearers have sought to foster this understanding in the human collective for thousands of years. Australian Aboriginal culture has a special understanding of the relationship between the spiritual and the earthly and the sacred bond that exists between all beings. They refer to this as Kanyini. In South Africa, the concept of Ubuntu embodies a universal bond that connects all of humanity.

Andromeda teaches us about connection and how we evolve and grow together. It is important that the individual has fulfilment, but that can only happen in concert with the fulfilment of all beings and never at the expense of another. When a soul is in divine conversation with Andromeda, it indicates deepening connections and a more profound and expansive sense of belonging that will reach beyond the obvious ties of family and friends. It is about soul belonging — feeling connected to the planet, to the stars, to a team of spiritual beings from many realms, and to the great plan of love that is unfolding for the benefit of all. Andromeda helps us claim our rightful place in the tribe of Spirit. Once that happens, the resources, helping hands, opportunities to fulfil our life mission and everything else that comes our way, can be astounding.

When Andromeda speaks to your soul, your spiritual and physical horizons expand. There will be opportunities to connect with new people and different worlds. You will also assume greater spiritual responsibility for yourself and those in your care. You may attract a growing group of souls to guide and assist through your own spiritual journey. Andromeda Galaxy embodies the consciousness of maturity. It empowers you to really be yourself without trying to impress anyone or comparing yourself to another. Instead, you simply trust in the movement of your soul.

The star medicine of Andromeda Galaxy is also for those who consider themselves late bloomers. These souls need plenty of time to come into their own, because they have a deeper and more expansive purpose that cannot be quickly realised. This star guide steadies us with the patience and serenity required to persist toward a goal, understanding that all things come in time and a greater purpose can require more groundwork and a stronger foundation before other steps can fall into place. Andromeda often asks us to delay immediate gratification for wider-reaching success. You may see yourself as a late bloomer, but Andromeda knows your influence can be long lasting and expansive. So, the attitude you bring to your work and your choice to cultivate goodwill and positive intentions for all beings is incredibly important — especially when working with Andromeda Galaxy star medicine.

THE CRYSTAL ANGEL OF COVELLITE

Dark and lustrous like a scrying mirror, covellite facilitates penetrating vision that helps us glimpse behind the veils that protect secret spiritual knowledge until the soul is ready to receive it. This crystal teacher leads us beyond the compelling but distorted lens of the ego, which tends to run a constantly narrated script that creates distance between us and our immediate experience of reality. It helps us attain the presence and awareness required for accurate vision and genuine higher understanding.

Covellite leads us right into own shadow. At a certain level of spiritual maturity, we will embrace this, even though we may not always enjoy the process. That is because we realise that the problem of ego in the world is actually the problem of ego within. To resolve the pain that we experience outwardly requires us to resolve our inner pain. If we do not, then we will continue to project it onto 'bad people' in the world. This may give us temporary comfort, but ultimately it keeps us trapped in suffering. Paradoxically, perhaps, we can only become free from that which we lay claim to within ourselves.

As an emanation of the Earth Mother, covellite holds her wisdom, grace, truth and compassion. This stone can help us journey into the darker recesses of our being without becoming overwhelmed by what we find there. When we connect with the hidden parts of our being, we discover what is going to help us most. Remember, every unknown aspect of self is within our shadow. Unless we are already completely integrated with our own divinely enlightened nature, when we are willing to look into the shadow, we will find our wounds. We will discover our divine beauty, presence, power and light, too. It is often the deep witnessing of our wounded state that allows for healing to take place, so the spiritual blessings meant to come out of those challenging experiences can begin to unfold. Covellite helps us understand that hidden in the darkness is the switch to turn the lights on.

Many humans have had to endure painful secrets in their lives. Sometimes those secrets are driven so deep that they lie forgotten, until they demand acknowledgement through illness, broken relationship or other suffering. Covellite helps us recover lost knowledge, whether it be the recollection of past lives or of a truth essential for present-life healing. It is fearless, kind and honest — all the qualities that make it a perfect ally for a divine detective, committed to authentic and total self-knowledge and enlightenment.

Through this process, covellite helps us find our true purpose and place in the world, because it is only when we really know, accept and embrace (with some soul swagger) the truth of who we are that we can naturally manifest our higher purpose, and in doing so, attract all that we want and need for spiritual fulfilment.

SPIRITUAL GUIDANCE: THE HIDDEN HELPFULNESS OF BROKENNESS

A new friend I made at a spiritual group I had been attending for chanting and meditation came to visit me at home. She walked into my house and stopped short. I gazed around to see what had shocked her so. I couldn't see anything out of the ordinary. Eventually she said, "I am so surprised — you are so ethereal, yet your home is so ... tribal!"

She had met me in a spiritual context, in a group where I had swanned about in floaty dresses and chanted Sanskrit mantras. Thus, she had formed the expectation that visiting me at home would be like walking into a New Age bookstore. I confess, that was a pretty apt description of my book collection at that time. However, even with all the New Age books, meditation music, my crystal 'family' and incense, she saw something I had not really noticed before. My place did look like an African homewares store had exploded in it.

The earthy tones, handmade furnishings sourced from local artisans during my travels and my preference for things that look slightly raw, textured and natural, did add up to a tribal vibe. My friend loved crystals and interior design, so she responded to aesthetics with sensitivity. She easily noted the big, raw chunk of quartz resting on a rustic wooden table, in contrast to the perfectly polished sphere on a gleaming glass table that she may have expected. I had created that space unconsciously. It was only with her observation—astute as usual—that I realised I was using my home furnishings to help ground myself.

Her reaction when her expectations were so off the mark, gave me food for thought. I hadn't ever considered how much of a spiritual image people might conjure up about each other. After thinking about it a little more deeply, I realised that meant the ego conjures a spiritual image of ourselves, too. I began to wonder what we expect of ourselves when we choose the spiritual path. Do we think we have to dress or behave in a certain way? That we must appear 'spiritual' to others by not expressing anger, frustration or sadness?

There is a story about a monk who lost a beloved family member and was crying. With genuine puzzlement, another monk asked him why he was acting in such a way. The grieving monk replied, "Because I feel sadness." Which monk was more enlightened? The one who believed we should be so detached that we feel no emotion or the one who accepted that feelings and authentic human experience are part of his spiritual journey? My vote would go to the latter.

One of my beloved Tibetan Dzogchen teachers spoke about not making a show of spiritual practice. He cautioned against 'yoga clothes' as a fashion statement that can puff up the ego and undermine the true purpose of our efforts. Some of the practices he taught included the repetition of mantra. When alone the mantra is to be said aloud. If we are with others—perhaps we are doing our practice while our partner is in the house reading a book or meditating—then we respect that person and do the mantra silently or very quietly under the breath. If we are in public where the mantra might confuse someone, we adjust our practice accordingly.

This is not about fear, being silenced or making our spiritual practice less important than another's reality. It is about kindness, respect and wisdom. Spiritual practice is not meant to cause distress to others. It is a humbling antidote to ego-driven sense of entitlement. Demanding that others bow down to our spiritual journey can derail us from the path. Of course, we can set boundaries and commit to and respect the time needed for spiritual practice. That is important. But we don't allow our ego to grab hold of our spiritual interest and lead us to believe we are somehow more important or more evolved than those who don't seem to meditate, do yoga, understand what chanting is about, go to our church, donate to charity and so forth. Any kind of comparison is the work of the ego, and as such, it doesn't lead to true understanding or insight about ourselves or others.

Spiritual image is fast gaining currency in our modern society. Much that was considered fringe culture in the West, be it yoga, mala beads or meditation, is now on trend. However, mainstream appeal and effective marketing don't necessarily equate to a growth in genuine understanding. If that were the case, the explosion of yoga-wear sales would correspond with an explosion of kindness, wisdom and enlightenment on the planet. I hold great hope for us as a collective of awakening divine beings — I just don't pin that hope on the sales of yoga pants.

If anything, I have found that a growth in spiritual image can mean it is harder to be free from ego-attachments and outer trappings. This is not so new. The stories of Jesus overturning trade tables in the temples and admonishing those who prayed for public spectacle or to affirm their superiority over others, shows us the egoic lure of spiritual image has existed for a long time. It is something I am very aware of, working in the public eye and creating beautiful objects that enter the marketplace. This is challenging territory, to navigate with integrity and wisdom. I must be aware of my ego and rely on my guides and teachers to help me keep it real.

When I am enjoying my Tibetan tattoos or the creation of videos for Instagram, I bring myself back to the reasons why. Is it devotion, humility and love that is infusing my experience, or is ego creeping in? One can never be too careful around such matters as ego can play spiritual dress-ups all too convincingly. We must be willing to snatch those mala beads right out of its clutches as soon as we realise what has happened.

If good is to come out of exposure to spiritual images—and yes, I am an eternal optimist who believes we can generate goodness out of any experience—then it will be an increase in discernment. As deception, unconsciousness and confusion increases, our wisdom and insight must increase even more so, so that our spiritual light can continue to thrive. We can develop an ability to sense purity, or its absence, beyond the right words or convincing appearance on the surface. We learn to trust what we feel rather than what appears to be. The more we rely upon the wisdom of the heart rather than the rationales of the mind, the less likely we are to be derailed from our spiritual path. That is how we keep the balance of light on this planet for the benefit all beings.

This process is most tricky when we encounter a particularly charismatic spiritual image. On one occasion, a post of a beautiful-looking man who is successful in his chosen metaphysical field found its way into my social media feed. Stylishly dressed, he gazed out to the sunset in a contemplative pose, as though the camera had captured him in a moment of great vision. One of his spiritual quotes was printed across the bottom of the image. Everything about the image was designed to depict an evolved being who was destined to lead others.

My response was immediate and visceral. Despite its surface beauty, there was something toxic about the image. I didn't want to move closer to this person energetically. In fact, I wanted to get away from that image and that person's energetic broadcast as swiftly as possible. I pondered the difference between this reaction and my response to those who had become spiritual teachers in my life — which was an instant and open-hearted desire to be close to them as my heart melted with gratitude for their presence here on Earth.

I decide whether I want a spiritual teacher's influence in my life based on my innate response to their energy. I don't count the number of books they have written, the number of followers they have on social media, how famous they are, what people say about them or what controversy has or has not followed them. I look at them—in person, in video or in photograph—and listen to them and allow myself to feel the effect of their being on my own. If I melt and soften and feel the deeper presence of my spirit, it's a thumbs up. If I instinctively recoil—even if I cannot explain why—I move on. I ignored my intuitive responses a few times in the past and it was to my peril. I have learned not to ignore such instincts.

I felt this social media image was holding the teacher up as something he was not yet able to be. It was ego dressed up as something else. This can happen easily enough when we are navigating the strange waters of social media with the intention (one assumes) of connecting with people we can genuinely assist. When the ego is at work, the motivation can be far murkier. The ego may be seeking admiration, validation, the sense of power that comes from rescuing people, to feel special or superior, and so forth. Being a spiritual guide for others means doing whatever work we can on ourselves to keep any negative potentialities in check. It wouldn't be appropriate or respectful to delve into an analysis of that person, beyond my instinctive choice to step away.

It is an interesting time to be alive. Much is being learned about the use of images. They are used in visualisation to precipitate healing, realisation and creativity. Every day we are exposed to a slew of images through social media, advertising and cinema. Some are beautiful, some are profoundly disturbing, and then there are what I call *pretty poisons*. An image can look harmless but be far more noxious than one would first suspect. Violence can be hidden in an image, but still be felt and still evoke pain. However, blessings can also flow through an image and elicit healing, spiritual protection and grace.

Interestingly, an image does not always affect us the way we think it will. Our dream images teach us this. At first, something that appears to be all sweetness and light may suddenly unveil destructive tendencies. A ferocious dream animal may be a compassionate protector, keeping you away from something that could harm you. That is why we need wisdom.

This type of wisdom comes from stepping back from the notion of 'this is what good looks like' and 'this is what evil looks like' and learning to drop the notion of good and bad altogether. Instead, we come to embrace all that feels authentic for our spiritual growth and move on from what doesn't with firmness and compassion.

This applies to the images we create and choose to communicate to the world and those we consume through media. It is also relevant for our dreams where unique and healing images are created by our inner being every night, whether we remember them or whether they seem meaningful. When we recognise images as visual food for the soul, we can make informed choices about how to better care for ourselves.

Attempting to mould ourselves to images of perfection can cause secret violence within because it denies our right to be living human beings. Images of unreal 'perfection' are unhealthy but like their junk food equivalents are abundantly available for mass consumption. Images where everything is edited and groomed to appear a certain way will pop up on social media and as with the example I gave above, we need to be discerning.

I believe there is a hunger for what is real — perhaps, at a deeper level, we recognise authenticity is not only nourishing but rare. One of the videos consistently viewed on my Instagram feed is of me with no make-up on, in fluffy slippers and tattered old harem pants, collapsed on the ground in hysterical laughter after the filming of an oracle card demonstration went slightly awry!

I also know it will take time for this naturalness, this overcoming of the deathly grip of perfectionism, to seep into our culture more readily. Recently, I heard of a young woman who committed suicide. One of her family members confided to me that the family never talked about challenges, everything had to appear perfect. She also described the young woman as beautiful, talented and with so much going for her. I privately wondered if that perception was part of the problem — that perhaps she wasn't allowed to own her darkness and had to suffer in silence until she eventually expressed her suffering in a final terrible act.

When we are taught (as most of us are) that to earn love, respect and any other good thing we must act in a way that makes us attractive to others, we begin creating an image or false self before we know what we are doing. That is why we think we are that false self.

I could relate a little to the young woman who took her life. The false self I had unconsciously adopted over the years was based on a need to be perfect in various areas, so I could be worthy of attention, time, love and respect. It didn't work so well for me. The attention I earned was based on 'perfection' and for the attention to continue, for the feeling of self-worth to be sustained, the perfection had to continue as well. It was a lonely, exhausting way to live that generated self-loathing rather than the love I was seeking.

It took years of inner work for me to become conscious of what I was doing and even more years to be ready to accept myself. I had experienced painful criticism of my appearance, my body, my choice of clothing, my voice, the way I spoke, how I thought and even what I felt, from various sources over a prolonged period. Curiously, the qualities I now consider my greatest strengths and assets and the ones most openly admired by others, are the ones that were once the most attacked and invalidated. It wasn't until I learned to summon the sacred inner rebel and love myself no matter what another had to say about me, that I could begin to free myself from a distorted self-view. I welcomed the love, respect and appreciation that flowed into my life following that change, but I didn't rely on it for validation. It was simply a bonus.

After some time and preparatory inner work, I was ready to confront the parts of myself others had considered unacceptable. I needed to be able to bear witness to the judged parts of me and still love myself, rather than plunging back into the pain of rejection. To foster the ability to love and accept myself, I began by acknowledging and embracing the qualities I felt were positive such as my courage, determination, compassion, independence, vulnerability, generosity, wisdom, kindness, patience, ability to love and contagious sense of humour.

On its own that was not enough for me to feel healed, alive and able to manifest the sort of life I wanted to live. It was a good start, but I still sensed a lack of full vitality and aliveness. It felt like I was living in half of my house while the rest of it was shackled and closed. I was curious about what was in those other rooms. Learning to claim the brightness of my being had made me so much happier, but I knew I needed to face the rejected parts of me and to see if I could love them, too. That part of me was hidden and cloaked in shame, but she was still alive. She wanted out of the rooms where she was banished, and I wanted her to be free.

The shadow or hidden self never goes away, even when we refuse to acknowledge its existence. At some stage, we must deal with it. We can do this by choice or by the force of circumstances beyond our control (the Universe's way of telling us we are ready to face it, even if we don't agree!). We might think we can keep the shadow self tucked away, but it is always operating in our lives. It can wreak havoc in those hidden rooms and cause self-sabotage in many ways. You may wonder why releasing that crazy negativity into your life would be a positive move. Yet, once claimed and accepted, that energy is healing. When the distortion of shame falls away, the authentic aspects that remain are essential to feeling alive and living as freely as we wish.

Anger can transform into healthy boundaries. Rejection wounds can become compassion. Sadness can transform into wisdom. It takes courage to face our darker self, but when we do, gifts emerge from the process. There is a sweet spot between pushing our minds to tackle something we are not yet ready to face and tenaciously avoiding the pain when we know it is time to deal with it. One way to get to that place more swiftly—and peacefully—is to recognise that neither our judgements nor the judgements of others are accurate. When we think everything that appears to be good is actually good or everything that appears to be bad is actually bad, we end up confused and may miss the guidance the Universe is providing.

In the animated film *Kung Fu Panda,* the good-hearted panda Po, is a great fan of the famous Kung Fu Masters of China. His heroes are plastered all over his bedroom walls and he acts out fight scenes with his action figures. Elaborate fantasies relating to the awesomeness of his heroes dominate his dreams and daydreams. Becoming a Kung Fu master seems an unlikely destiny for an overweight, unfit, food-obsessed panda, but what is in his heart is the key to his destiny. Circumstance conspires, and Po ends up in an elite school of Kung Fu, alongside his heroes. His fate as the great warrior who will save China from the clutches of darkness is acknowledged, but no-one can see how that could come to be. It seems ridiculous, really. Even the greatest Kung Fu Master of all cannot see how it will work out. However, unlike everyone else, he has complete trust in the workings of the Universe.

As it turns out, Po becomes a great Kung Fu warrior by harnessing the very factors that had seemed to make that an impossibility. Panda lacks the qualities that makes his Kung Fu idols so great. Tigress has ferocious power, the snake has speed, the monkey has agility, and the praying mantis has delicacy and precision. Po is good natured, gentle, ticklish, slow and clumsy. What he does have is a big heart with a lot of passion — most of which is expressed through his obsessive appetite for delicious dumplings! These are the qualities his teacher exploits to teach Po focus and speed. He builds his fitness by making Po chase after the dumplings he so desires. The master helps Po fulfil his destiny, without changing or rejecting what was first considered to be his weakness. Through acceptance, those qualities become the source of his remarkable success.

Some years ago, I came across a charming story from spiritual teacher Anthony de Mello. Each day, a man carried two pots to the well and back again to provide water for his family. One pot was perfectly formed and never lost a drop. The other was cracked and dripped all the way back from the well to the house. It was not able to deliver as much water to the family as the other pot. The cracked pot felt sad about this and one night, it asked to be repaired. The water bearer compassionately told the cracked pot to pay attention to the path as they walked to and from the well the next day. The cracked pot did so, and the man asked it what it saw. The cracked pot said, "I saw a row of flowers growing on one side of the path." The man replied, "Yes, those flowers grow because of the water you drip on the way home each day." At this, the cracked pot felt happy, useful and complete. What it had viewed as a flaw was a valuable source of beauty.

Like the cracked pot and the Kung Fu-obsessed panda, the Divine wants us to pay attention to our 'flaws' — not because there is something unworthy there, but so we can free ourselves into a clearer vision of who we are as we embrace everything we have to enjoy and share with the world.

HEALING PROCESS

You may like to dedicate this healing process to a situation, a quality or trait of your body, mind or personality, or to anything happening in the world around you that is difficult to accept. If you are choosing to dedicate the exercise, consider how you would describe your dedication simply and clearly, then place one hand over your heart and say aloud:

> *I choose to dedicate this healing process to obtain wisdom, healing and enlightenment about … then express your dedication in your own words.*

If you are not dedicating the exercise to something specific, simply begin with the instructions in the next paragraph.

Place a hand at your heart. Rest your hand there as you relax. Visualise or intend that a softness of love is glowing within your heart. You may see, sense or feel this as a colour. Let it be. When you are ready, say aloud:

> *I call upon the Crystal Angel of Covellite and the star teacher of Andromeda Galaxy. May your wisdom, healing presence and unconditional love bless me and all beings with true enlightenment. May we accept and embrace all of life as a teacher that helps us become compassionate and wise. May the darkness of unresolved pain be embraced as a healing path to spiritual awakening. I take shelter in your grace and I discover and express my authentic self. I open my heart to release judgement and to gently discover the depths of my being, so that I may be free. Please guide me in this process through the highest wisdom for the greatest good. May all beings discover their true nature and fulfil their spiritual destiny. So be it.*

Bring your awareness back to the light in your heart. Allow the light to flow, move and generate healing according to an inner wisdom. Meditate on that light and rest for as long as you wish. You have completed your healing process.

CHAPTER SIX

SOUL CONNECTION, INDIVIDUAL ECCENTRICITY AND SURRENDER TO A HIGHER PLAN

STAR GUIDE: OMEGA CENTAURI

OMEGA CENTAURI IS THE LARGEST known globular cluster. When viewed with the naked eye, it looks like a fuzzy star, but it is actually a collection of nearly ten million stars orbiting a galactic core. The stars are around 12 billion years old — almost as old as the Universe itself! These stars are tightly bound by gravity and are very stable. Even toward the end of their lifespan, as each star darkens and fades from view, they remain bound to each other in a deeply enduring connection.

One of the teachings Omega Centauri shares with us is about the enduring nature of soul connection. Some spiritual guidance on this theme came through during a mentoring session with a woman who was struggling with the nature of her relationship with her son. She wanted to be close to him, but the anger he was carrying created distance between them. Her higher guidance spoke to her of allowing her son to have his experience, even though it seemed to thwart her desire for loving closeness. The message focused on the nature of their soul connection and spoke of the love that endured between them, irrespective of what was unfolding on their individual human journeys.

Allowing her son his experience, didn't mean she couldn't experience a deep and loving relationship with him. She was encouraged to drop deeper into love, to a soul level, where she could feel the connection she desired while affording herself and her son the freedom they each needed to take their human journeys and process their feelings in their own divine timing. That soul love would always be there between them. It was there before they incarnated as mother and son, it will be there throughout this incarnation, and it will continue when they are no longer mother and son.

Omega Centauri helps us connect with the enduring nature of love. In turn, we are helped to let go of possessiveness and the need to 'cling'. It helps us love in a way that is freeing for ourselves and our beloveds. We can delight in closeness and feel the same love flow in the spaces between us, too. We can realise a love that lasts beyond the lifespan of a human or an animal by recognising the bonds of love at a soul level. This realisation gives us the freedom to forgive and to live and let live. We remember that true love frees us and our beloveds.

Omega Centauri is by far the biggest and brightest globular cluster in the Milky Way galaxy. This ancient soul group holds around ten times the stars of an average globular cluster and is the size of 4 trillion solar masses. Omega Centauri helps us realise the sheer power and vastness of the Universe and of our own soul. When we recognise the presence of the divine mountain, it puts our earthly problems into context as being smaller and less intimidating molehills. We gain perspective by acknowledging there are powers in this Universe far greater than our own ego. This is not meant to make us feel unimportant or insignificant but is an invitation for us to relax into the vastness of a considerably evolved spiritual being.

If we haven't experienced a loving, capable and powerful parent who skilfully took care of us and was the safe haven of protection we needed as children, we may have learned that we need to do everything ourselves. Omega Centauri offers us the sense of having a loving elder who can shield and buffer us from life's ups and downs, so we can learn and grow without feeling completely alone or unprotected.

Omega Centauri is not only massive, it is somewhat eccentric. It has never quite fitted in with the other globular star clusters that encircle the Milky Way. It has the unusual trait of being home to a diverse range of stars of different ages and types. This star teacher shows us that aspects of our being can be in varying stages of development, and that is okay.

I have met spiritually advanced souls who struggle with the basics of being human. They have such insight when it comes to higher worlds but managing their physical and emotional needs can be an utter mystery to them. Even highly evolved souls will have aspects that need to heal and mature. Giving ourselves permission to recognise this humbly, without undue shaming or feeling that we should have already mastered whatever our issues may be, can be helpful. It's hard to work on our issues if we are so ashamed of them that we pretend they don't exist! Omega Centauri teaches the soul that all parts of us are valuable — both the evolved and the broken parts (the broken bits hold the seeds of our continuing evolution). This is a great antidote to the mistaken view that as we grow spiritually, we are supposed to be perfect.

The non-typical characteristics of Omega Centauri have astronomers postulating that it was a remnant core of a dwarf galaxy before it was pulled toward the Milky Way in a galactic merger. Galaxy mergers are powerfully transformational events. In most cases, there is so much distance between stars that it doesn't involve a physical collision of the stars. During the merger, especially in the later stages, each galaxy becomes so affected by the approach of the other that the stars lose their memory of their previous orbit. Astrophysicists refer to this as 'violent relaxation'. Galaxy mergers also trigger a creative surge and an extreme amount of star formation takes place. Thousands of new stars can be created each year.

Connecting with Omega Centauri on a soul level suggests a life-changing encounter with a greater spiritual power is imminent, or already happening. This could be an encounter that you don't consciously recognise, like a deeper soul connection with a guru or guide on the spiritual planes. It could be a connection with a teacher in physical form, an earthly group or a community that will radically change the course of your life.

Maintaining a sense of authenticity as an individual while being open to the positive influences of other sources takes some skill. For this, you need to recognise your own truth as well as wisdom greater than your own. You don't want to lose your self-possession and inner balance completely, but as you open yourself to ideas and energies, you are likely to feel stirred up within until those newer energies are integrated. Parts of your personality or life may change with these encounters, sometimes dramatically, but the essentials will remain intact. This change may entail loss, but much can be gained from this process — such as a major increase in creative energy and vitality, the assumption of a new role in your life and finding a new place in the Universe. Remember, no matter how much you or your life changes, the real you is always going to be the real you. You do not have to fear losing your authentic self. It is always there, within.

Omega Centauri supports the soul when smaller desires need to be sacrificed to realise a greater plan and higher purpose. This can simply mean that the ego needs to bow down to the soul. If we understand what is happening it can make the process easier to go through because we don't misinterpret not getting what we want in that moment as meaning we will never experience fulfilment, peace, love, joy and happiness. Instead, we recognise that the Universe is saying, "Not yet." Perhaps some other things need to happen first, or it is not to happen that way because there is a better way for you. This can be hard for the ego to take, but this understanding brings great relief to the soul. Knowing a wiser hand is steering your course brings the sense that you can take shelter in a greater divine being. You may have had to play lone wolf, be a hermit, always be taking others under your wing or be a source of strength for those around you. This star teacher helps you learn how to hold space powerfully for others, and how to be held yourself.

Omega Centauri also reminds us to cultivate a healthy relationship with the past. We can acknowledge our past experiences for the powerful wisdom we acquired through them, without remaining attached to old thoughts, belief systems, memories or viewpoints. We can accept that everything serves for a time and can then be released so a new orientation to the world can emerge.

Finally, this amazing star teacher reminds us that our uniqueness and powerful wisdom can be the key to our belonging, rather than a cause for jealousy, separation or distance. When we allow ourselves to gravitate toward what feels powerful for us, we will find our place and our purpose, even if they are not what we first expected them to be.

THE CRYSTAL ANGEL OF ELESTIAL QUARTZ

Elestials are quartz crystals with natural terminations over the body. They often have skeletal plates that build upon each other on the surface. Elestials can have incredibly detailed etchings on their faces, too. They are also called 'crocodile quartz' or 'skeletal quartz' which gives a sense of their appearance. Their outer layers emanate a raw and very physical energy, and the inner nature of these crystals is highly refined and subtle, though powerfully healing.

Elestials can generate in cathedral quartz formations, also sometimes referred to charmingly as a 'light library' quartz formation. Unlike quartz clusters, where many termination points grow in various directions out of the main base, cathedral quartz demonstrates multiple termination points that have grown side by side in the same direction. Essentially, it is a single-bodied crystal, arising from the one base, with distinct terminations at the apex. If there was ever a crystal to teach us that the one and the many are the same, this would be it. These crystals help generate harmony and common purpose. They help us focus on unity without losing respect for individuality. They can alleviate divisiveness in group consciousness and be deeply healing for all types of communities including families, meditation groups, nations and humanity as a whole.

With intricate layers and complex surfaces, elestials often resonate with people who feel they are a bit odd, have a lot of depth and are quite complex beings. Every elestial is unpredictably unique — rather like human beings. These are the divine rebels of the crystal world, true to themselves while providing a sublime gateway through which we can immerse ourselves in the loving unity of higher consciousness.

Elestials come in many colours — clear, brown, violet, yellow, white, and no doubt, others I have not yet seen. All elestials can ground us in our bodies and simultaneously open us to higher frequencies, but I find the smoky quartz elestial does this particularly well.

Elestials sometimes grow self-healed formations. This occurs when a crystal has been damaged, perhaps the movements of the earth broke its attachment to the mother crystal, and it repaired itself by growing natural terminations over the fracture point. These can be remarkably powerful crystals to use for self-healing as we transform the wounds in our soul into sources of greater energy and power.

Elestials are known as great healers and connectors to Mother Earth. When we are touching the elestial, our fingertips and palms (and feet or other parts of the body including the forehead and heart) can take in the healing communications encoded in the stone. It teaches us how to receive information in a non-verbal and instinctive way.

This stone is especially valuable for those of us who have never comfortably fit in to society or the family and seek a union with the Earth Mother to experience what it is to fully belong.

SPIRITUAL GUIDANCE: STAR SEEDS

In a sense, we are all born of stars. However, certain souls need to remember and fully embody their 'star signature' in order to fulfil their divine destiny. It is part of their higher purpose to do so. I refer to these unique souls as star seeds. Many of us want to help humanity in a meaningful way, feel some sort of connection to the stars and acknowledge that stardust is part of our genetic composition. Star seeds embody all of this. They are also compelled by a sacred inner purpose to elevate consciousness on this planet by discovering, being and expressing their authentic star nature. They are meant to be living, breathing, meditating, laughing, healing star medicine in human form. In that sense, they are something like human crystals. They vibrate with the frequencies of a greater spiritual intelligence and emanate healing energy for all those open to it.

Star seeds incarnate with a soul mission to help our planet in some way. This may be through living and shining their unique vibration, through completing a task or series of tasks or through a vocation as a healer, teacher, activist, guide, all-round sacred rebel and so on. The clue is in the name: star *seed*. They are here to plant seeds of love, higher consciousness, wisdom and light which can grow and develop into a nurturing part of the earthly ecosystem.

I stumbled across a comment on a YouTube video which I felt was a great summation of the star seed soul in the earlier phases of their experiences on Earth. The person wrote that they had been contemplating their life and the many issues in the world and thought, "I must have been out of my mind to come to this planet!" The person then noted that their higher self answered, "Yes, you were! You were in your heart."

When star seeds remember that love brought them here, and that love will guide, protect, inspire and support them, they begin to fall in love with their lives. That is the game changer that shifts their focus from painful experience to personally fulfilling spiritual purpose.

Star seeds can utilise their eccentricity, their differences, the ways they don't fit in to the current paradigms on this planet to better understand what it is they are bringing into play. What they have, and others don't understand, is missing in the human collective. With great courage, they eventually embrace and commit to their earthly experience, and proceed to broadcast their dissonant, unconventional and ultimately healing frequency.

The dissonant frequency of the star seed is actually harmonising. It is a corrective sound for the soul. It helps retune those trapped in the discordance of fear and delusion, so they can align their soul with the pure song of the Universe. It creates union. It's not unlike how healing it can be when you see a performer in concert and everyone knows the songs and sings along. There is a sense of kinship, unity and connection. It can be uplifting and powerful. Imagine that to the power of ten times infinity and you have what is possible when we align our soul notes to the heart song of the Divine.

You see, the dissonant frequency of the star seed is the true note. It is only from the perspective of those trapped in lower frequencies that the sound of the star seed seems strange, off-key or unwelcome. If you joined a choir that was singing off-key, it would take a lot of courage to sound your voice and stay true to the real note! They may all tell you that you are doing it wrong. You may fear that you will be rejected from the choir, judged or gossiped about. If you know what is true, have a great passion for the healing beauty and power of music, and you understand the benefit it would bring to the choir if they learned to sing the true note, then you could find the courage to proceed with your task.

Other healers, lightworkers and of course, other star seeds, typically recognise their frequency for what it is — corrective and healing. Mainstream consciousness will not always be so accepting and embracing and that is exactly why that different frequency is needed. Those trapped in fear need love, even if they resist it for a time — in fact, when they resist it is when they need it most. Fortunately, star seeds who have the courage to stay true to their own note long enough will eventually attract those rare friends who understand that their wonderful weirdness is actually wisdom.

Star seeds often have a subtle inner understanding that they are somehow profoundly different to others. I don't mean in the usual way where we acknowledge our inimitable quirks and qualities as being part of the many common traits we share as human beings. That would be like saying we are all 'soul flowers' where some of us are more like roses and others are more like slightly odd (but still beautiful) birds of paradise. Star seeds feel their difference is deeper and more pronounced. They don't feel like a type of flower, but another species altogether! Star seeds can feel as though their experience of life on Earth is like watching a very foreign reality television program. There will be times when they do not relate to the way most humans behave. I have often said that I find it weird to be human. It is such a strange experience to me. I am more familiar with it now, after forty or so years of practice, but whilst I completely accept and acknowledge it, deep down I still find it to be a curiosity. It can be absolutely delightful, but bizarre, nonetheless.

This may lead to the idea that star seeds are aliens, but I don't feel that is correct. To me, the star seed soul is a human being, with cosmically exotic flavour. I have had some interesting encounters with extra-terrestrials in unexpected, inspiring and sometimes amusing ways. Whilst they were beings from the stars, they weren't star seeds. Aliens or extra-terrestrials are more like visitors to Earth, rather than part of the local population. No matter how much a star seed may feel like an alien (and I've certainly had that feeling in the past) they are still human beings and part of our human family. They are more akin to a twelve-string guitar than a regular six-string, or a harp or a bassoon! But they are still musical instruments in our earthly orchestra.

When I was in my early twenties, I had a psychic reading with a well-respected angelic channel. She told me several things that were so helpful at the time. Like most star seeds, I can recognise when a higher truth is being stated — it just rings true. So, when this psychic said I was not meant to be here on this planet, that my being here was some sort of mistake in the worlds that I came from, I recognised a lack of resonance, a lack of truth. I believe the Universe is wild and unpredictable. I believe it can seem like chaos in play. However, I also believe in the invisible and graceful workings of a higher order intelligence. I don't believe in 'mistakes'. Even exceptionally talented psychics don't have a 100% strike rate, and I trusted my own intuition and wisdom enough to take what resonated from the session and cast the rest aside, with gratitude for this woman's talent and time.

I mention this experience because if that sort of belief—that you could be placed somewhere in this Universe by mistake—existed in her mind, then it will exist in other minds. Given that star seeds often feel out of place for a portion of their life journey, that belief could take hold and make their ability to embrace Earth, trusting that they will be graciously and generously hosted here, much more difficult and painful than it needs to be. It's important to emphasise that you can be a star seed *and* feel very much at home here on Earth. Many star seeds have a powerful love for nature and the earth — that love is part of what brought them to this planet for their life mission.

I remember a star seed soul telling me that he went for a psychic reading but when the psychic opened the door, so he could come in, she simply stared at him. Then she screamed and slammed the door shut in his face! A few moments later, the front door opened to this startled star seed once again and the psychic somewhat sheepishly said, "Sorry, I just saw you as a star person and freaked out, but it's okay now."

This soul already saw himself in that way, so he wasn't bothered by it at all. In fact, he was quite comfortable with who he was at a soul level. He had a sort of dignity about him, a sense of quiet inner confidence that came from embracing who he was at a deeper level. Before you become concerned that as a star seed people might have the same reaction to you, relax. Most people won't see anything like this psychic did (nor behave like she did!). This was a most unusual situation, but I want to mention it because there was something so interesting about this man and how he comes across to others.

He was an attractive, ordinary-looking human being. When I first met him, I noticed there was something about him that I couldn't quite articulate, and yet it was there — a quality of 'otherness' and difference. He just resonated at a different frequency. In his day-to-day life, people were drawn to him and obviously found this quality of his to be most appealing. He wasn't particularly warm or friendly. If we were going to 'animalise' him, I would say he was more like a cat than a dog in personality. Yet, when he went out with friends, people would consistently want to sit next to him as he 'guessed' their star signs. Apparently, he was never wrong, and given the high level of development of his third eye chakra, I believe that.

His self-acceptance gave him a naturalness and ease. His enjoyment of his higher consciousness gave him a 'royal' quality without him considering himself superior to others. He had a spiritual magnetism which people responded to and which made it easy for him to attract what he wanted in life, including financial support, work opportunities and friendships. His subtle strangeness never got in the way of his earthly success and spiritual growth. His respect for his own being was mirrored in the way others felt toward him.

I wanted to describe this soul to you as a contrast to the stereotyped star seed experience based on rejection, loss and disconnection. This is not a dismissal of the pain star seeds can experience, especially in the earlier phases of their lives. I have given a voice to some of those challenges below, to help those who are courageously dealing with such circumstances be more able to process them. Rather, I share this star man's example here to show there is a way for such beings to thrive with love and abundance on the earth that does not involve trying to change one's true nature. It is about creating a loving and respectful attitude toward who we are. This may mean unlearning or reinterpreting earlier experiences which may have framed our talents or abilities with fear and suspicion.

Star seeds have incarnated to help the earth and, at some level, most people (not always consciously) do recognise that and gravitate toward them and the light they emanate most strongly when they are just being themselves. Each one of us is special and valuable, and yet for the star seed, the recognition of that value often starts within our own hearts. It flourishes in the world around us but only when we choose to see ourselves as beautifully dignified in our eccentricity and uniqueness. As with any soul, we may need to embrace a healing journey before we can get to that inner place of lovingly claiming ourselves.

Not all star seeds come from the same star system. There are differences in the qualities of a star seed who identifies closely with Sirius and those who relate to the Pleiades or Arcturus, for example. No matter which star system they hail from, every star seed will spend a portion of their lives asking, "What on earth am I doing here?" (pun intended!). Like a plant that has been (lovingly) re-potted because it could grow well and add beauty to a new garden bed, their roots are in shock for a time. So, star seeds can have an inexplicable feeling that they are supposed to be somewhere else or that they have been uprooted from where they once belonged — even though they are in the right place for them.

Star seeds will eventually develop a sense of belonging and kinship with a global soul tribe that includes humanity but also encompasses other beings of wisdom and love throughout the Universe. They will make the Universe their home, even whilst in a human body here on Earth. For star seeds that have reached this state, nationalism, culture and other types of categorisation are relevant as part of their journey but are not essential to their identity. Typically, they will find more meaning in experiencing their identity as a universal being of light than as a member of a nation, church or political group, for example.

Star seeds will not forget who they are or lose their beautiful differences, but they eventually relax and let go of the feelings of shock, grief, disorientation and confusion and regain a sense of rightful place. This gradually happens as they step into their journey with the understanding that they are meant to be here and that it can be interesting and fun for them, too. They learn how to relax and be themselves. They also recognise that while their task may be challenging, the Earth Mother really wants them here and will support and provide for them, so they can fulfil their spiritual mission. Once they get their heads around the idea that they are meant to be consciousness transmitters in whatever way feels most authentic, joyful, empowering, free and beautiful to them, everything begins to flow.

Some star seeds are more sensitive than others. Some find that being on Earth feels heavy and dense compared to their natural lightness of spirit. They steadily adjust and settle into the substance of Earth and learn to rest in its deep stillness and restorative slow vibration. Star seeds learn that 'low' and 'slow' are not the same thing when we are speaking about the earth energies. Connection to the earth can slow down the fast-workings of the mind and allow a star seed to gain clarity, peace and wellbeing. This will enhance their quality of life and their ability to attract whatever earthly abundance is required to support their divine purpose. Their spiritual empowerment grows through their attunement to earth energies.

Some star seeds fiercely express truth with a clinical detachment that allows them to cut through the collective confusion of human wounding and get straight to the real issue. Some have a far gentler way of speaking and find the idea of confrontation difficult as they do not want to cause any harm to another being. Learning that honesty can be expressed with kindness is helpful for both these types of star seeds.

Some star seeds feel solitary and reclusive at times. They may struggle with human relationships, until they learn to remain true to themselves while accepting the different vibrations and ways of being that other humans can embody. Other star seeds are involved in their work and relationships but can sometimes feel more like an observer of the world, rather than an active participant. They can feel slightly removed from humanity even though they are happy to be here making their contribution. In their meditations and dreams, star seeds may feel that they are transmitting their observations about the consciousness on Earth back to their star home — a bit like a school report to help other beings better understand how they can further contribute to spiritual education on Earth.

For many star seeds, the emotional life of a human being with its changeability, density and intensity can be a startling and strange discovery. While they relate to the high-frequency emotions of love, joy, serenity and peace, denser emotions like anger, grief, fear, guilt, hate and shame may seem foreign at first. Eventually, as the star seed becomes accustomed to the nature of existence on this planet, they learn that all emotions can teach us something useful when we work with them wisely. They learn not to run away from such feelings but to work through them. They realise their light is not going to be extinguished by emotions and that they can settle themselves by listening and responding calmly. Emotions can then become a healthy aspect of being human and a way for communication to flow between the body, mind and spirit.

Star seeds can also find the 'slow' process of manifestation frustrating. Some carry a soul memory of being able to instantly manifest with thought. The earthly manifestation process, where thought needs to translate into practical physical steps can seem unduly burdensome. As they develop commitment, discipline, and constancy (three traits star seeds learn from being in a human body) they can become masterful manifestors of uniquely beautiful creations that bring spiritual light into this world for the greater good.

Ample solitude can be helpful for a star seed. As star seeds are generally quite old souls, and by that I also mean 'big' souls, they can take in a lot — like a larger-than-usual receiving dish. In a lot of ways, they are travellers in a strange land. Something those more acclimatised to Earth wouldn't bat their third eyelid at, the star seed may find deeply disturbing or profoundly moving and need time to effectively digest it. Without time alone as needed, a star seed can feel overloaded, agitated or become prone to depression, anxiety or outbursts of rage. A star seed can resolve most of the challenges of emotional adjustment to life on Earth through time alone, preferably in nature, perhaps with a journal, and with complete permission to just be. When they are ready, they will 'rejoin the human race' with more understanding and energy.

When a star seed child is living in a family who are not star seed souls, and they are expected to keep up, to do what they are told and to fit in with the family way of things, it can cause problems at the time and later in life. They will need to unlearn that constant activity is desirable and move away from any negative connotations about rest, such as it being laziness or non-productive, for example. This can be a tough nut to crack in our modern culture that tends to normalise the 'always on' nature of technology, as though our bodies should be the same way. We can lose the taste for rest and how beneficial it is on all levels. Yet, all souls need space to become their own true self, to develop a balance between authenticity, individuality and socialisation. They need time to figure out their rhythm for rest and activity. I feel this is almost totally askew in the majority of human beings, not only star seeds, and is the root cause of so many health problems on physical, emotional and mental levels. Giving ourselves permission to experiment with rest and rediscover the joy of it, not to mention the overall increase in productivity and energy that it creates, can reverse so much damage and provide the fuel necessary for us to manifest the beauty that is within our souls. Meditation can be a wonderful practice for many reasons, one of which is that it is an activity where discipline and rest meet and enhance our connection to our natural self.

When a star seed child is not given space to be in their rich inner world to process things in solitude, they may develop compensatory behaviours like zoning out, not listening or getting lost in fantasy or imagination. Their struggle to fit in to various social systems like school or the workplace will become greater without balance of that inner time out. When they are denied that inner time and still manage to overcome the difficulties of fitting in to a school or work environment, they often do so at the expense of their authentic self. They may forget how to trust and connect in the voice of their authentic self which is their intuition and instincts. Quiet time will help them reconnect to their authentic being, even during when they are dealing with ways of the world that could become dehumanising. Connected to their authentic selves, they can become part of the sacred revolution — the movement of awakening human beings who dare to live outside the norm to create a way of being that is more in tune with the soul and less about treating our human selves as machines to fulfil ego-driven priorities.

Many star seeds have a very gentle nature and don't like confrontation or anger, but every moment that they can get in touch with their sacred rage and shake off the confines of other people's opinions or demands is a moment their soul light can glow brighter and help them find their own way. It is important for a star seed to learn to reach out and ask for help from those who will encourage them to find their own truth and trust them to find their unique journey. They are not here to live according to established values and current paths, they are here to live something new, different and higher voltage in terms of light, love and wisdom.

There are many legitimate reasons for star seeds to feel positive about their life on Earth and to trust it is not a case of enduring it until it is over. Rather, as they learn to love and accept themselves, and assume responsibility for their life, the Universe will stand by them by offering support. They can then handle challenges more easily and find the peace, fulfilment and creative freedom they need to thrive. Encouraging this completely reasonable hope for their future can help them do the inner work they need so that all the good things meant for them can reach them more easily.

HEALING PROCESS

Completing this healing process in nature, in solitude, would be helpful. If you are not able to do so, you may be able to have some music with nature sounds playing in the background. If that is not possible, then you can tune into the power of nature by listening to the flowing sound of your own breath, as it moves in and out of your nostrils.

When you are ready, place one hand lightly over your heart. Relax and allow your awareness to become more introverted, more inward focused. You may wish to sense the quality of your heart energy. You may feel the beating of your heart or a subtler sense of energy, light and love that animates your heart. Be at peace with whatever you sense.

Imagine, intend or feel that you can summon generosity and full permission for your own heart to be truthful and free in its expression. Allow your heart essence to gently expand until you feel enveloped in it. If you wish to transform this exercise into a global healing—on your own or with others—imagine, intend or allow your heart essence to gently and freely expand until it envelops the earth and all beings within her auric field. You are giving a blessing, freely from your heart. The Universe responds to such actions in kind, blessing you in return.

When you are ready say aloud:

> *I call upon the Crystal Angel of Elestial Quartz and the star teacher Omega Centauri. I open my heart to the heart of the Universe. I open to receive an abundance of divine blessing. May I know my true nature through unconditional love, mercy and compassion. May I live authentically in harmony with the greater purpose for my life. May I open to truth, abundance, prosperity and peace, to fulfil my divine destiny as a beloved child of the Universe with balance, wisdom and authentic inner connection to my true nature. May all beings be blessed, through the highest wisdom for the greatest good. So be it.*

Imagine, feel, intend or visualise all the goodness of the Universe pouring into you, in abundance, generosity and grace. Simply intend to receive. You may like to sit or lie down in a restful posture with your arms outstretched to help this process. Allow your mind to rest in the process, so that no effort is involved. Naturally, once you have been filled, the excess will overflow into the auric fields of all beings in all realms, for the greatest good.

Rest for as long as you wish to complete your healing process.

CHAPTER SEVEN

STRATEGIC SOLITUDE TO REINFORCE YOUR LIGHT

STAR GUIDE: SPICA

THE BRIGHTEST STAR in the constellation of Virgo, Spica represents the ear of wheat that is held by the virgin goddess. Spica is the star of the harvest and resonates with abundance and plenty. It reminds us of the unlimited supply of divine resources that help us fulfil our potential. Spica is a binary star, and the stars are so close to each other that their mutual gravity has an effect on their shape. They are egg-shaped, rather than spherical, and complete a swift orbit around each other every four days. The egg is a powerful symbol for the feminine principle, signifying abundance, birth and creativity. The number four is a powerful signifier of manifestation. When Spica makes connection with the soul, it is a sign that manifestation is imminent, particularly when there has been a long or deep time of personal development and spiritual growth. Creative realisation and spiritual harvest are soon to come.

When working with Spica, we want to be sure that we seed and nurture what we want to reap when it is time for our karmic harvest. What kind of thoughts, intentions and ideas do we want to contribute to the world? We build those contributions day to day by living to inspire and encourage others or by tearing others down (and ourselves in the process).

Focusing on what we give, being open to a generous flow of blessings and being happy whether they are coming to us or moving through us for the benefit of others, is key to receiving the full grace of Spica. This is not about denying our more selfish tendencies but acknowledging that we vitalise that which we choose to focus upon. When we focus on generating goodwill in our hearts and encourage others from a place of fullness, we open ourselves up to a great flow of generosity from the Universe.

Increasing our practice of generosity means being more generous with ourselves and allowing the Universe to be more generous with us also. Remember, the sweetest fruit is at the top of the tree, meaning that working harder or climbing higher will bring a greater reward. I believe discipline and commitment are essential to manifesting divine life purpose, but I also take on something my mother instilled in me from an early age which is to work smarter rather than harder. To me, that means leveraging the divine support that is available to us, knowing that this is exactly what the Divine wants us to do! When we allow the way to become easier for us, we can grow and assist others on their path more effectively. Everyone wins.

Working smarter means the best outcomes happen when we put our efforts into the correct channels. Pouring ever more effort into things that won't get us closer to where we want to go just wears us out. It is like cutting down trees when you need to dig the well. You can triple your efforts, but the well will still be dry unless you put down the axe and pick up the shovel. So, when we feel like we are doing a lot of work for no harvest it may be a case of endurance and patience, but it may also be a matter of changing our approach.

If we persist with the way we think our path should unfold, rather than responding to the inner wisdom guiding us, we can end up blaming the Universe for the delays our own behaviours are creating. If we then misapply the notion of needing more endurance and patience, we can talk ourselves into continuing in our self-driven rather than divinely-guided path, and not make the progress that we could be making. I don't believe we need to subject ourselves to undue time pressures and rushing tends to get us nowhere fast, but I also acknowledge that human life is relatively short. We typically spend the first decades doing preparatory spiritual work before we can effectively help others. That only leaves a certain number of decades to do the work and there is so much work to do! So, we want to make the most of the lifetime we have. Even if you believe in reincarnation, you only get one shot at being the you that you are in this life. It is so valuable and precious. We don't need to force things to happen, but we don't want to block things from happening either.

I was mentoring a young man who had much promise as a healer. He was keen to step into that role and dedicated hours to practicing healing techniques each day. However, when I looked at his energy field, I saw an image of a car with the overfilled tyres on one side and those on the other side going flat. If he tried to drive that car, he would go around in circles at best. He firmly believed that with enough spiritual practice, his healing abilities and career would simply manifest. Whilst spiritual energy is incredibly powerful and beneficial, it is not meant to be a substitute for dealing with practical matters. It is a support and helps us approach physical-world tasks with more wisdom, grace and efficiency.

By persisting with his approach, the young man's development would become more and more lopsided and he would be increasingly disheartened that Spirit was not responding to his efforts. He couldn't hear that he needed to balance his inner healing with engagement in the outer world. Those steps were necessary to help bring his dreams to life because it would lead him right into confrontation with a deep wound around an absent parent that he was not yet ready to confront. That is okay. Confronting a soul wound usually needs deep preparation. Acknowledging that can feel humbling but it puts us in an empowered position. We work and progress with the understanding that when we are ready, we will tackle the next hurdle, and clear it. Spirit will help us do so. This man needed Spica to help him channel his efforts in a way that would manifest the worldly success his inner self wants him to have, for his own fulfilment and to help others, too.

Associated with both Mars and Venus, the planetary manifestations of masculine and feminine energies, Spica can help us integrate our masculine and feminine qualities, no matter what our biological gender may be. Spica is a celestial psychologist who helps us activate the sacred inner masculine qualities of discernment, clarity, boundary setting and action, and to strengthen the sacred inner feminine qualities of listening, intuition, trust in an unseen guiding force and patience. In harmony, Mars and Venus are creative, manifestation-oriented energies. Spica shows us how to channel the inspirations of the soul mind (from Venus) into action that leads to manifestation (with the energy of Mars). It is star medicine for making sublime ideas practical, so that they can be shared in the world.

The poet Ovid told the story of Astraea, the last of the immortals said to live on Earth with humans. When the world became corrupted by evil forces, she retreated into the sky to become Spica. The star is a symbol of her purity and a promise of her return in the Golden Age. This theme is echoed in Chinese astronomy where Spica is favoured as a special star of spring. The Hindus refer to Spica as Chitrā meaning *bright one* and associate it with pearls. Spica helps us understand that sometimes a strategic retreat can strengthen our position and reinforces our light, wisdom and inner knowing, especially if outer forces appear to be gaining ground and causing confusion or disorientation.

My grandmother used to say that sometimes you must be willing to lose the battle to win the war. Wisdom is knowing when you need to fight and when it is smarter to retreat so you can ready yourself to stand strong at a better time. Retreat can come from wisdom and strength, rather than fear. The Coptic people of Egypt refer to this star as Khoritos—meaning *solitary*—due to its isolated position in the night sky. There are times when solitude is the only way to recalibrate and reinforce our inner light. When the time is right for a triumphant re-emergence, we shall know it, and so shall it be.

THE CRYSTAL ANGEL OF APOPHYLLITE

Apophyllite is one of those stones that keeps popping up in my life. I absolutely adore it, so I don't mind at all. It can be pale green, grey or white, sometimes with a silvery sheen to it, and it is found in clusters of rhomboidal terminations.

Apophyllite integrates spiritual light with the physical body. This is a priceless for all of us trying to live true to our spiritual nature without restraint or distortion. Although this is a powerful stone, I have found it works well over the long term by subtly increasing spiritual energies. I have had pieces of apophyllite in my home for years and it continues to build a field of quietening energy by radiating a peaceful divine presence. Even when there is noise around my home, there is a field of silence and peace within my little sanctuary, increased through my meditation practice, how I choose to live, and with the loving assistance of the Crystal Angel of Apophyllite.

Apophyllite works at the crown chakra to open our conscious connection to luminous forms of higher spiritual guidance — be it angels, realised spiritual masters or other unconditionally loving and pure divine beings. It brings peace where there has been disturbance and light into the darkness of suffering, especially where there is a feeling of disconnection or abandonment by the spiritual worlds. Even when we really love Spirit, unresolved pain can create an unconscious distrust. Apophyllite gently brings this to light, soothes away pain and promotes unconditional trust in the Divine. It opens the higher chakras to experience the Divine as an attentive and responsive wisdom that is always flowing in our lives.

Soothing and protective in any environment, apophyllite is peaceful enough to have in one's bedroom where it can work as you sleep to bring spiritual light through the astral body and boost protection and spiritual progress during the dream state. This can be helpful for those who process a lot of information or inner psychic pain during their dreams or are troubled by nightmares. Such situations can be helped by asking the Crystal Angel of Apophyllite to be present and to protect the relevant person and their sleeping space across all realms of existence with divine light and love.

White apophyllite is particularly attractive to the angelic realm and holds a pure angelic frequency itself. Having a piece of apophyllite in the home is akin to placing a welcome mat at the door for angelic guides. I especially like this stone for children as it holds purity, unconditional love and encourages a total trust in the light that can be missing from the hearts of those who have suffered abuse and neglect, in this or other lifetimes. Apophyllite helps us reconnect with our innate light, expansiveness and spirit, to cast off unnecessary suspicion and fear and remember that peace and divine presence is always in our hearts.

SPIRITUAL GUIDANCE: PRAYING LIKE THE DIVINE BADASS YOU ARE

There is a Chinese proverb that goes something like this, "Four ounces of energy can divert the force of four thousand pounds." This is demonstrated in Chi Gung practice where the force of a powerful opponent can be diverted and even used against them. Someone who understands this can obtain victory, even against powerful opposition, not by meeting force with force but by allowing the energy to flow and then redirecting it. This proverb alludes to the difference between force and power. For peace-loving lightworkers this teaching brings hope. You can be powerful without turning to aggressive tactics. You don't have to resort to weapons at all. You can have a positive influence in the world by learning how to use the tremendous power that resides in your consciousness.

We explored the idea of working smarter rather than always striving harder earlier in this chapter. Without commitment, discipline and effort, we may never take the steps needed so that we can come to the end of our lives feeling we have matured and given the best of ourselves to the world. But, if we use a hacksaw when a toothpick will do the job, we waste energy and are likely to create unnecessary damage.

In a world that cleaves with passion to the notion of 'go big or go home' the beauty and power of the small can be overlooked. I am a big-picture person with bold dreams of what I would like to create and share with the world, so I would not typically encourage myself to think small. However, I have found that it is the small steps, the simple adjustments, the willingness to plod steadily along that leads to creation itself. It is the little things that make big things possible.

Countless people tell me they feel they are destined for great things in this lifetime. Yet, they struggle to show up or to take care of their bodies day to day, for example. Often this results in chaos. They cannot understand why they cannot achieve the greatness that is in their hearts. If we focus on the big picture and forget about the small, essential steps, we may begin to doubt the heart's vision. It is a back-to-front, cart-in-front-of-the-horse recipe for frustration.

We must be willing to give up the attachment to flying high, to ground and to attend to the day-to-day steps to make progress. It's simple but not always easy, especially when the daily tasks lack the shine and bliss the grander vision evokes within us. This is when we must be smart and remind ourselves of the big picture. We connect to the inspiration and use it as fuel to get us moving on the daily steps instead of a reason to avoid the work and float off into fantasy. I do believe we need some fantasy in our lives to enthuse us with creative ideas. It can be incredibly good for the soul! However, the soul cannot create on fantasy alone. The more grounded we are, the more attentive we are to simple routine, the more our dreams can come down to earth and take flight. We need wildness and whimsy with a balancing dose of practicality. It is as simple as asking, "What can I do right now?" And getting on with it!

The simple daily steps are whatever you need to do to take care of your body, mind and soul. They will vary for each of us depending on our passion and purpose. You are worth the time and energy it takes to find out the type of lifestyle that suits you. Discover the mix of meditation, relaxation, exercise, sleep, nutrition, solitude, socialising and challenge that suits you. This might seem self-absorbed, but until you figure out how to meet your needs, you are not going to be particularly skilful at helping anyone else meet theirs.

It might not seem that these small steps matter that much. However little changes to daily routine, like regular exercise, drinking enough water or an extra thirty minutes of sleep, make a big difference to our wellbeing and our capacity to effectively undertake spiritual practices. So, you could find out where you can buy healthy food in your area, set up a water filter in your home or research what cleaning products have the least amount of damaging chemicals for your body and the earth. You could commit to meditating each day, even if it is only for five or ten minutes, and maybe even play with loving that you have that time for yourself rather than seeing it as a chore. It's a good idea to choose one or two changes and proceed a little bit at a time, rather than attempting to overhaul your life in one go. It all adds up and creates a solid foundation. When the foundations are good, they can handle a high-rise building. A firm foundation will support you through the challenges of manifesting a beautiful soul vision, whether those challenges are external obstacles or a need to reframe your mindset.

There is a lot of information—and misinformation—circulating these days. Your intuition can help you sort the wheat from the chaff. As we try what feels right and cast aside what doesn't, we come to realise that figuring out how to live well to maximise our divine potential can involve a lot of trial and error along the way. What works for one and what suits another can vary dramatically depending on personality and the soul phase each is going through. We are all unique. Living in a way that brings out our best is exciting, but it comes with the price tag of taking responsibility for ourselves. Some people are scared to do that. They may need to learn to trust themselves or to realise the courage and strength they have within. With small daily steps they can liberate themselves from societal conditioning and step into a freer lifestyle.

Most people in the modern world need to learn how to sleep, rest and repair their bodies and minds so that they are not running purely on stress. However, it can be easier, or at least more familiar, to stress out than to learn how to relax and trust and let things flow. Yet daily relaxation is so worthwhile, even if it is just a few minutes before and after eating a meal, or part of our bedtime routine to promote quality sleep. Rest contributes to our happiness, energy levels and wellbeing, and the people in our lives benefit when we are in our soul zone and have grace, love and energy to share. Tuning in to your needs and doing your best to honour them (without creating more stress or inflexible, impossible to-do lists in the process!) is part of how we fulfil our contribution to this planet.

The hidden power in apparently small or insignificant actions is evidenced in prayer and the cultivation of goodwill. These two practices—along with meditation and doing your inner work—are perhaps the most powerful means by which you can contribute positively to the world.

Those on a path of personal healing and spiritual growth may already understand the importance of their thoughts. My first spiritual teacher said the power of a negative thought in the spiritual worlds is the equivalent of throwing a piece of furniture around the room! Some years later I came across the idea of thought correction, where you 'clean up' a negative thought when you notice it. A fantastic idea! You can do this in several ways: visualise it being purified with violet light, make a heartfelt mental apology (especially if the thought is directed toward yourself or another), and/or stop the thought in its tracks and replace it with another thought (or a giggle).

Where I live on the Northern Beaches it is not unusual for people to walk barefoot from the beach into the post office or a café. One morning at the post office, a barefoot local was collecting his parcel from the counter and I noticed a thick crack in the sole of his heel. It was the deepest heel crack I had ever seen. I worried for a moment that it could be a danger to his health. I realised where my mind was going and instantly shifted my thinking to affirming his health and vitality and brought my attention back to the present moment — and away from that man's feet!

Sending out positive vibrations is an easy way to generate goodwill and develop mental control. I have heard people say to their loved ones, "Oh you look tired, you are going to get sick if you're not careful!" I call this the 'care curse'. It is where a negative idea is unintentionally directed at someone you care about. When we clean up our words, they can become a blessing. Instead of stating a negative, we could ask, "What delicious form of self-nurturing are you planning for yourself this week?" We have the same intention—to express care—but when this come from a place of love and empowerment, rather than fear or negativity, we can plant the seeds for a beautiful and positive outcome.

Some emotions, like jealousy, may evoke thoughts of wanting another person to fail. The ego may not like to see them shining so bright or that life seems so easy for them. They might stand for something that goes against what the ego thinks is correct. If they appear to fail, then the ego might believe they have done a terrible thing and deserve their comeuppance. This sort of thinking is most painful for the one doing the thinking. Ill will—whether it seems justified to the ego or not—is a form of spiritual sickness and a thief of the heart's joyful vitality.

The antidote is simple. Ask yourself if *there another way of looking at things.* If you feel inspired, you can even find a way to be grateful because you learned something and became wiser and stronger through the experience. You can trust the Universe to sort out everyone's karma, so you don't have to. You may be able to find the compassion in your heart that helps you remember when you were not at your best and needed forgiveness, so you can summon the goodwill to let someone else off the hook. In this process, the person you are freeing from negativity is yourself.

There is a Buddhist teaching something like this: The Buddha asks a man who had been held captive if he has forgiven his captors. The man says he has not, because what they did was unforgivable. The Buddha says the man is still captive, but in a prison of his own choosing.

Consciously using our thoughts for goodwill eventually leads to a willingness to trust that the Universe is working for the good of all beings, including ourselves. Essentially, we are reprogramming our emotional patterning through our intention. We begin to loosen the grip of fear-based impulses such as distrust, defensiveness and control and become more aligned with natural flow. We gain energy and lose stress, which means our inner resources can be dedicated to things such as the discovery and expression of our higher purpose.

A couple of years back, I had a sudden and clear thought that it was time to sell my car. This startled me as I hadn't been thinking about it at all, but I felt excited about the thought and asked the Universe to assist me with the process. A day or so later, I parked outside a grocery store that I didn't usually frequent. I didn't know why, but I just wanted to go in there. As I got out of my car to walk toward the market, a woman approached me on the street. She said she had her heart set on owning a pink car just like mine. I was stunned silent for a moment and then I told her that I had just decided to sell it. I gave her my number and she called me that afternoon. A few days later she took it for a test drive with her son. She told me she felt safe driving the car and at home in it as it had, "really good energy." Considering all the chanting I had done while I was driving that little pink car around, I could understand why!

When she decided to buy the car at the price I asked for, it was surprisingly emotional and healing for both of us. That car had seen me through five or so years where there was a lot of love and some very painful experiences of loss. Along with the car, I was letting go of a layer of attachment to my past that I didn't realise was there until the moment was upon me. It was unexpectedly freeing. I suspect this was part of the reason for the nudge to part with it.

There was healing for the new owner, too. She told me this was the first time she had bought something just for her. In a family of big men, her little pink car would be for her! There was sacredness in the transaction for both of us. We both gained something of value in the experience — we both let go of the past and we were both supported. We both expected the car market to be tricky and time consuming, yet this was simple, swift and a win-win for all involved. This is an example of goodwill between myself, the new owner and the Universe. When we trust the loving power of the Universe within us, things can work out beautifully with grace. A combination of prayer, trust and listening to our intuition can work wonders.

I have experienced this phenomenon of prayer and goodwill creating amazing outcomes with several students in my online healer training program. These souls recognise the power of prayer and don't hesitate to ask for support in the online student forum whenever needed. The group responds with prayers that come from a place of faith and a willingness to work together for a greater good. It has supported some extraordinary healing and divine intervention.

As part of the online healer training, I often feel a trainee on the inner planes and without knowing the specifics, know that I need to pray for them. I don't usually mention this to the trainee in question, unless Spirit guides me to do so for some reason or other. On several occasions, the trainee I have been 'anonymously' praying for has piped up on the online group the next day sharing that they had a mentoring session with me in a dream or some other healing event has taken place for them. I know the outcome is connected to the prayer process.

I am public about my belief in the power of prayer. I don't believe you have to belong to a religion to pray — it is for everyone. All you need is some sense of a higher power. This may be your higher self, the Universe, a loving higher being or spiritual consciousness. Even when you aren't sure such a consciousness exists, a willingness to try prayer is enough. I never found this to be a particularly controversial belief, certainly not compared to some of my other beliefs (which are normal and obvious to me but can be startling to others). Nonetheless, some people take great offence at the suggestion prayer could be helpful, and angrily declare it is useless. I suspect that reaction has to do with unresolved trust issues and anger about perceived abandonment and betrayal by the Divine in this or other lifetimes.

Some people even argue, erroneously in my opinion, that prayer is a substitute for doing something real and useful. In my experience, prayer is profoundly motivational. It has the blessed effect of helping us surrender our fear, paralysis and doubt, and in doing so we become clearer, more energetic and able to act from a peaceful and trusting place — which leads to far better outcomes than acting from fear.

When we pray, we are saying to the Divine, "I am with you, let's do this, you lead, and I'll follow." There is a beautiful explanation of the original meaning of the word obedience which comes from the word *obedere* which means *to listen, to hear, to not turn away*. When we surrender through prayer, we are asking a higher power to show us the way to the best outcome for all. We are telling the Divine that we will listen and will not turn away. This takes courage because Spirit is something of a wild card. You never know what it is going to do, but you can trust it is based in unconditional love. It's not always easy to bear witness to divine guidance, to hear it, to accept it and to love it. Have you ever known something to be true guidance and yet felt unable to take it on? Have you taken the hard road only to realise later that if you had followed that guidance everything would have been better for you and everyone involved? I certainly have! Prayer is advanced spiritual intimacy with the Divine. For something some people say does nothing at best, it takes a lot of soul and spiritual muscle to wrestle our minds away from ego assessment and be willing to unconditionally trust the Universe to do its thing without trying to control or resist it.

Our resistance to trusting divine guidance is partly because we project our unresolved psychological baggage onto the Universe. If we are new to the idea of goodwill, we may not have seen it in action. We don't realise that in giving to another, we are allowing the Universe to give to us, too. You may have experienced 'instant karma' in your life, where something you do or say comes back to you (for better or worse) almost immediately. You might have cut in front of someone in traffic (intentionally or not) and then had someone cut in front of you (intentionally or not) just moments later. You may have done something nice for someone for no other reason than to help them out, and then had a lucky break come your way from a different source. So, it is with goodwill. When you generate it for others, you generate it for yourself. This may also be viewed as the law of karma, the law of attraction or the reality that there is no separation, no 'I' and no 'other' so what we emanate we give and receive simultaneously.

Until we have some real-life examples of how much the Universe can support us when we are open to it, we may find our old wounds are more compelling. This can make it hard to trust in the inherent goodness of the Universe. We may believe that opening to the Universe and becoming more trusting will not bring us what we want or that we could get exactly what we don't want! We may feel we will have to give up too much and not trust the sacrifices could lead to our deepest happiness. We may not know what love really is until we begin our journey into conscious relationship with the Universe. We may not understand the power of the deep spiritual goodness that pervades life until we practice goodwill and see where it leads. Because of this, we must be willing to take a leap of faith and give it a try. Practice before proof. Faith before evidence. Willingness to continue even in the absence of immediate results. To grow spiritually, you really do need to have a toughness within that protects the softness of your heart and allows it to grow and open in love, again and again, no matter what. Lightworkers, priestesses, star seeds and healers really do need to be divine badasses.

We may not realise just how powerful energetic work—such as prayer—can be in our physical lives. I often quip that God is more powerful than the real-estate market, because the Universe has been responsible for finding me places to live when finding a solution by more earthly means seemed impossible. The Divine has found ways through so many obstacles that I have become a firm believer that the Universe can and will do whatever is necessary for each one of us to fulfil our destinies. We just have to learn how to trust it. Prayer helps us be more conscious of our connection to divine consciousness, so trusting it feels easier.

It is important to connect to your own prayer practice, in your own way. It doesn't need special words or phrases and can simply be a chance to settle down and speak from your heart to the Divine, the Universe, your higher self, the angels or other divine beings, such as our luminous star teachers or the Earth Mother. Think of it as speaking to the best friend you'll ever have. You don't have to be formal, you don't have to hide yourself or your true feelings, nor do you have to know how things are going to turn out. You simply have a loving conversation about what's going on and where you need help. Then, you stay open to how that help will show up, because it most certainly will. There is the saying that prayer is speaking to the Divine and meditation is when we listen to the Divine speaking to us. Any truly satisfying conversation has a balance of both.

When you add the small act of prayer to your daily routine, the ability of Spirit to deflect unnecessary obstacles, to protect you and your loved ones, to surround you in a field of grace and to support you as you manifest your life purpose is truly palpable and deeply reassuring. In turn, this gives you more confidence and courage to take the leaps your heart guides you to take, knowing the open arms of the Universe are always ready to catch you. You will begin to recognise when good will or prayer comes into effect. There have been times when some accident or other unwanted event should by all rights have happened, and it simply hasn't. I have felt the bubble of protective grace around me and been so astonished and grateful for it. May all beings come to know this generous grace as it shields them on their divine life journey, nurturing them to fulfil their sacred destiny.

HEALING PROCESS

Rest your gaze upon the crystal mandala for the star teacher Spica and the Crystal Angel of Apophyllite. Do this with softness rather than a hard focus, allowing your vision to relax. Imagine, intend or visualise a soft crystalline light emanating from the mandala and moving very gently into your eyes as the most delicate wave of light. Allow it to wash so very delicately behind your eyes, inside your ears (it may tickle a little!), and then gently and smoothly flow out through the nostrils. If you wish, you can close your eyes whilst this happens.

When you are ready, gaze at the mandala again with soft vision which may feel clearer now. Allow the gentle light emanating from the mandala to flow as a delicate wave to wash so very gently in through your eyes and out through the back of your head and through each hair on your head. It is cleansing, refreshing and peaceful. It carries any negative thoughts away with it. You can close your eyes whilst you allow this if you wish. Rest for a few moments.

When you are ready, say aloud:

I now give thanks for the unconditionally loving blessing of Spica and the Crystal Angel of Apophyllite for mental

cleansing, protection and peace. I give thanks for the healing
of my mind and heart so that I am open to more effortless
manifestation and the flow of goodwill, goodness, generosity
and grace through the highest wisdom for the greatest good.
So be it.

Place your hands in prayer at your heart and bow your head to your hands for a few moments. Feel the soft loving wisdom of your heart as you surrender your mind to your heart. Does your heart want to speak to the Crystal Angel of Apophyllite, the star teacher Spica, the Universe or some other divine being? Give your heart permission to say its prayers for yourself, for your loved ones, for all those in need in our world. Remain open with hope and trust the outcomes will manifest themselves with divine grace.

To complete your healing process, rest quietly, perhaps in meditation, for as long as you wish.

CHAPTER EIGHT

DARK INITIATIONS INTO FREEDOM AND LIGHT

STAR GUIDE: POLARIS

POLARIS, KNOWN AS THE NORTH STAR or Pole Star, is positioned in line with Earth's axis almost directly above the northern pole. It is almost motionless with the other stars of the northern sky rotating around it. It is a fixed point from which to navigate. In the Hindu Puranas, Polaris is personified as Dhruva meaning *immovable* or *fixed*.

A key message of Polaris is to stay strong to your soul course and not allow external influences or circumstances to sway you from your focus on your inner guiding light. It reminds us that when we keep following our soul star, making it our true reference point, everything else in the outer world will unfold around us in accord. When we try to change the outer world to fulfil our inner vision, we can end up feeling lost and disconnected from our authentic being. When Polaris connects with the soul, it encourages us to remain open to the guidance of the Universe, to be flexible on how our journey unfolds and to be true to the deeper meaning and inspiration that guides us from within. It guides us to stand our ground whilst all else moves around us. Polaris helps us manifest our true inner light, so that it can guide others — even if we are not formally coaching or mentoring others. Someone living their truth is incredibly inspiring and can indirectly help others find the inner permission they need to march to their own beat and live their own journey.

In the medieval period, Polaris became associated with the Virgin Mary's constant, protective and guiding light, as she watched over those taking difficult voyages, and as such was referred to by one of Mother Mary's titles, *Stella Maris* (Star of the Sea). In esoteric astrology, the Tibetan ascended master and spiritual guide known as Djwahl Khul teaches that Polaris is a major star of direction. Its physical expression as a navigation guide is an outer representation of its inner purpose as a guide of the soul. Polaris is a steadying influence for those who feel swept away by the tides of social pressure or family expectation. An example could be feeling guilty and pressured to continue in the family business while their soul yearns to embrace a different path. It can stem the tide when we have drifted off course. It helps us remember our real selves when we have become busy, perhaps for a long time, trying to be everything to everyone and thus have lost touch with who we are. It is a consistent, fixed and brightly shining reminder that our true selves are just the same — always within us, always constant.

When Polaris makes a connection with the soul, it can indicate a major change will be bringing us back to our true path. In Western mystery traditions, Polaris is associated with the first ray, which is a ray of light that embodies the higher will of the Universe. When divine will makes its presence known in our lives, it can feel like a realignment, a reorientation and sometimes, from the ego's perspective, a destructive force that undermines our ideals and plans. That's why some astrologers associate Polaris with negative forces and disaster. When the first ray is blasting divine will into our soul, the things our ego has been plotting may suddenly begin to fail, whilst the soul becomes stronger and our false self begins to crumble under the greater spiritual weight of the authentic being that is emerging from within.

There is a promise of real happiness once the dust settles, but when it is underway it can feel like a challenging onslaught and a lack of control. It may show up as a failed career or a broken marriage that shatters our view of the world and plunges us into seeming chaos. Yet, when we tune into the soul, we can sense that we have been climbing the wrong mountain. Before we could waste any more of our precious time, we were kicked off the mountain and firmly nudged toward the path we were destined to take this lifetime. The chaos can save us from far greater unhappiness and destruction later on.

In Western occultism this 'chaos' is considered necessary for soul growth. It is believed that the soul goes through a process when it incarnates. When the soul enters a body, it is 'lost' for a while, tricked by the compelling illusions of this world that have us believe we are separate beings who can prosper through exploitation and greed. The soul forgets its real nature and is caught up in lesser pursuits, becoming confused by glitter and believing it is gold. Eventually there is a turning point, a shift whereby the soul realises these lesser pursuits are not all they were imagined to be and cannot provide anything real or meaningful. It is ready for the next stage of the spiritual journey — the path of return. The soul becomes interested in deeper meaning and spiritual reality. It is seeking truth and Polaris is the star guide that supports the soul in its process of reorientation as it transitions into spiritual maturity.

Polaris is also considered the cosmic guardian of the etheric spiritual centre Shambhala, which in Sanskrit means *place of peace*. Referred to in Hindu and Buddhist traditions, as well as in the Ageless Wisdom of Theosophical teachings, Shambhala is the spiritual dwelling place of a group of enlightened beings that emanate peace. In the Ageless Wisdom, these beings are seen as ascended masters who work for the good of humanity, bringing through divine will and higher guidance.

I have worked with these guides and seen them in action. They help humanity in so many practical ways especially through the evolution of various systems on Earth such as business, finance, education, health care, politics and the arts. They do this by encouraging our spiritual progress and bringing out the best in our human nature whilst fully respecting our free will. They are truly exceptional and fully realised beings that do a great deal of work on Earth and actively assist those who want to help humanity evolve through their life work as healers, high-minded politicians, musicians, filmmakers, educators, medical professionals, business people and so forth.

Esoteric teachings hold that the spiritual paradise of Shambhala cannot be sustained on Earth at this time — it is simply too much spiritual potency for a world largely trapped in delusion to be able to fully receive and integrate. We can understand this through the story of the three rabbis that entered a room where God dwelled. One became enlightened, one became insane because he couldn't yet handle the enormity of the divine presence and the other dropped dead, presumably because it was too much for his body to handle at that time. Shambhala holds the divine presence in trust for the earth, until the vibration of the human collective has matured spiritually and become ready for Shambhala to be made manifest in the physical world. So, it lies in wait, retracted into the etheric plane, drip feeding through those souls that are able to bring through light, until we can handle that level of divine voltage in its entirety, as a collective. At such a stage, humanity can become enlightened by it rather than the less desirable responses that befell the two less fortunate rabbis!

When Polaris is connecting with a soul or we feel inexplicably drawn to it, the soul is receiving communication from the enlightened ones, guidance for its path and purpose, and we may feel it is not our personal preference but rather a higher power that is directing our life path in important ways. This experience could be about loss, but often it's about beautiful new opportunities opening up and encouragement to express your soul gifts.

This star teacher is a celestial reminder that if we get stuck looking for spiritual fulfilment through the physical world, we can miss out on what is real and helpful. When Polaris resonates in our souls, we are getting a message from the Universe to focus on healing the inner to shift the outer, not the other way around. We are inspired to stay true to our path and to trust that the beautiful vision of our souls will manifest according to higher wisdom and divine timing.

THE CRYSTAL ANGEL OF BLUE HALITE

Halite looks like a stunning crystal but is a form of salt that is dissolvable in water. You would have an unpleasant surprise if you tested this assertion by washing it! This happened to a colleague of mine when I worked in a healing centre in inner Sydney. A lovely pink halite was literally washed away in a much-regretted cleaning frenzy. Halite is physically delicate. It manifests in an array of beautiful colours including soft, fairy-floss pink and the baby blue of a clear summer sky. Halite can be a reminder to let yourself be healed by colour and to allow nature to bring happiness and beauty into your heart and mind.

As a form of salt, halite has some powerful healing properties that belie its ethereal nature. Salt has spiritual significance as a protective and purifying agent. It deflects negativity and curses (which I define as directed negative thoughts and/or actions) and functions as a disinfectant and preservative — two healing qualities that are essential for life. In alchemy it represents the earthly or bodily plane and evokes healing and protective qualities on all levels, both subtle and physical. Metaphysically, Halite is a dissolving agent for negativity or unhelpful behavioural patterns and can be useful in the purification of mental suffering and for cleansing the mind and soul.

Halite can be particularly helpful when we have experienced a deluge of negativity. A difficult day, a bad week or a streak of ill-fortune typically means the soul is stuck in a rut of negativity and needs a good wash to help it shake it off and settle into a more spiritually protected state.

Blue halite is particularly cleansing for the mind. Sometimes when the mind is going through a purging process as part of healing, many thoughts, memories and fantasies arise. Sometimes these fantasies are extremely negative or destructive and can frighten the body with dark or violent imaginings. In reality, the mind is trying to process unresolved pain — nothing more. Blue halite can soften this and open us to supportive opportunities for healing. It might help us attract an integrative medical specialist who can balance the function of the body's neurotransmitters or a trained therapist who can provide the emotional support required for swifter, more gentle healing.

Blue halite can support the throat chakra to process psychologically painful material and use it to gain wisdom, insight and compassion. In turn, this increases light, peace and healing in our minds. It is a gentle and effective stone for transforming dark imaginings into a healing gateway for greater wisdom and inner peace. It is as reassuring as a bright-blue midsummer sky after a terrifying stormy night.

SPIRITUAL GUIDANCE: CRISIS IS CONSCIOUSNESS ATTEMPTING TO BE BORN

Dealing with our pain can sometimes seem all too hard. I hear this in the frustrations of spiritual aspirants who struggle with health conditions. They may have experienced a trauma in childhood that lodged itself, unprocessed, in their bodies. The tissues have become diseased and need healing. The source of the problem may be obvious abuse which they can recognise. It might be the subtler kind, where everything seems okay on the surface, but the body is telling the truth about the depth of the wounding. It is crying out in physical, emotional or psychological pain, begging for the truth to be uncovered, held in compassion and then allowed to release. Even when we have worked on these issues for some time, there can be more work to do. This work can take a toll on the body and mind. There will be moments when we waiver, when our faith doesn't feel quite so strong or we fall prey to doubts and fears. We may wonder if the work will ever end — if we will ever be free from the struggle.

If we have had more time in pain than in wellbeing, and I know many people for which this is true, we need extra faith in a reality we don't recall or have never experienced. In such cases, it can seem like asking a person who was born in darkness and has lived through a constant night, to believe in daylight and a brightness they have never seen. It might seem fanciful and unrealistic to them, even though many others live in the bright light of day without a second thought. To keep hope in something we are yet to experience requires courage and a willingness to admit it could be a bit nuts to trust in something you have never known, but it's more enjoyable to be a potentially nutty optimist than a depressed pessimist!

I went through those kinds of challenges for quite some time in pretty much every possible area from health, finance and work to my love life. I dreamed of the possibilities I wanted to live and was working toward them as best as I could, but I had never experienced them nor seen them in the lives of those around me. I wondered if what I was dreaming was a realistic possibility that could manifest as I grew in to it or an unrealistic fantasy.

I was once in a relationship that had me wondering whether my notion of what love could be like was completely unrealistic. When I left that relationship, the parting words of my partner were that he hoped I found what I was looking for, but he didn't think I would. I wondered if he was correct. Right or wrong, I knew I had to leave that relationship anyway. Some years later, after a lot of inner healing work, I did meet a man who loved me in the way I had always dreamed of.

From the perspective of others, the new man in my life was a great guy but the world is full of great guys. They were happy for me, but they weren't anywhere near as shocked as I was that someone like this had shown up for me. From my perspective, this man was as rare as a Sasquatch and I was sure he had dropped out of the sky (via a dating app) as a divine dispensation triggered by a blessing from a Tibetan yogini I had met! Either way, I had stepped out of the darkness into the astonishing revelation that what I had dreamed about concerning matters of the heart could exist.

I have had similar experiences in many areas of my life. In each instance, I held enough faith to keep working on myself and taking steps toward what I wanted for myself even when I wobbled and wondered if I was delusional rather than optimistic. I would rather take the journey and see where it leads, than give in to the devastation of doubt and despair. Having been through this process in many guises, some lasting for decades, I know only too well how much of a mental and physical challenge it can be to weather the storm of an ongoing inner crisis — even when we have faith that what are feeling is birthing pains.

Our mindset has so much to do with how we can move through crisis into new consciousness and new reality. Even in my darkest moments, I believed the Universe was urging me forwards in growth. I didn't know if I would have to sacrifice my cherished dreams through that growth process, but even if it did come to that, I trusted it would somehow be for the best and bring great blessings and happiness for all. After going through that process a number of times and experiencing the liberation that healing brought me, I could finally understand how it was that people who had been through profound challenge—perhaps as a difficult illness or loss—could say it was the best thing that had ever happened to them or that it had given them their life back. They were acknowledging that a more loving and authentic existence had been born to them through crisis.

Whether we see something as a blessing at the time it occurs has little to do with the ultimate outcome. There have been plenty of times when I have been forced to deal with the very thing I was wishing away. And, it led me to outgrow old pain and to blessings and became the very thing for which I felt profound gratitude and awe at the greater wisdom of Spirit.

Our spiritual path can teach us how to love our physical body rather than judging or feeling it has failed us — even when we are confronted by a health issue. I am compelled to mention that loving and respecting the body does not mean turning it into an object to be worshipped and used for power through seduction or exploited to get what our ego wants! Loving, respecting and honouring the body as a beautiful creature to be in relationship with is based on kindness and generosity, not what we can get out of it.

We are not prisoners to what others—including medical professionals—think is possible. Spirit may have different plans for you than your doctor expects. I have experienced healings in my body that have shocked medical professionals and holistic practitioners. These healings didn't happen through Spirit taking away the situation. Remember, when we ask Spirit to take something away, we are in ego. When we ask Spirit to show us the way, we are in soul. We cannot heal or grow from ego, it is a false foundation. When we are in soul, growth and healing become possible through a higher wisdom of spiritual grace. Such healing may or may not involve curing the physical condition. Often it will, but I also know some souls with physical burdens to bear this lifetime that are part of their spiritual journey, and yet they have undertaken such a profound healing journey that their suffering has transformed them so that they hold tremendous compassion, and have become truly radiant, light-bearing souls on this planet.

In esoteric astrology, Saturn relates to karma, grounding, life, structure and the body. We could imagine Saturn making a commitment to our souls saying, "I've got you, I'm holding you, be in your body, I'm already there ready to support your life and your growth."

Saturn, with its stunning rings, can be likened to a divine playpen. It is a boundary at the edge of a world or a reality within which we can safely grow. It is the home ground we can come back to and is connected to our spiritual home for this lifetime, our bodies.

Saturn is often referred to as the *Initiator*. One of his more impressive and intimidating titles is *The Dweller on the Threshold*. Saturn conjures testing experiences in our lives to ensure we have enough maturity to handle increased spiritual power and freedom with wisdom. Otherwise, it might be like putting a baby in the driver's seat. Too much responsibility on the shoulders of someone not equipped for it leads to disaster! Saturn is the challenger but also the protector.

Part of how we grow from spiritual baby to spiritually licensed to drive is through the Saturnian school of gravity. This is the physical field of gravity that helps hold the world in form, so we can move through life and grow stronger through that process. It is also what I call *astral gravity* or the weight of habitual consciousness that can pull us into old habits of negative thinking until we grow too strong and it loses its grip on us. This is what we feel when we begin to assert a new way of living or thinking that is inspired by Spirit, feels right for us, and then resistance arises. It can feel as if the old way and the new way are at odds or even that the old way somehow sabotages us by pulling us back down into unhelpful attitudes.

This is the pull of astral gravity. Anyone who has gone on a healthy eating kick only to inhale a pizza can attest to its power to influence our choices! Any time we try to change our physical reality, even when we are wisely working on our inner healing as the source of the change, we encounter Saturn's spiritual bootcamp of astral gravity.

You can't really have a healthy relationship with Saturn if you are blaming others or the world for your woes. Do others and the world have an influence in your life? Sure, but you have the power to decide how you are going to respond to that. Saturn is not an indulgent energy in that sense. He demands that we find our strength and use it. This is how we gain spiritual maturity.

We can fear Saturn's spiritual training before we realise that the testing, limitation and challenge eventually give way to greater skill, freedom and happiness. However, if you have experienced the physical body or the physical world as a scary, unsafe or unpleasant place to be, then Saturn's teachings—which are about getting into the body—may feel confronting. That was the case for me, as I had a lot of unprocessed emotional pain stored in my body which I was only ready to begin dealing with in my twenties.

As I went through that process, increasingly willing to be present to my pain and suffering, giving it a voice in my journal or expressing it creatively, I discovered something. There were entire worlds of subtle beauty and spiritual light within the body. Until Saturn pushed me into it, I had no idea how extraordinary the body was and how essential it was to befriend, claim and inhabit it so we can make spiritual progress, but also for the sheer delight, wonder and amazement of its inner realm.

Of course, it wasn't all hearts and flowers. Living in a world where the sacred feminine is so often ignored and derided can feel like hell on earth for our bodies. The pain that is our own and the pain that belongs to the collective of which we are a part (and not apart from), begins to rise. As we bring our awareness into our bodies and allow them to become more conscious, they demand to be heard. It is important to remember two things in this process.

First, we need to find a way to give what is arising in the body some non-judged, free expression. Dance, toning, singing, art, writing, poetry, music … anything that allows us to move through the emotional release rather than numbing or distracting ourselves from it will be helpful. The body is designed to take in, process, digest and distil the useful stuff that supports life and eliminate the rest. If we give it a chance, it can do this on an emotional level, too. Secondly, when we allow the body to release what it has been holding, it is free to receive more consciously loving input.

Saturn carries out his healing grace through gravity but also through sacrifice. Now I don't know about you, but 'sacrifice' is not a word I tend to respond to with a gleeful and embracing attitude! At best, it's more of a begrudging acceptance for the greater good. However, what I've most often been asked to sacrifice was not something I particularly wanted to hold on to anymore. Its funny (and/or disturbing) just how much pain our ego can create around letting go even when we are letting go of something we don't want.

One example of Saturnian sacrifice involved giving up a spiritual identity I had been unconsciously holding on to. I believe this was asked of me, not so I would no longer see myself as a spiritual being, but so I could become freer and more authentic in myself and my spirituality.

On a quiet afternoon, outdoors on a bushland property in northern New South Wales, I was sitting on a plastic chair opposite a healer who was sitting on an equally uncomfortable and unattractive plastic chair. We were meditating quietly together with the intention that he would do a soul healing for me. After some time had passed, with eyes closed in meditation, I had a vision of a burning white sun. It was dull white with a pale grey corona around the edges — a living star. Despite the softness of the colours, it was so luminous that I could hardly gaze upon it without feeling I would be blinded. I could hear the crackling of energy as it poured off this sun. I sensed there was tremendous nuclear power within it — a type of divine furnace churning away. I also felt that it was very old, toward the end of its lifespan, actually. All these impressions dropped into my consciousness and tears poured down my face as I suddenly realised that I was looking at my own soul. I had never seen nor imagined it in such a way before. This vision had come from an entirely new, previously inaccessible place within my awareness.

Eventually, as we emerged from the process, I asked the healer what he had been doing. He told me he had been cleaning away an image that I had been holding on to — that of a priest. He said it had been hard to clear, and he had to put some spiritual muscle into it! I instantly understood. He had cleared away my unconscious attachment to a spiritual identity (that of the priest or divine intermediary) and as a result, I could suddenly experience my soul—beyond any identity—in a new way.

The archetype of the priest, perhaps experienced in another lifetime, and the priestess, which I had identified with so strongly in this lifetime, had become an unconscious attachment for me. I was holding on to it and it was obscuring my spiritual progress. It didn't mean I can't be a priestess this lifetime, but I cannot invest my ego in it nor make it more important than my soul path which may ask me to let go of that role and serve in a different way at some point.

Since that healing my soul still expresses itself through the role of a priestess. It is authentic, yet it is no longer how I define myself as a spiritual being. I experience my inner spiritual being as beyond identity and my soul will use certain roles to fulfil its purpose — that may be a healer, a teacher, a priestess or something else entirely. This is the benefit of the Saturnian sacrifice. It asks us to give up something we may think is holding us up but, is holding us back.

The more refined the consciousness we are aiming for and the more it is at odds with mainstream culture and/or our own upbringing, the more Saturnian training and spiritual strength needed to overcome the astral gravity. This is akin to how a plane takes more energy and power to get off the ground and ascend than it does to cruise at its new altitude.

Although my work is a labour of love, it *is* a labour. Even with the light, inspiration, grace and flow of so much of my work—perhaps because of that—the grounding, disciplinarian and earthing quality of Saturn is very much a part of my life. Without it, nothing would get finished. I have learned to embrace Saturn's qualities to take care of myself. I use discipline to write, but I also use it to switch off, to balance and to prevent myself from becoming completely overwhelmed by the many projects I have in play at any given time.

I remember unintentionally shocking one of my colleagues when she was talking to me about how much she loved writing. Given that I was already published, and she was hoping to be, she expected an inspirational response. Usually I can authentically deliver on such expectations, because my work is something that I consider an incredible blessing. However, in this instance she was talking about the process of writing itself and my reply was, "Really? I don't like it at all!"

She seemed crushed! So, I hastened to explain that I love that my writing helps people and I am always satisfied—very much so—with the end result because it feels like a precious soul creation. I find translating spiritual concepts into words for the benefit of others deeply fulfilling *but* the writing process itself, is not something I relish. It takes a toll to process so much information. My body rebels at sitting in one position at a computer to write. Writing requires a great deal of mental focus which tends to pull a lot of energy into my head which can create tension that I have to work on releasing. Physically and mentally, writing is a lot more demanding on my body than most people expect. There are times when I would much rather be doing yoga, cleaning the house or watching Turkish soap operas on Netflix, than performing the mental gymnastics required to pull a book together. That doesn't mean that I don't treasure the opportunity to do it. It just means that it has its challenges. My colleague was nonplussed and disappointed, but I wanted to be honest. I've lived through the frustration and despair of feeling trapped in work that I hated, so I know how precious a gift it is to dedicate your life to work you deeply love, as I do. Yet, that doesn't mean your life is suddenly free from challenge. It just becomes a challenge that you are willing to go through for a greater cause of the heart.

I once dated a man who was jealous of my lifestyle as a writer. He was in a job he didn't much like, living in a way that created stress and resented that I was happy with my work and how I lived my life. I puzzled over this for a while and tried to help him. Could he retrain? What field would suit him? Eventually I realised that way of thinking was unnecessary and ineffective. What mattered was whether he would open to life and to his own inner experience and allow himself to grow. If he did that, the Universe would be able to guide and provide all the other information that was needed. We often think life purpose is something that we do, but it is an authentic way of being — something we become. He didn't understand that if he was willing to pay the price, which meant dealing with his inner world, he could live a life that brought him more joy, too.

Saturn is always asking us to grow. We can work with him, so he becomes a soul friend who shows us how to open doors to all the blessings the Universe wants to generously bestow on us or we can see him as an intimidating bearer of issues we'd prefer to avoid even if that means living a less vital, alive and authentic existence.

I see some highly creative, very inspired people who haven't done the work to make friends with Saturn. They suffer because of it and are easily mired in procrastination or by the addictive high of the new idea and lack the follow through necessary to birth it in the world. When ideas that are special and could help people fail to launch because of a Saturn deficiency (or Saturn avoidance), it means that every one of us misses out.

The funny thing is that once we get over our Saturn aversion, we can learn to love his simplicity and quiet, methodical, step-by-step approach to getting stuff done. The days when I can just plod along are treasures for me. I love public appearances, workshops and stage performance, all the light and joy and vibrancy are amazing. Yet, the quiet days in my yoga pants, doing some writing, tending to the laundry when my body needs time out from a computer screen, have a healing restfulness about them.

Making friends with Saturn means trusting in the bigger picture of what the Universe wants for us. When we believe that pain is a pathway through which we can find more wisdom, then we will be more willing to go through it. We might even learn to become a radical optimist, believing that every situation has a positive end in view, even if we cannot see it at the beginning. Then, so many of our fears about the world and our safety can dissolve which in turn leads to less pain as we take our life path. We feel supported and that we are generously nurtured to our fulfilment. We just need to do our part and know that Spirit is with us, in us, every step of the way. We are willing, and we are hopeful. We may then find that our wildest dreams can manifest in ways that are more beautiful than we could have imagined, even on our most radically optimistic days.

HEALING PROCESS

Begin by grounding yourself by gently moving your body. Sense the connection between your feet and the earth. Make a more conscious connection with your body by being present in the here and now. You can do this by touching your body gently, focusing on your breath and paying attention to and sensations you may feel in your body.

You may like to narrate what you are doing aloud, to help ground you in the present moment. For example, "I am touching my arm. I am wrapping my fingers around my wrist. I am standing in this room, breathing, now." This is a form of mindfulness that can increase your physical consciousness and connection. Take your time to practice this for as long as you need.

Once you feel grounded, say the following invocation:

> *I call upon the luminous star teacher Polaris, guardian, guide and protector. I call upon the healing and cleansing energy of the Crystal Angel of Blue Halite. I am willing to be cleansed on all levels of my being, with mercy and grace. I open to purification and protection through unconditional love. I open my heart to the guiding light within so that I*

may live my truest calling in life. I accept, embrace and lay claim to my earthly life as an expression of my soul journey. I accept the blessing of life to fulfil a sacred purpose. I open to all divine assistance based in unconditional love, to support my spiritual growth and earthly fulfilment, according to the highest wisdom for the greatest good, so be it.

Take a moment to feel as though there is a fine white line of spiritual energy that sits like a spiritual spine in the centre of your physical spine. As you relax and breathe, the Universe provides a gentle healing adjustment to that line of energy deep within your spine, so that you are oriented authentically to your own being.

Imagine, feel, visualise or intend that as this takes place, you can gently release any energies from your mind, body and soul that are not in harmony with your true alignment with the Universe. You can gracefully allow these to simply drift away from you, without needing to consciously recognise what those things may be. Rest into this process for as long as feels best for you.

When you are ready, place your hands in prayer and close your eyes for a few moments. You have completed your healing process.

CHAPTER NINE

BODY WISDOM, ISOLATION, CONNECTION AND FREEDOM

STAR GUIDE: FOMALHAUT

FOMALHAUT IS ONE OF THE ROYAL STARS of ancient Persia, said to hold the frequencies of the archangels. Associated with Archangel Gabriel, this star teacher is known as the *Watcher of the South* and as a spiritual sentinel that watches over the stars. This divine being is very aware of what is taking place on Earth and actively intervenes for our spiritual wellbeing. Archangels have a protective quality and a higher purpose to guide beings into alignment with divine will, truth, unconditional love and wisdom. The Royal Stars of ancient Persia, resonate with the archangelic frequency, are guiding lights and soul friends to all of humanity.

Fomalhaut is known for having a profound influence on human affairs especially at a global level. With its broad range of influence, the star wisdom of Fomalhaut moves humanity forward. The spiritual progress Fomalhaut evokes focuses mainly on healing through cultural development. Those of us working to heal cultural issues have a special relationship with this star teacher. This healing work may centre around becoming more conscious within a family, a national culture or Western society more generally. It may also be concerned with business, religious or industry culture (such as in banking, health care, education or the arts). We may not think of ourselves as being cultural-consciousness workers, but if we are seeking to overcome ego and bring out the higher-minded qualities of an industry, then this is one way we can describe our life purpose. Similarly, if we are part of the consciousness movement in Western culture and seeking to integrate technology with wisdom, to honour the feminine and integrate spirituality into the material side of life, then we have an especially deep connection to Fomalhaut.

Some time ago the position of Fomalhaut in the Earth's sky was different. At that time, this star teacher was the stellar marker of the winter solstice and was associated with the worship of Demeter in the Eleusian Mysteries. These sacred rites were based on the themes of death and rebirth. This star guide holds the codes for accessing the healing wisdom inherent in a spiritual winter which includes darkness, loss and endings, so that new life can be born. Fomalhaut, as Archangel Gabriel, announced the imminent birth of Christ to Mother Mary. A connection with Fomalhaut foretells the coming of profound change, brings a divine promise of new life through the transformation of darkness, and is a sign that out of any darkness, great light can and will eventually emerge. For those who have suffered great loss or feel called to a higher purpose of a global nature, Fomalhaut provides strength, wisdom and encouragement — especially in the most challenging times.

This star is also a bearer of blessings. It is associated with good fortune, eminence, and can indicate fame or public profile in connection to one's life purpose. This may be on a global level or within your community. When Fomalhaut connects with our soul, we often have a spiritual role of some significance to play in the greater community. One's profile may be more visible or one's work will have a far-reaching impact. We can relax into a sacred task as a guide or light for others as we surrender our ego attachment and trust in the divine wisdom that decides all such matters. In any position of leadership, Fomalhaut can help us be humble, authentic and to ground ourselves in spiritual practice whilst inspiring us to act for the greater good.

This star guide shines in solitary grandeur. Fomalhaut appears isolated in the sky, but it has two distant stellar companions. Before their discovery in 2013, Alpha Centauri (who we meet in Chapter Eighteen) was recognised to be the widest double star in the sky, with its companion Proxima. Fomalhaut now holds that title. Fomalhaut and its companion stars are an astonishingly huge system. One companion star in the system, Fomalhaut C is located so far away that it is in a different constellation. That is nearly three times the distance between Alpha Centauri and Proxima.

This brings us to another therapeutic quality in the transmission of Fomalhaut. It helps us learn how to recognise and sustain sacred connections, even over great distances. This star guide is the master of long-distance relationships. Fomalhaut can use this special star medicine to help those that feel isolated or need a high degree of solitude to fulfil their life purpose for reasons which may not be immediately apparent. It assures us that even when there is an appearance of isolation, the subtle connections of relationship are somehow still in play. Those connections may not be obvious. We may recognise the connection at a purely energetic level and give ourselves permission to be sustained by that inner sense, even if the outer evidence of relationship is not always there.

Trusting in what we feel rather than what appears to be, can be challenging. There have been times in my life that have been 'peopled' with many groups of friends, a partner and an abundant flow of social opportunities. There have also been times when all of that seemed to be pruned back and I experienced a high degree of isolation which had its blessings and its challenges. During those times of solitude, the relationship I felt with the Divine was even more pronounced than usual. I have always felt Spirit present with me as a loving friend, but during that time of unofficial retreat, it really felt as though the only 'person' I could call on for loving relationship was God. This solitude taught me a lot about my ability to trust and rely on the spiritual source and these lessons remained with me when life shifted, and human connections increased once more. During phases of relationship shedding where a karmic cycle has ended, and the soul is taking a breath before opening a new chapter, there may only be long-distance or purely spiritual relationship sustaining the soul. It is not always easy to recognise and be nourished by such subtle connections, but Fomalhaut helps us realise those relationships are still real and can have a powerful sustaining effect for the soul.

When we are going through a phase of feeling alone or that the relationships we have are mostly on a spiritual level, Fomalhaut reassures us that no matter how isolated we may seem there are loving beings who *are* connected to us. We are held in a sacred bond even when no-one recognises it. When Fomalhaut connects with the soul, it often indicates the imminent discovery of a meaningful connection that was not previously recognised. Forthcoming relationships will be with souls who have a longstanding connection but have not yet met on a physical level this lifetime. When it is time for those souls to reconnect, the full history of their sacred bond will be felt.

A connection to Fomalhaut can also raise our awareness of the far-reaching influence of spiritual light in our lives that reassures and brings a sense of clear inner guidance. This star guide helps us realise the effect our spiritual light has in the world and that it is farther reaching than we imagine is possible. Our ability to make a palpable connection with others is not limited by physical distance. Our light can travel far and wide to touch the souls of those who resonate with the same truth that moves our own hearts. We have soul friends in many outposts of the Universe. We may not always know they are there, but the bond between us flows with divine light, love and wisdom.

THE CRYSTAL ANGEL OF MOLDAVITE

This crystal is said to have originated from outer space. A meteorite struck the earth and the fusion of earthly and extra-terrestrial energy was captured in this forest-green stone. Moldavite is a particularly helpful crystal for star seeds and those wanting to deepen their conscious connection to high-frequency and loving non-earthly beings. It can promote constructive relationship dynamics in all ways, between all beings and across all dimensions. It is a stone for love, peace, higher consciousness and harmony.

As such, moldavite supports conscious collaborations that bring out the best in all concerned. It can help us navigate our connections in the world, so they work for the greatest good, cleaning out the subtle distortions of ego that can arise without us realising. For star seeds who struggle to deal with the ego-based drives that can bring pain to human interactions, moldavite is a constructive ally. It arouses the soul, quiets the ego and helps anchor our relationships in a higher consciousness of generosity and respect. It is up to the individuals in question to decide how they will use their free will—to honour soul or ego—but moldavite is there as a cosmic cheerleader to encourage us to choose the higher path.

Moldavite is a powerful stone of synergy. When the collective energy is more than the sum of its parts, we have synergy. It creates new fields of potentiality. On a practical level, this means moldavite enhances the effectiveness of other stones and amplifies the energetic fields they create. It is wonderful for group work, families, soul tribes and other communities that need to work together for a greater purpose while honouring everyone as individuals, too. In that sense, it is a stone for humanity.

The supply of genuine moldavite from authentic sources cannot seem to meet demand. There is a growing amount of fake moldavite, sometimes with forged certification, showing up in gem shows and on various websites. Unless you are a specialist, with the knowledge and apparatus used to accurately identify the mineral content of a crystal, it can be hard to know whether you are purchasing genuine moldavite. This is especially so for online sales where you don't get a chance to hold the piece to feel if it connects with your energy field.

If you are drawn to something, I tend to feel there is a reason and that you can work with it — even if it is not what you expect it to be. It also seems that learning to work with crystal angels is increasingly important as it ensures a connection with the authentic frequency of the relevant stones. So, if you are drawn to moldavite and are uncertain if you have a genuine piece of this tektite, or even if you have no physical piece of it in your collection at all, the Crystal Angel of Moldavite will help you make the desired connection to the true wisdom and real healing energy of this stone.

SPIRITUAL GUIDANCE: THE SECRET WISDOM OF ADDICTION

We live in what I consider to be an addictive society. Mass consciousness fosters a false type of reality that is based in fear, greed and self-serving instincts, and stimulates the ego, harms our bodies, ignores the soul and distorts our minds. That false reality then judges us mercilessly for struggling with the issues it created. It is a negative loop that can overtake human beings and plunge them into the realm of ego where the light of Spirit can seem like nothing more than fanciful nonsense. However, no matter how much ego seems to take over, the authentic self is still deep within us, expressing truth. Sometimes the only way for the authentic self to break through the layers of shame, ridicule, confusion and pain is to communicate its truth via an addiction. The addiction itself is a messenger that can help us realise our inner selves are speaking to us.

Bikram is a hugely popular yoga practice in the West. I have heard it described as yoga for addictive personalities. Whether that has a grain of truth to it or not, it does help us understand that the addicted human being is far more commonplace than we may realise. There are the more culturally recognised addictions such as to drugs and alcohol, but we could classify most of the human population as addicted to thinking, for example (there are times when I would certainly include myself in that category).

Addictions can be behaviour based, such as with self-harming, or they can manifest in attachment to certain objects such as cigarettes, food or even people who our unconscious psychological projections transform into objects of emotional or psychological fixation. Addiction can focus upon objects—consumables, wearables or collectables—and turn those objects into surrogates for unmet inner needs. Those needs are healthy and natural and important. They are for authenticity and honest intimate connection. Yet, they are consistently dismissed and denied in a society that inflates the importance of appearance, perfection, social image and status, and locks the soul into unnaturally inflexible identities such as always needing to be the provider, the mother, the caring one, the responsible one, the strong one, the one who listens, or the weak, sick or useless one.

There is no place for authenticity in the unconscious demand for the soul to perform according to externally imposed identities that have little to do with its natural and evolving state of being. When a man cannot be loved for who he is but afforded conditional regard when he supports his family financially or a woman is recognised as having creative value only when she bears children and looks a certain way, then the soul is put under a pressure to conform. The soul needs to live and express itself free from constraining, deadening stereotypes, and so can be silenced through such pressures. The soul's true voice—of pain and despair at such a situation—often emerges through addiction to exercise, being busy, appearing productive, one's social media image, alcohol or to an obsession with a personal trainer or celebrity, for example. By embracing the secret wisdom of an addiction, we can find new ways to express the healthy needs of the soul, such as through art, journaling, therapy or dance. The journey from silence to sacred rebellion and creative expression takes great courage and consciousness, it is also our pathway from addiction into authenticity.

A drug addiction is likely to have a more serious and intense nature than an addiction to yoga, but the prominence of addictive behaviour speaks to a broader cultural need for the expression of soul truth. Our souls are collectively telling us that mass culture, the modern world in general, is failing us at a spiritual level. We need to change how we are living. We need to find our inner truths, take our soul journey, and engage the courage to defy cultural norms and birth new ways of living that honour the soul. This secret inner wisdom of addiction needs to be heard.

It is not enough to know this intellectually. Unravelling an addiction is a journey. It is the same journey we take when we connect to our authentic self and allow it to express freely and without judgement. It is a spiritually demanding task. We need to stop fixating on the addiction and listen for the story beneath it.

A woman came to me for mentoring in despair about her eating patterns which were creating a heavier weight than she felt comfortable with and in turn contributed to a negative feeling about exercising her body. She was trying to adopt the conventional wisdom of willpower whereby she would magically feel better is she would just go on a diet and go the gym. "Being thin feels better than anything tastes," as the expression goes. It was all such unhelpful advice! It only shamed her into feeling like a failure and compounded the problem at hand because it didn't get to the core of the issue. It was like the Rumi parable of the man who was looking for his house key. He lost the keys inside the house but was looking for them outside because the light was stronger there. Listening to the loudest voice, rather than the wisest voice, rarely helps us find our way.

This woman's addiction stemmed from her lack of mothering and being truly nourished. Her body was telling her this, but until she stopped looking outside of herself for the answers, and instead sought out her own authentic experience, she would not be able to break the pattern. Once she identified and processed the mother wound, she would feel more nurtured, mirrored and received by herself. She would be repatterning her ability to mother herself in a way that actually met her needs to be seen and heard with respect and care. She would no longer need food in the same way. Her relationship with her body and being would feel more loving and positive. The natural desire to care for her body could develop and she would have a more enjoyable experience of exercise. The negative loop would become a positive spiral. It all starts with an authentic inner experience. To go there, we need patience, commitment, wisdom, and often, the help of experienced professionals, too.

Addiction can help us take in more when there is a sense of lack or to push the world away when it all feels like too much. Addictions arise when those behaviours become our standard response and we are unable to evolve into more effective, healthful or honest approaches. It can be difficult to accept life as it is. We can try to distance ourselves from it with judgement or make it behave according to our ego desires with fantasy projections. We can believe that if we could just have that item or do this behaviour, then everything will be as we wish it to be.

It is important to acknowledge when something is toxic—especially if it seems harmless on the surface—but I don't believe in shaming. I don't think it is helpful. Negativity and criticism are hardly going to help us love ourselves out of an addiction. Addictions can be very resistant to healing because they tap into some of our deepest and most vulnerable wounds. But we can remember that love is stronger than fear.

I do feel that looking for the underlying truth is helpful. This truth is always trying to break through. We can more readily access it with a sense of curiosity, non-judgement, and compassion. Addiction is trying to say something real, healthy and helpful, but the message was not 'allowed' for some reason (most likely due to social conditioning, mass consciousness and/or childhood programming/circumstances) and so has become rerouted into unhelpful behaviours.

When an addiction focuses on taking something in—like cigarette smoke, alcohol, food or drugs—it suggests a deep hunger hasn't been met. Oral-based addictions often present in those who have not experienced being mothered in a healthy, nourishing and supportive way. This doesn't mean addicts didn't have mothers who loved them — perhaps, they did. It does mean the love they needed, the mirroring, the presence, the giving, wasn't there to the degree it was needed to provide a rich inner fullness. The child's sense of true self didn't feel nourished.

We can try to deal with addiction using willpower. However, if we use it to control the behaviour rather than to deal with the underlying issue, it is a bit like laying concrete over a burst water pipe. It might stop the water for a time, but underneath the pressure will be building, wearing away the stopgap from within and in time there will be far more to deal with than the original burst water pipe. The *Tibetan Book of Living and Dying* describes it this way, "Whatever you do, don't try and escape from your pain, but be with it. Because the attempt to escape from pain creates more pain."

It sounds simple, as truth is, but that does not mean it is easy to action. To successfully unravel an addiction, there must be acknowledgement that it is in effect and is in some way blocking us from living more fully, enough self-love not to shame ourselves for it and a powerful desire to connect with the underlying truth of why it is there. Until we can see how addiction is preventing the fulfilment of deeper needs, there is no motivation to do anything about it.

Allowing myself to have needs was one of the first steps in my healing journey around addictive tendencies toward people, objects, and behaviours. I had learned to be hyper-independent and self-reliant. In moderation those traits could be useful but in excess they kept me cut off from people and unable to be nourished by the human love and affection that can only flow when we are open to it. I needed to recognise that the need for human affection is a healthy one and that it's okay to need help, love, respect, connection, to be listened to and to be accepted as I am without judgement. I had to be okay with having needs and admit that I am not completely self-sufficient.

On the spiritual path, there can be the confusing belief that a connection to Spirit can be perfectly fulfilling so we won't need people anymore. I have not found this to be true. As my connection to Spirit deepens, my ability to be with other humans has become healthier and more loving, free and generous — both in giving and receiving. I became fairly skilled at recognising the needs of others early in life but learning to recognise my own needs only came through my journey into personal growth and spiritual development. The quality of my relationships improved markedly when I allowed my authentic self—with her natural needs and desires—to be the one doing the relating.

When we don't allow ourselves to have needs, we cannot know what we need. Without that self-knowledge, we cannot understand what an addiction is trying to fill in us. Once we figure out the need, we can accept it and look for alternative, healthier, non-addictive ways to meet that need. While the only way a need gets met is through addiction, you are unlikely to be free of its hold over you and your life cannot be fully and truly your own.

The more complex we are psychologically and emotionally, the more likely we are to need time for ourselves, so we can figure out our needs and wants and get creative about how to meet them. The less our parents were able to understand and meet our needs (which has more to do with their emotional and psychological skillset than their love for us), the more compensatory behaviours we will have adapted to try to deal with the gap between what was needed and what was given.

The pain that arises when we begin to unravel addiction and our unmet needs is the sort of pain we need. It is the type that can push us to heal. Delving into this pain can stimulate inner gifts and qualities we didn't know how to access before. Even when truth is uncomfortable, it brings us freedom and relief. It alleviates internal psychic pressure and defensiveness, so we can relax into healing and become more trusting and open to the Universe and its flow of abundance. Loosening the grip of addiction by getting to the core unmet need is different to attacking the addiction as though it is the problem. That is like cutting up credit cards thinking that will solve a shopping addiction.

I imagine it a little like the fairytale of the *Princess and the Pea* with a modern upgrade. Let's say a sensitive princess is lying on her many mattresses and there is a pea wedged beneath them. Although that tiny pea doesn't seem like much, and she can only vaguely sense it beneath the pile of mattresses, it is enough for her to end up sleeping in a slightly strange position to avoid pressure on her spine. Eventually, that slightly strange position starts to become an issue by causing certain postural muscles to cramp. After a while, she starts to bend forward, until she gets a cane to help her walk. She might go to the chiropractor to fix her posture. But, until the pea is removed from under those mattresses, she is going to keep creating secondary issues.

We must heal the primary issue. When we try to heal an addiction by dealing with the secondary issues, we are using willpower and diets or budgets or whatever it is that is enforced from the outside. If the ego tells us that we lack willpower, then we might go to a personal trainer to fix it. When we listen to our authentic needs, we can go deeper within, until we become aware of the 'pea' and figure out how to remove it. Take the pea out and our behaviours change because the original stimulus no longer there. Healing can now happen.

When it comes to addiction, becoming aware of and removing the pea often begins with a therapeutic connection with a trained professional who can see and mirror you with compassion, patience and a friendly regard. In this safe environment you can learn to trust and be vulnerable enough to be yourself in a more aware way. You may learn more about your childhood and who you can be once you address certain wounds and the soul evolves into new patterns of being. A weekend workshop may be a good starting point. Consistent and caring relationships are often the best medicine because addiction stems from a flawed connection with others and with yourself. A consciously held, authentic relationship can be enough to dislodge the grip of an addictive behaviour, so a new way of living and loving can come into being.

The Universe is willing and able to help all genuine seekers with all issues, including those that are the most apparently impossible to resolve (please re-read this sentence!). So, there is no need for despair, although when we confront childhood programming it may at times seem like it is too much to process. It is important to stick with the healing process even if everyone around you says, "If it hasn't happened yet, it won't happen."

If I had taken such advice—and plenty of it was given over the years—then I wouldn't be writing the books, oracle decks, music and meditations that are published by Blue Angel in abundance. I'd be sitting in an office somewhere, in chronic physical pain and emotional despair, unhealthy and profoundly unhappy. I can see how my life would have gone in a vastly different direction if I hadn't kept faith. There were times when I wondered if I was nuts to keep trusting that things would somehow come together for me if I continued to listen to my heart and follow my soul star. I have nothing but gratitude for the stubborn attitude that kept me from giving up.

When our self-healing journey requires much more love, attention, courage, money, time, energy or support than we have ever received before, it comes with a hidden blessing. It is a chance to make a commitment to ourselves in a way that no-one else ever has. This can be transformational on so many levels. Instead of bemoaning the time, energy and money we need to give ourselves, we can use the need for that investment as a way to affirm to our bodies, our minds and our entire beings that we are willing to commit, be present, be patient, be kind, care, be responsible, show up, honour and respect ourselves. We are valuing ourselves, even in our vulnerability or apparent brokenness. When we take the healing journey, we are practicing active love. We are healing through what transpires on the journey, but also by simply taking the journey.

As you begin to value yourself, certain destructive behaviours—which are chronic in our addictive, stress-based modern society—begin to lose their appeal. One such behaviour is being in constant stress. As you begin to love yourself, the comforting and soothing aspect of love emerges, and you start to feel safe, grounded, and peaceful. You start to sense the connection and support you have from life and the Universe. You would have had this 'base' if love had been more consistent, unconditional, supportive, accepting, protective and encouraging when you were a child. When we have this sense, we are naturally more relaxed. When we relax, we can deal with stress more efficiently. We can more readily provide the body with what it needs for healing and repair, so we are more able to heal physically, too.

You'll also start to feel what that level of health feels like and will naturally be more drawn to relaxed, warm, encouraging people rather than those who are anxious and uptight. You'll choose your company more wisely and start to notice that your energy transforms the energy of those around you, not intentionally, but as a positive side effect of your connection with your relaxed inner state.

A drummer who for some time worked on my *Divine Circus* dance music project, told me that he loved to hug me because it instantly calmed him and made him feel good. His stress simply melted away. It was not through anything other than his response to my connection with my own being. As a drummer he was well-connected to his body and sensed these things acutely.

Of course, the opposite has happened too!

At the end of a workshop, I can be so filled with energy that I use a discharging process to release it all. This begins to happen within the first few minutes of the close of a workshop, but the full discharge can take some hours or even days to complete. On one occasion a woman came up to hug me at the close of a workshop, before I had even had the chance to energetically disengage from the group. She flung her arms around me and nearly fell over. She was completely overwhelmed by the amount of electricity flowing through me. From that moment onwards, I became much more aware about taking care during any 'hugging process' that happened after teaching! Our physicality can affect the physicality of another so when are working with our bodies, we are also helping other bodies, too.

The vagus nerve is a trip switch into deeper connection with our needs, especially our physical ones. For those who are willing, it can be engaged for unravelling addiction or to enhance wellbeing. The vagus nerve has multiple branches that diverge from two stems in the back of the brain, extending into the abdomen, touching your heart and most major organs along the way. You can connect with it by placing your hands—or one of my favourite things, a cold pack wrapped in a towel—behind your head where the base of the head meets the neck.

Visceral feelings and gut instincts are intuitions transferred to your brain via the vagus nerve. This mind-body feedback system works between body and brain, and from brain to the organs. It lets your body know whether you can relax, rest and digest or whether you need to be alert and ready to deal with a situation through fight or flight. The latter is triggered in modern life far more often than is needed, simply due to stress. Watching an action movie or having a fearful thought can be enough to trigger a stress response in the body. The response created by the parasympathetic nervous system, commanded by the vagus nerve, is the polar opposite. It slows us down, lowers heart rate and blood pressure, and takes us into a state of repair, healing and restfulness. This doesn't mean we become couch potatoes. In this relaxed state we tend to be more effective, even in physical pursuits. Ask a sports professional with a long-term career how important rest is for their overall performance! It also allows us to go into deeper states of rest when we sleep or meditate which again promotes healing on emotional and physical levels.

Deep breathing—with emphasis on a long, slow exhale—can get the vagus nerve functioning optimally, evoking its positive effects. We can do this at any time, not just when we register a need to relax. Practicing deeper, slower breathing throughout the day can be beneficial, especially when we find ourselves caught up in stressful thoughts about the future. Calming ourselves with breath makes us present and aware which is the best place from which to make decisions. If I catch myself getting caught up in some mental episode of stress-creation, I like to make myself laugh by saying, "Vagus, baby!" (rather than "Vegas, baby!"). To laugh, you need to breathe. It helps us reconnect to the breath and in doing so, become more present.

Slowing and deepening the breath with a thorough exhale and a pause at the top of the inhalation and the end of the exhalation, is an ancient yogic practice for calming the mind. It also tones the vagus nerve. Tuning in to your vagus nerve by using my playful mantra (vagus, baby!) or by placing your awareness at the back of your skull can be enough to bring you into a more relaxed and present state. If you are working on finding the truth underlying an addiction or an answer to a troubling matter in your life, shifting into a relaxed state of presence and awareness is so helpful. Though this practice, you are demonstrating that your needs and feelings matter enough to you that you are willing to slow down, be present and pay attention. The Universe has been patiently waiting for those moments, so it can slip the answers to your prayers into your open, receptive awareness. This is often the very same moment that we suddenly realise how brilliant we are and that we have finally figured something out.

HEALING PROCESS

For this exercise, it is helpful to find a place where you can settle yourself and relax without interruptions. If possible, lie down on your back. You may wish to have a pillow or cold pack wrapped in a towel to place behind your head. Your body may cool down as you unwind, so have enough layers so that you can remain comfortably warm. A slightly darkened rather than a brightly lit room can support your relaxation process. When you are ready say the following prayer aloud:

> *I call upon the Crystal Angel of Moldavite. I ask for your healing energy, your synergistic power and your unconditionally loving wisdom. I call upon the star teacher Fomalhaut, for your radiant transmission of higher will and creative power to assist soul evolution. With mercy and compassion, please help me see, feel and release any emotional and mental blockages that are preventing me from relaxing into trust and receiving all the blessings the Universe wishes to bestow upon me. Please help me connect with the energies in the spiritual and material worlds that truly support my authenticity and fulfilment on all levels. Through unconditional love, in honour of the highest wisdom for the greatest good, so be it.*

Now it is time to relax. You may wish to place a cold pack wrapped in a towel (so it is cool rather than cold) behind your head where the base of the skull meets the neck. You could also use a soft pillow. Work with however your neck and head feel most comfortable, but try to have your chin pointing downwards slightly, to subtly elongate the back of your neck. You may wish to lie on your back with your arms and legs slightly apart, palms facing upwards. Close your eyes and allow yourself to breathe in and out, resting, drifting off into meditation, or a nap, for as long as you choose. Try to remain as still as possible to enhance the power of this process.

When you have finished your resting meditation or nap, place your hands on your heart. Imagine, feel or intend that the Universe is gently filling your heart until you are completely nourished by divine love. It is soft, gentle, powerful and healing.

Take your time to emerge from your restful posture, as you patiently and lovingly ground your awareness back into your body with gentle physical movements. You have completed your healing process.

CHAPTER TEN

FROLICKING IN THE FIFTH DIMENSION

STAR GUIDE: ARCTURUS

ARCTURUS IS INCREDIBLY OLD, over 7 billion years old and much older than our Sun. When our Sun evolves to become a red giant, it might become a star much like Arcturus is now. Edgar Cayce, the sleeping prophet, referred to Arcturus as one of the most advanced civilisations in this galaxy. He believed it existed in the fifth dimension, meaning that it resonates at the same frequency as Shambhala, the abode of the ascended masters that we learned about in Chapter Eight.

In ascension teachings, the fifth dimension is a reality totally immersed in spiritual unity and wisdom. The name Arcturus is a Biblical name that translates as *gathering together*. One way to recognise the workings of Arcturus in our lives is through the love, connection and oneness that unfolds. This forms the basis of fifth dimensional consciousness within a human being. When we experience fifth dimensional consciousness, we do not suddenly lose ourselves and become enmeshed in each other. Rather, it means dwelling in a state beyond the realm of ego, nestled into the inner nature of the Higher Self and eventually as a fully realised, enlightened spiritual being. There is the acute awareness that we are all connected and the ego ideas, such as profit at the expense of another being, are insupportable. Cayce saw Arcturus as a spiritual model for humanity's evolution. It supports the human collective in readying to integrate Shambhala and the higher levels of spiritual consciousness into our world for the spiritual benefit of all beings. It is a star guide with optimism about the potential for spiritual progress within humanity. We are a collective of ascended masters in the making.

In that sense, Arcturus is a star teacher especially for star seeds —and those who hold a higher consciousness within and are shining it as a light to guide humanity forward. For star seeds, lightworkers, priestesses and other spiritual practitioners who are accustomed to a higher frequency of light (like those born in clean country air who struggle to adjust to higher pollution levels in a city) connecting to Arcturus can bring some relief. Connecting with this star guide can help us access higher states of consciousness than are readily available on Earth at this time.

If we ate at a restaurant that only used unhealthy ingredients, we would only be getting a certain level of nourishment. What we were eating may cause more harm than good. If we changed to a high-quality service that worked with organic foods and understood how to create genuinely nourishing and life-enhancing meals, then our nutrient levels would increase accordingly. Arcturus provides spiritual food for the soul, in the form of high-level consciousness that fosters a much higher frequency of being.

This star guide serves us truly nourishing energies so that we can benefit from fifth dimensional awareness in practical ways in our daily lives. Arcturus helps us make wise choices on where we seek our nourishment, so we can feed our spiritual selves with high-quality frequencies that have a positive, inspiring, uplifting and healing quality on our consciousness. It teaches us to recognise higher consciousness not by appearance (which can be misleading) but by the effect it has on our being.

This guided-from-within approach is the basis of the Arcturian wisdom of respecting capacity with kindness. When you force a body to go from a diet of processed foods directly into a fasting state, you can cause grievous harm. Yet, for a body that has spent years purifying and preparing, that same fast could bring many health benefits. It is not about whether fasting can be useful, but what suits the circumstances.

This can apply to diet as well as how we nourish ourselves with exercise, spiritual practice, the things we watch in the media and the materials we read. Arcturus helps us discern what it is that will help us make progress. For some that might be upping exercise and for those recovering from exercise addiction or adrenal issues, it might be stepping down the physical demands on the body so that it can heal. Arcturus reminds us that there is not a one-size-fits-all approach to living well and fulfilling our destiny. At some point, we will need to trust ourselves and find our own way, by following our inner wisdom and taking responsibility for our decisions and the effects they have on our bodies and our lives. This can free us from any guilt or shame we might feel for not matching up to societal ideals about how we should live. It also gives us permission to afford others the respect and encouragement that can help them figure out how they want to live.

Arcturus is a type of spiritual gateway between Earth and higher levels of consciousness that provides what is needed to stimulate humanity on the evolutionary path whilst regulating the flow of spiritual light coming to the planet so we don't burn out too quickly (like the unfortunate rabbis we met in Chapter Eight who went bonkers or dropped dead from witnessing a spiritual mystery they were not ready to receive). Part of the wisdom that comes with genuine spiritual power is kindness. The light and energy are shared with compassion, mercy and based on individual ability. Burdening a first grader with a master's degree math problem would not be kind nor useful. It would create confusion and set up inaccurate and unnecessary negative beliefs about one's ability. When there is less of a gap between what is shared and the current ability of the recipient, it can stimulate curiosity and put one on the path toward fulfilling one's divine potential. Wisdom has kindness built in.

Arcturus can help us realise that more is not always better and that the steps to divine realisation are graced to us as we become ready, willing and able. This knowledge can inspire confidence when our tasks seem more than our minds can handle and patience when we hunger for more but need to master what we are already working on.

Compared to our solar system, Arcturus moves at tremendous speed (estimated at 122 km/s). Rather than moving the same way as the general stream of stars, it cuts perpendicularly through the disc of the Milky Way. As a star guide and elder guardian, Arcturus reveals that the unique soul path and the swiftest way to make spiritual progress are not often in sync with what the mainstream—or our logical mind—may think is best. Arcturus, the patron star teacher of sacred rebels everywhere, stirs the soul to break free from the pull of the crowd and swim across the currents toward its destiny, even when no other appears to be taking that path and the progress is guiding one into unfamiliar territory. When one is in connection with divine wisdom, there is joy, rather than fear, in marching to one's own beat.

As it cuts through the galactic disc, Arcturus will reach its closest point to our Sun in around four thousand years. As it is moving in its own unique trajectory, sight of this star will eventually fade from earthly view in around a million or so years. Arcturus teaches us not to hold ourselves back just to stay in connection with known worlds. Radical progress can mean venturing into unknown territories where new communities and the renewal of purpose awaits. It also means that certain relationships or life situations can become more intense for a time, before fading away from your life altogether. Arcturus encourages us to trust in the greater guiding spiritual direction that charts our course. When Arcturus connects with the soul, you are being given a spiritual fast-track which will take you beyond the world you have known.

CRYSTAL ANGEL: STIBNITE

A striking looking stone, stibnite appears grey-silver with a metallic finish and long blade-like formations. Stibnite looks like a crystal aerial or antennae and one of its primary uses is picking up higher-level frequencies and detecting and removing lower-level attachments in the energy field. I have found that attuning to new frequencies can involve an adjustment process like that of a plane rising in altitude. As the shift begins, there can be some turbulence and the transition doesn't always feel stable. Eventually, flight at the increased altitude steadies and the continuing journey feels more comfortable and 'normal' at that higher state.

Before that adjustment can happen, there must be an understanding of which altitude you are 'reaching for' so the pilot (your higher self) can chart a flight path based on those coordinates. This is where stibnite is so helpful. Stibnite helps increase the strength of energetic signals so that you can gain a clearer reception, tuning in to that new transmission more clearly and easily, like making it easier to tune a radio to a new station.

For the mind, body and soul, that means higher frequencies become familiar pathways that you can tune in to for nourishment, guidance, and energetic support when bringing through a new way of being. The new frequencies and the patterns they create will become increasingly imprinted in your energy field. This is a bit like when you save a radio station you regularly listen to, so that you can press a button to tune straight in to the broadcast. Stibnite amplifies this process, making it more powerful. It supports our energy body to recognise and replicate new patterns of thought and establish body-memory patterns for the new beliefs. Each belief system has a feeling pattern that manifests itself in our bodies. This is sometimes obvious in our posture, movements and facial expressions. Stibnite makes that entire process more conscious for us, and if we use our intention to work with it for healing, it will help us upgrade our beliefs and cement them in our energy field.

This crystal is a cosmic mirror for conscious manifestation. When working with stibnite, or any crystal or amplifying spiritual practice such as Chi Gung, meditation or yoga, it is important to remember that we need to be in harmony and authenticity with ourselves to manifest what is helpful and needed. There is no point using stibnite to attract higher-level guidance if our bodies are giving off fear because we are yet to embrace some form of inner work. If we are yet to heal abandonment or betrayal wounds from our past, we may feel tremendous distrust and whatever we broadcast could be confused at best, and stibnite would amplify our negative expectations along with the positives.

However, even a worst-case scenario can be put to good use. If stuff comes up for us, we can use our increased awareness to make changes, so we are ready to resonate with the goodness, grace, love and plenty we may wish to attract into our lives. Stibnite is again our ally in broadcasting the sort of frequencies that allow us to 'be what we seek' and kick the law of attraction into action in our lives in a positive and enjoyable way.

SPIRITUAL GUIDANCE: SWIMMING IN THE OCEAN OF CONSCIOUSNESS WITHOUT DROWNING IN IT

Many of us who are on a spiritual journey feel profound compassion for the suffering of other beings. I remember a movie where one of the characters would cry at the plight of ants. The struggles all beings generally contend with caused him considerable personal distress. He was portrayed as a ridiculous character in the film, but I could relate to his sensitivity. I recently saw a meme on social media of a group of people standing around someone who had collapsed on the floor in a crisis of despair. The quote was, "When you accidentally step on your dog's paw ... I don't know what to do! My entire brain is hurting right now!"

Tibetan Buddhists understand the torment that can arise in the face of suffering. They use various cleansing practices to let go of the anguish they experience when another being is harmed, even if it was done unintentionally. Feeling moved by the pain of other beings is not the issue, but we do need to deal with these experiences wisely, so they don't incapacitate us. They may otherwise leave us feeling helpless or overwhelmed. They might inspire us to dive in to rescue others, only to drown in the suffering and lose the sense of peace, equanimity and compassion that makes us useful. We need spiritual skilfulness and understanding so that our efforts are effective and don't undermine our wellbeing as we strive to help others.

It's no good signing up as a lifeguard at the beach, if you aren't strong enough to swim in the ocean. Lifeguards are trained on how to swim across a rip tide and navigate dangerous currents, so that their passionate purpose can be fulfilled. We don't want courageous beings drowning due to overenthusiasm and under preparation. Those precious souls can help so many! Comparably, we need to become more aware of how we could unintentionally trip ourselves up and sabotage our progress even when our intentions are noble. This usually begins with a recognition of ego, which can be a humbling, disconcerting, helpful and empowering experience.

A successful artist had won many awards, but the one she set her mind on had not yet been granted to her. Rather than recognising her ego was doing what egos do (finding ways to be miserable and believe they are being denied) she took it as evidence the Universe wanted her to do something else with her life! When I asked her if she felt passion, purpose and love for art more than anything else in the world, she agreed wholeheartedly. She was relieved when I proposed that rather than being a genuine message from the Universe, her ego could be suggesting she stop being an artist as a temper-tantrum protest against the organisation running the art prize she so coveted.

Then there was the exceptionally talented writer who wondered if the Universe was asking her to sacrifice her passion for writing. I suspect she may have felt this way because her parents needed her to perform as they wished to satisfy their own ego wounds, rather than to be herself, which was dreadful narcissistic abuse of her personhood. She was willing to give up her passion, if Spirit was asking it of her. In truth, no such thing was happening, and it was such unnecessary pain to even consider it. The distorted ego was projecting her unresolved abuse onto the Universe. I assured her that the Divine never asks us to not be ourselves. The only things we give up on the spiritual path are connected to the false self of the ego, because it inhibits the realisation of our true divine nature. However, until she could recognise that writing was from her heart, and that she didn't have to keep repeating the sacrifice demanded of her in childhood, she would vacillate between trusting in her talent and worrying that it—and she—was not enough. Eventually she did make that leap, her talent was freed and as a result was duly acknowledged by industry experts as being genuine and considerable.

These stories might seem silly, but my own past had plenty of angst along similar lines — that's how I learned these lessons. During my own wilderness years, which lasted nine or so years, I wanted to share the work I do now, in the way I do now, but it just hadn't happened yet. I didn't know if it ever would happen, yet I believed in the authenticity of my offering. The dissonance between vision and reality was profoundly painful. I was learning to let go, trust and endure. On a practical level, the publisher who would eventually assist me in so many ways, including the publication of my work, had yet to start his publishing company. The ego can say what it likes and make circumstances mean things they do not. Sometimes however, we just need to wait for time to run its course and for things to fall into place according to a higher order of divine timing.

Whilst we don't want to dither when we need to act, as others will benefit from our progress, there is no point trying to rush the journey. Sometimes delay is the Universe giving us a red light, so others can be where they need to be. We all get green and red lights — that's how everyone can get to where they need to be safely. If someone needs to arrive at a destination before we can get there, according to a greater wisdom that understands how everything can work out, then it makes sense to bow down to that. We may need to learn how to discharge the frustration we may sometimes feel (to that end, I suggest robust singing and dancing!). We are not alone in our journey, even if it seems like at times, nor are we forgotten. There are always other factors at play, other people, other aspects of divine timing at work. What we view as delays are part of divine progress just as much as what we view as flow.

It isn't until we know ourselves and feel valued for who we are (perhaps through therapy, healthy relationships, spiritual practice or a combination of all these things) that we will be able to stop torturing ourselves with doubt and confusion about our purpose and whether or not it will ever happen. Our fundamental purpose is to be ourselves. As we do that, it becomes natural to live in a way that reflects, awakens and expresses our passions. We let go of the need to know it all in advance, and start living with more trust, figuring out the wisest approach to our challenges as we go. Your life and expression of your higher purpose may not happen in the way you expect, but the more you let go, the more opportunity you give the Universe to show you a beautiful and attuned way to experience deep fulfilment.

We all have an internal navigation system, and it knows how to guide us on our unique life journey. Unconditional trust is the key to living that guidance. It's how you walk the path created for you by the Universe. I sometimes hear clients say that if their higher guidance just gave them a map, they would follow it. They are still learning that their heart holds the map and as they trust in its guidance, it will all unfold perfectly according to divine timing and a higher plan.

As we work on our own consciousness, trust, love and faith in the goodness of Spirit guiding us always become more natural for us. If we must overcome some major trauma around trust due to childhood wounding, for example, it shows we have more powerful trust muscles than those who have not had to work so hard. Part of the higher purpose behind karmic struggle may be to prepare us for taking greater leaps, in total trust and peace, later in life. This will bring benefit to us as well as the many other beings who only learn to trust the Universe because they trust us and see that we trust the Universe. Trust can be a wonderfully contagious wisdom.

There are teachings on the effect higher and lower consciousness have on our being. Yogananda, the Hindu sage, speaks in terms of magnetism. A small amount of high-level magnetism can be overcome by more intense but lower-level magnetism. This is what happens when our truth and love seem tainted or overwhelmed by the greater intensity of fear or hate in those around us. We can be like the lifeguard that starts to drown. We need more skilfulness and practice to strengthen our spiritual muscles and increase and sustain our higher magnetism. After removing ourselves from that field, we may find cleansing ourselves through meditation, spiritual healing or devotion (such as chanting, sacred ritual or time spent in nature to reconnect with our true inner nature) can again bring us into the higher vibrational frequency of our spiritual magnetism and no longer subject to the hate, fear, greed or whatever else was expressing itself in that fear-based consciousness.

Fortunately, it also works the other way, and that is the basis of spiritual healing. It is why we can feel so uplifted in the presence of certain people, why I break into a grin when I see a picture of the Dalai Lama and why my heart melts whenever I think of Mother Mary, even for a moment. If fearful people come to us for help, and our vibrational frequency of love is greater than their field of fear, our love can transform their fear and uplift everyone in the process. Instead of everyone feeling down and depressed, everyone feels amazing.

It is a question of which force is stronger at the time. Some souls can remain in their peace-affirming truth in the face of tremendous force to the contrary. They radiate extraordinarily strong, high-level spiritual magnetism. Mahatma Gandhi, Nelson Mandela and Mother Teresa are some well-known examples. The soul can become so aligned with higher magnetism that standing strong and true, even in the face of millions of people's fear, can change reality through the presence of the divine light within. So inspiring!

Some sensitive souls, often known as empaths, tend to pick up the feelings of others. At times, they may find it difficult to distinguish between the feelings that originate within them and those that 'belong' to others. Empathic ability can be a great asset for insight and healing when one learns to govern it rather than have it overtake one's sense of self. It often develops when non-existent parental boundaries lead a child to unconsciously assume the role of mirror to the parent. Here, the child senses the parents' emotional needs and tries to meet them, rather than the parent being the guardian and mirror to the child, faithfully reflecting the child's reality so that they learn to feel safe, trusting and present with their own innate sense of self. This sort of soul is the most likely to want to help others unconditionally as they have been trained to serve from childhood. Until those childhood issues are resolved, they are also the people most likely to get lost in the suffering of others. These are also the souls who can most easily receive spiritual presence. So, the potential to become well connected to Spirit, able to remain in that truth and even tame negative energies with their presence is also there.

If a sensitive or empath doesn't work on their boundaries and give themselves the right to be individuals who are not always at the beck and call of anyone in need, there will eventually be an experience of what nurses refer to as *compassion fatigue.* This is where you become too exhausted to give any more of yourself to anyone. It tends to heal itself with some restoration and *me time.* When it has progressed for far too long, an extended healing period may be needed to recover from the depletion that comes when compassion is not extended to yourself as much as it is to others. If you burn yourself out in five or ten years of dedicated service, rather than flourishing through fifty plus years of service, where is the greater benefit for anyone?

Sometimes the only way to heal compassion fatigue in such a way that it doesn't happen again is to break the cycle of self-neglect and learn how to give to yourself. A client described this to me in a beautiful way. Her acupuncturist had told her that she was so used to being an empty cup, that whenever she got just a little bit of energy she felt fantastic and promptly gave it away to someone or something. She had to learn what it felt like to be full and to give from a place of overflowing, rather than depletion. As she was not nurtured as a child, she had no idea what it meant to be kind to herself. When I described ways to do this, she duly took notes. It broke my heart to see such a giving, generous being needing to learn how to be good to herself as a mature woman. However, she has a beautiful heart and much wisdom and is learning that enjoyable spiritual lesson now and making great progress.

Those keen to offer a light to humanity need to know how to hold our own when faced with the daily onslaught of negativity and fear in the media and the subtle yet pervasive conditioning used to manipulate the human mind and purse strings through advertising. Even if you don't watch television or listen to the radio except for carefully selected programs, there are ads on the back of taxis, the sides of buses and bus stops, wrapped around telegraph poles and in the material that relentlessly finds its way into our letterboxes and email account, on the websites we browse, on social media and even on our workout clothes. Visual commercial branding has become insidious noise in modern culture, and it has an effect.

In the modern world, not drowning in lower consciousness takes more than boosting our wellbeing and helping others effectively in the process. It is about waking up and connecting to our discerning inner knowledge and making conscious choices.

Recognising the vast extent of the conditioning that plays itself out in our minds has become increasingly challenging. It is easy to be swept along in the fear-based consumeristic madness that has us constantly feeling anxious, needy, denied, deprived and uncomfortably overfed and undernourished on all levels. However, we can take steps to help us feel present, grounded, full and loving. The people who think they are fine and believe they are unaffected by the system, are the most susceptible to this modern madness because they don't have the awareness to recognise the issues at hand. As Krishnamurti put it, "It is no measure of health to be well adjusted to a profoundly sick society."

There's a phrase in the news industry, "If it bleeds, it leads." I encourage the intelligent research of world events, but we need to look deeper to the causes that have led to terrorism, for example, rather than create further divisiveness, hatred, fear, judgement and blame by making it about *us and the horrific other*. When the media reports on a terrorist activity it has a global reach. The media influences the human collective, for better or worse. Whether we happen to watch that particular broadcast or not, we need spiritual strength to choose how we respond to the emotional waves that are triggered within the human collective.

I remember standing in line at the post office while a reported terrorist attack was discussed. It seemed that almost everyone in the queue had been up watching news reports all night. They regurgitated the fearful messages they had heard on the news and declared that the city where the event occurred was a terrorist hotspot. The fact that nothing of the sort had happened there previously apparently meant nothing. Given that nothing has happened there in the years since, that viewpoint may now have been dismissed. One can only hope as it's hardly the sort of reality we want to empower by lending our voice to it.

It might not seem to matter once the deed is done, but how we respond to events can inflame or diffuse them. How they are reported and talked about can either contribute to rising global hysteria or soothe it. News reporting on terrorist activities is just one example where mastery is needed to bring a higher magnetism into effect. The end-of-the-world hysteria of Y2K and the onset of 2012 are some other examples. It is easy to write these emotional reactions off as ignorant hysterics, but I believe an unconscious, displaced but otherwise genuine fear of destruction, was triggered. Weapons that can destroy our planet now exist and the human beings who have access to those weapons are not always pure of mind. Living in a world where such weapons are created in the first place suggests that bringing calm, loving spiritual magnetism into our hearts and minds for the greater good is a valuable ability.

When the mainstream media gives its typically depressing apocalyptic takes on the latest activities of terrorist groups, it instils fear in the human heart and induces anxiety in the mind. That is, unless the soul is strongly connected to a spiritual magnetism that is more powerful than the collective belief system. Wisdom is the only answer to this sort of fear-inducing manipulation. This wisdom involves taking a beat, checking our reactions, discerning the deeper truth and making a choice about being the light. Terrorist groups can lay claim to events, especially those with high-profile media coverage, regardless of whether they were involved. Like any bully, generating fear makes them feel powerful. Focusing on who did what or why can become a fear-inducing distraction from our true spiritual task.

Studies have found a curious commonality between the people who joined certain terrorist groups in the Middle East and those who joined other types of cultic groups. The common thread is a sense of displacement. The study found that many of the people who joined extremist groups did so when they were not living in their home country. This infers that an unfulfilled need for belonging is a significant motivator for joining such groups. I have found this to be true in my experiences with cultic spiritual groups, too.

We have an opportunity to do something constructive when faced with negativity in the media and the fearful, obsessive reactions it tends to evoke. When we recognise that there is a need for compassion, spiritual intervention and healing, we can respond in a way that attracts, generates and shares these qualities. We build our own positive magnetism by choosing what we focus upon and doing our part to create a sense of community and belonging with our words, actions, attitude and prayers. This not only responds to the immediate situation but begins to unravel the reasons why terrorism exists in the first place. We can strengthen the presence of love and extend a sense of belonging to each other that is increasingly inclusive, not restricted by cultural, geographical, political or religious boundaries. In doing so we are grassroots spiritual activists working together to uproot the insidious weed of disconnection that allows something like terrorism to fester in the human collective. May we remember our power to contribute, create and be wise in our expression.

Whilst I have an inner fire about this state of affairs, I am by nature an optimist. When we have a willingness to live differently and a little bit of courage to face the unknown and seek out something better, the Universe generously meets us with all sorts of unexpected help. I was so deeply moved by the intelligence, beauty, effectiveness and wisdom of the many higher beings of divine love that helped me find my way from darkness and ignorance back into the light of my true soul nature that I channelled an entire healing modality—which I teach as an online healer training program called *Soul Guidance and Sacred Mentoring*™—to help others strengthen their own divine magnetism. It is a practice that helps us grow our soul, so we are strong enough to hold our own whilst we are also held in love. We can learn how to have a positive effect on lower magnetism, which in turn helps us all.

Radiating a strong and high-level spiritual magnetism requires a healthy connection to the divine realms of spirit and a healthy connection that is grounded in the body. You may have an incredible song in your soul that could heal many people, but for that to happen, those people must be able to hear it. You need to sing it! We need the body to take the inner beauty and share it with the world.

One year there was a lovely trainee in *Soul Guidance and Sacred Mentoring*™ who was a yogini. You'd think all that yoga would have guaranteed she was in her body, but once she progressed to module three in the training, which involves connection with the divine feminine through the various faces of the goddess, she realised that she used to ground with her head, rather than through her body. Not long into module three, while in a simple yoga pose, she felt the lower half of her body for the first time. What an amazing and courageous breakthrough!

Tantric Buddhism teaches that you can only become enlightened through the body. To build our consciousness so that it can withstand the negative magnetism of fear, we need a strong base on the earth — a strong sense of self that can consciously choose how to think and behave according to inner values. For a star seed, this can bring relief. Instead of feeling aversion for the body and the earthly life, we can recognise them as opportunities to increase our spiritual enlightenment. We don't need to avoid the earth and our bodies to frolic in the fifth dimensional consciousness of loving unity. The exploration of unity consciousness benefits all beings and it can actually happen through connection and integration of spirit and body. It helps star seeds find a spiritual home here on this planet. Not a home away from home that must be tolerated, but a true divine home where Spirit and Earth are united and creating love, light and wisdom through an awakening human being. May all beings be graced with the spiritual blessings that gently awaken true higher consciousness within.

HEALING PROCESS

Begin your healing process by saying this prayer aloud:

> *I call upon the Crystal Angel of Stibnite and the unconditional loving grace of star teacher Arcturus. I ask for assistance in opening up to the universal Bodhisattva of compassion and wisdom to release my attachment to suffering in the face of suffering. I open to your instruction for building higher spiritual magnetism in my mind, body and soul, to stand true in divine wisdom and radiate spiritual light with unshakeable confidence for the spiritual benefit of all beings. Through the highest wisdom for the greatest good, so be it.*

Place your hands in prayer at your heart. Imagine, intend or visualise that there is a great silver-grey angel, the Crystal Angel of Stibnite, reaching out on your behalf to amplify the healing frequencies being offered to you from the Universe. A beautiful light of compassion is flowing from the heart of the Universe into your body, mind and soul, bringing comfort and reassurance and filling you with positivity and strength. This is peaceful. It asks nothing of you other than to enter the softness and peace of this light. The more you relax into it, the stronger you become. It is strength without tension or force.

Rest in this feeling for as long as you choose.

Then imagine, feel or intend that this feeling of peaceful strength fills you entirely and begins to gently overflow. It is slow, thick and substantial, perhaps like lava from a volcano, luminous, richly nourishing, warming and healing. It is flowing in all directions and attracting all beings who can benefit from that outflow to become warmed, healed, empowered and blessed by divine goodness.

Be with this process for however long feels best for you.

Meditate or add your prayers for the blessings for all beings to know peace, compassion and freedom. Then rest for as long as you need.

You have finished your healing process.

CHAPTER ELEVEN

THE COSMIC PRIESTESS

STAR GUIDE: ALCYONE

ALCYONE IS A BLUE-WHITE GIANT and the brightest star in the constellation of the Pleiades. Over the ages, the Pleiades cluster has been spiritually significant to many cultures including the Australian Aborigines and the Lakota of North America. Some cultures, such as the Hopi, Cherokee and Mayans, shared the belief that their ancestors heralded from the Pleiades. Others, such as the ancient Egyptians, revered them as cosmic midwives who helped to birth a higher consciousness on Earth. In Greek mythology, the Pleiades embodied many faces of the sacred feminine and honoured them as muses, priestesses, mothers, lovers, and midwives.

Humanity has marked the passage of the Pleiades for thousands of years, acknowledging the special relationship between these stars and the earth. Many star seeds feel a meaningful connection to the Pleiades and sense that part of their soul journey involved some sort of spiritual evolution through that star system where they soaked in the energies of love and feminine wisdom. Their preparation in the divine feminine training ground of the Pleiades, readied them to bring that wisdom to other civilisations including those here on Earth.

In esoteric or soul-centred astrology, the Pleiades are a cosmic chakra around which seven other solar systems revolve. They have a significant spiritual influence across many worlds and the earth is just one of them. At a spiritual level, the Pleiades are a source of electrical energy for our solar system and support the spiritual path of our Sun in harmony with Sirius, another star guide we will meet in this book. Occultists hold that the sun, the Pleiades and Sirius form a cosmic triangle which is an expression of celestial sacred geometry that serves a higher purpose for many beings.

A triangle is the most stable and solid structure in sacred geometry and down-to-earth, construction geometry alike. In building, triangular structures within square or rectangular frames add strength for weight bearing. Any force spreads evenly through all three sides. Similarly, the triangular formation in energy work adds strength, stability and an ability to bear more weight, pressure and dynamic fluctuations without collapse or loss of structure. This increases the amount of divine electricity that can be received in spiritual work and thus allows higher consciousness to be sustained for longer periods and with greater stability. A spiritual synergy can then occur so there is greater output with less effort than if the three beings created their part of the output separately.

The Pleiades is significant for the soul as it demonstrates the art of spiritual synergy through conscious, high-level collaborations that allow for greater manifestation for all. Our souls can take this in and learn to re-enact it. This may mean effectively working with others for the advantage of the collaborators and the benefit of those who use the sacred creations that come from the collaboration. It can also mean learning to integrate disparate aspects of our lives and harmonising different energies to support and nurture each other.

Alcyone is the central star of the Pleiades and is in Taurus, the astrological ruler of the throat. The Western mystery traditions view the Pleiades as the cosmic throat chakra and the supreme paragon of synthesis. Synthesis is the art of integration. It unites different elements into a seamless new expression. The trick with synthesis is preserving the original qualities of the individual elements. Otherwise, it can be like mixing different coloured paint together and ending up with brown goo and no sense of what has gone into creating it. It is not a particularly appealing outcome either. An example of a successful synthesis could be a superb meal, where the flavours combine and enhance each other, but the individual elements are still smelled and tasted. Nothing stands out in an overpowering way, nothing is overwhelmed by anything else and no component is lost either.

Synthesis is not a matter of doing a bit of this, and a bit of that, or throwing a bunch of ingredients together—whether ideas or food items—and hoping for the best. It requires an ability to sense interrelationships and understand which ingredients can work with others and in what proportions. A friend of mine once described her husband's approach to cooking as aspiring to (but not quite attaining) synthesis. He tossed several herbs—some suited to Thai food, some to Italian and others to Mexican—together and the end result was not so good! A genius in cuisine fusion will know how to combine aspects of various cuisines so that something new and delicious is created. Another example are healers who want to combine spiritual modalities without first developing an ability for meaningful synthesis. As a result, their treatment may lack continuity and flow as they jump from one modality to another. It's all a bit of a muddle for the practitioner and the client.

Synthesis is a soul art that requires spiritual intelligence and the creative integration of diversity and unity. It helps us reconcile the disparate parts of our being and our lives to bring a feeling of wholeness into place. Instead of feeling pulled in different directions by work, relationships, children and our need for a healthy lifestyle, synthesis allows these elements to become seamless parts of our person and our life. Through synthesis, our inner and outer aspects don't compete, they complement each other. With synergy, strength in one area leads to strength in all areas, not depletion or diminishment.

We can develop this talent with the help of the Pleiades. It utilises the throat chakra, the centre through which we discern. It is also where we create sound, the spiritual basis of manifestation. The throat chakra is an organising and prioritising aspect of our energy field, and the same goes for the throat chakras of massive cosmic beings. Including one huge enough to have an entire constellation—such as the Pleiades—as its throat chakra.

The Pleiades has a special soul relationship with those who want to successfully blend modalities (or cuisines!) or who have a life purpose that involves creativity and higher expression. This often manifests through integrating a range of disciplines such as music, philosophy, shamanism and crystal healing or science, medicine and art. Connecting with the Pleiades at a soul level can help us synthesise successfully when working with different disciplines or on a more day-to-day level of being a mum, a wife, a healer and a woman who needs a cup of tea and some downtime to remain sane!

When we work with the throat chakra to access synthesis, we become more able to live our complexity and honour the many and varied facets of our being from a place of simplicity. We learn how to be the tree, whilst acknowledging we have branches, a trunk, roots, leaves, fruit and birds that like to dwell in our energy field, also. As our spiritual ability to synthesise increases, we become capable of inviting increasingly diverse elements into our energy field without losing our simplicity, focus and clarity.

We can begin to strengthen the throat chakra by noticing what we think and what we speak and making choices that align with our integrity. That can start by ditching the thoughts that induce feelings of stress and being pulled in multiple directions and cultivating the idea that all parts of our lives are interwoven and can enhance each other. We can learn to live in a way that is more balanced and more honouring.

Alcyone is the stellar bearer of the feminine energy. She is the cosmic priestess connecting us to the Pleiadean light and our own inner feminine knowing. Feminine knowing, in men and in women, is the intuitive, instinctual sense of truth and wisdom which is not subject to logic. It is not irrational but grounded in an authentic connection to reality. It is non-rational as one doesn't need to go through steps of deductive reasoning to get to it. Alcyone helps us connect to that feminine wisdom, supporting and encouraging us to speak our truth, whether it seems logical or not. Some of the greatest insights we can have may seem to make no sense at the time but be revealed as extraordinary wisdom later.

THE CRYSTAL ANGEL OF MENALITE

This rare, chalky, coloured stone is round, smooth and in its natural formation looks like a blob of cream solidified. The quintessential feminine energy of this stone makes me think it should be called femalite rather than menalite! The stone can also go by the spelling of 'menilite'.

This is a stone of simultaneously powerful and soft priestess energy. The priestess is the guardian of the sacred feminine wisdom, the wise woman and the natural shaman who stands between the worlds. These may be the worlds of spiritual and physical manifestation (which appear separate to the mind), or the worlds of past and future, the child and maturity, or the mind and the heart. Like the throat chakra, the priestess is a portal through which apparently opposing energies meet and become integrated. The cosmic priestess is an old soul who works with the star energies of the cosmos for greater wisdom, light and healing. She supports the spiritual growth of the soul like a skilful gardener who supports the natural life process of a plant, from seed to sprout to flower and so on.

Menalite helps us feel the strength and wisdom of the priestess energy within and to plug into the inner wisdom of cycles with patience so we can understand the bigger picture. This is helpful when we are processing loss or dealing with uncertainty or impatience about our progress.

The Crystal Angel of Menalite reinforces *goddess gnosis,* sacred knowledge of the divine feminine. Menalite is a gentle and soothing reminder that progress does not happen in an instant, but over many moments. Manifestation and spiritual growth do not occur in logical and linear ways, where one step obviously leads to the next and we always feel like we are moving forward. The feminine wisdom of menalite helps us remember that the natural cycle of growth is just that — a cycle. It spirals, and this movement confuses the mind, but is understood and trusted by the heart. When we recognise that we can be making excellent progress even when it seems nothing is happening, we can relax, refocus our efforts, refuse to give up and surrender to divine timing.

This priestess stone is a guardian of transitions and a helpful grounding and protective agent. It can smooth out rough surfaces in our auric fields and our minds. Even when it seems like we are taking a great leap into the unknown, menalite encourages us to remember that at a deeper level, everything is connected, and even dramatic change can be seamless and graceful. It also helps us internalise and synchronise divine timing, so we no do not feel frustrated or out of step with what is happening and what we wish to have happen.

SPIRITUAL GUIDANCE: GAIA IS THE
HIGH PRIESTESS FOR THE HUMAN SOUL

The sacred feminine knows how to grow things. She is a divine creatrix without compare. We only need look at the diversity, strange beauty and extraordinary interconnection of all beings in the natural world to see her creative handiwork and gain a sense of her wisdom and skilfulness.

One of the reasons so many people struggle to live a life of soul connection is that the conveniences of modern culture can be so inviting and comfortable that we forget about the ways of the natural world. We can keep the lights on, play computer games or watch movies all night, and so forget the purpose of night for replenishment and inner reflection. We forget winter is about shedding and renewal, because we can put on heaters or jump on a flight to a warm destination and continue life pretty much as we did in the summer months back home. We can click a button on a computer and have a parcel arrive on the doorstep the next day as if by magic. Modern society has its advantages, no doubt about it. However, it can also disconnect us from the wisdom teachings of the sacred feminine as they are embodied in nature. If we are thoughtful, we can minimise the harm that modern conveniences do to the soul and maximise its potential for enhancing the soul (an example of the latter, which I am passionate about, could be using social media to offer uplifting messages of hope).

From an early age we are typically conditioned to think first, lead with logic, ignore feelings (from which intuition emerges) and ignore or override the needs of the body (where our authentic instincts emerge). We learn only to take steps when we feel in control of the outcome (rather than to live with trust in the unknowable workings of the Universe), to be afraid, to look out for ourselves (and maybe our family) above others, and so forth. What a stressful way to live! It disconnects us from ourselves, our spirituality, each other and nature. No wonder modern society is groaning under the growing weight of diseases and disorders of mind and body. It couldn't be otherwise under such spiritually dysfunctional mainstream conditioning.

The way out of that conditioning is the way into the body. One of the important outcomes of this process is that we learn to stop abusing our bodies. In a culture that celebrates certain ways of living, and refuses to acknowledge it as abuse, this can take a lot of courage. You'll be stepping outside of the mainstream. You will see people in complete denial. I was speaking with my beauty therapist recently about how I was trying to *pick my battles* with the chemical load on my body by using cleaner cosmetics, organic food and the like. We talked about choices that could ease my burden, without having to give up my love of nail polish! We decided that low-chemical formulas would do the trick.

She then told me about a couple that ran a successful cleaning business. Since they started the business, their financial state had improved dramatically but their health was deteriorating equally dramatically. I asked her whether they had considered the cleaning products could be causing symptoms through allergic reactions or toxic overload. She said the couple didn't believe there was a connection.

There is plenty of science to support the effect of chemicals on our health. It is not new or controversial, yet there are still people who will say phooey and continue to live as though it is not true for them. In this example, the couple didn't want to deal with the inconvenience of this truth. They could have a successful business using chemical-free products, but they were not willing entertain that possibility as it would mean sacrificing financial gain for physical wellbeing. So, they denied it was even an issue. We live in a society where many others would see that as an acceptable choice.

Unplugging from mass consciousness is not something that we do once and its done. It is a continuing reorientation process. We can plug back in without realising, cajoled by cultural pressures which we have internalised and unconsciously accepted. When there is pain, we can see it as a sign that we need to rebalance by tuning in to our bodies and making different choices. We can then unplug from conditioning and connect with the authenticity of our being. Our lives are then back on track and we will feel as though we are in possession of ourselves once more.

I noticed my abuse of my feminine being when I was doing things society would applaud me for. I was careful with my diet and pushed the limits of what I thought was possible for my body with exercise. I decided to work with a personal trainer. I later realised that he was driven by physical perfection and a kind of body domination, which he tidily (and I think misleadingly) summed up as mind over matter. He had a massive following. He was nice looking, vital, friendly and a great guy, but during classes tended to scream, "Punish yourself!"

This was funny at first. Eventually, I realised that he dismissed every sign that the body needed rest as something the mind could overcome. As I became addicted to the high of intense exercise and used it to maintain an unnatural thinness for my body, I became unwell. I ran myself—quite literally—into deep adrenal burn out and a chronic fatigue that made walking with the groceries from the car and up the stairs to my apartment absolutely exhausting. Yet, I still forced my body to train and didn't take time to rest.

Looking back, I realise how ridiculous that behaviour was, but it took years of self-healing and changing the way I related to my body to understand health from a place of self-acceptance, wisdom and natural balance. Some fifteen years later, the things I learned so painfully are starting to emerge in mainstream medical understanding, but there is still plenty of that dissociated drive in the name of 'health' to be seen at my local gym.

This problem in the human collective was a problem I needed to deal with in my own nature. As I took those awkward first steps to disengage my own power drive, to stop pushing myself into exhaustion and learn how to rest and give to myself, my boyfriend at the time criticised or dismissed my needs. When I struggled with the inevitable weight gain of no longer overtraining and excessively dieting, even though it was part of a process of becoming healthier and wasn't excessive, he suggested that I exercise more and said he preferred my thinner physique. This was hard because I preferred being thinner too but was trying to love my body enough to put my health above my vanity. I needed to unlearn my childhood programming that gave appearances far too much value. To add insult to injury, as the expression goes, the people who were still in the overtraining mindset concluded that I had lost my considerable willpower. They had no idea that it took more willpower than I had ever summoned before to stop myself from behaving in the old ways and figure out what really served my wellbeing.

My dreams were wild during this time. My inner wisdom was trying to help me understand what was happening so that I dealt with the real problem and didn't just fix my adrenals and go back into overtraining again. My soul wanted me to transform my relationship with my body, and to heal the mental pain that had led to treating her as a whipping post for my ego needs in the first place.

I went through a terrifying series of dreams that featured various assassins determined to murder me. I eventually realised that my relationship with the personal trainer and my boyfriend would need to end, but that the real murderer in my dreams was not someone outside of myself … it was the part of me that was killing off my soul, my body and my feminine wisdom. I had to learn the difference between loving how my body looked and just loving my body. I learned to listen to her, so that if my mind was pushing, I would back off. I wasn't always so skilful in this and my mind could get enthusiastically caught up in creative possibilities and create overly demanding schedules. However, most of the time, I was able to adjust my daily life, so it was more supportive of my body. I also learned to let her guide me in overcoming mental fears and delusions by letting her show me what she was capable of. I came to trust in her strength and respect her frailties. One way this happened was through a deepening yoga practice, where over the years her abilities grew in ways I didn't think were possible. In honouring the vulnerability of the sacred feminine, we also discover her strength.

When I was ready to leave my very short-lived corporate career behind me, I went about preparing for my successful transition into working as a psychic. I drew on all my experiences of working in law and consulting and such and created a strategy. I came up with ideas for workshops and sessions that I could share, created and distributed flyers and placed some ads. It never occurred to me that it would be anything other than an effective transition from corporate to consciousness-raising.

However, *nothing happened.* There was a lot of nothing, for quite some time, until I realised *something.* Spirit couldn't lead me if I was going to be the director. It wasn't a matter of doing what seemed destined to succeed. It was about being moved by my heart to create genuinely and authentically. I had to switch from the rational, logical and directive mindset to the non-rational, intuitive, guided-from-within approach. That meant doing things without guarantee and no idea if they would appeal to people or generate the income I thought I needed, but simply because they felt right. There would be no successful transition, manifestation nor soul rebirth into a different life, without feminine energy. That meant trusting in ways that my mind couldn't always legitimise or understand. Eventually I learned that this was how the feminine liked to work. She was a free-spirit and had little interest in being restrained by what the mind thought was possible.

Being in nature is temple-time with the earth goddess, Gaia. To me, she is a high priestess of the soul because as we live in her realm she teaches us how to empower, grow and enlighten the soul. If we allow her, she will show us how to cross the bridge from head to heart and from egoic mind games to soulful intuitions. She reinforces the wisdom of trusting the divine feminine intelligence that is within our own bodies and knows how to grow and heal things.

In my twenties, I learned a healing modality from a man named Bill. Although the modality was not something I ever chose to use professionally, there was a teaching that he repeatedly shared which really resonated with me, "Your body knows how to heal a broken bone." He was using this sentence to get us to realise that as healers we were working with the intelligence of the body that was already a great healer. We were not creators of healing but facilitators of healing — like gardeners who create an environment conducive to growth. This perspective can help us take the false burden of ego off our shoulders. We do not need to make healing happen. Instead, we tap into the growth energy within and allow the sacred feminine to do what she does be it transforming a seed into an oak tree or supporting a human soul into the fullness of its divine purpose on Earth.

A friend and I were reflecting on how difficult we sometimes found it to be held by other human beings, especially when we were going through deep inner challenges. It was not that we didn't know how to be vulnerable or to receive, but that the people in our lives didn't always have the capacity to hold enough space for what we were going through. It was too much of a stretch. So, we relied on nature to hold us when others—for whatever reason—could not. She was big enough to do it and we felt safe with her.

Ecopsychology recognises the innate connection between human beings and the natural world. To recognise and cultivate that instinctual connection in ourselves and others requires a willingness to learn how to respect the soul. The moment something becomes one-sided and linear, about profit above all else (which is not profit, but a recipe for eventual disaster), the soul is silenced. The soul is nourished and built through wholeness. It has a much broader view of things. The bottom line as something separate from the rest of the situation—an end divorced from the means—makes no sense to the soul. It doesn't experience life compartmentally.

When we look at the appalling, environmental damage done to our world, we can be at a loss to understand how those behaviours evolved, let alone continue. This is a symptom of lost connection. So many of us have lost our connection to our soul and with the sacred feminine nature she carries for all humans. When we live with soul, our experience of ourselves and our life intertwines with nature. Humanity's negative impact on the natural world, including the destruction of natural resources, is authentically devastating. This is not being oversensitive. It is being alive and real, as opposed to numb and disconnected.

When we begin to awaken to the divine feminine there is often a devastating uprising of difficult emotions such as hate, anger, repulsion and fear. These emotions might be directed toward ourselves or the feminine form of our bodies, our mothers, sexuality, emotions, women in general or men who are judged as effeminate. It might focus toward humanity at large. To process such emotion and distil wisdom and healing requires holding a non-judging space. To find this we generally need a connection with trained healing professionals who has an abundance of spiritual compassion. It is not always easy to hold one's centre in the face of such intense and long-repressed emotional content so that it can surface, have its voice, and be released. Letting ourselves be supported through such a process is wise.

There is a story about a Rabbi who was on a quest for awareness and spiritual growth. While he was in deep meditation, he discovered a level of self-hatred so violent and toxic that he felt as though he wanted to destroy his own body as it was little more than vermin. He realised that the experience of Hitler was not conveniently outside of himself, but within himself, too. There were times when I was confronted by a self-hatred so virulent that I was incapacitated and unable to leave the house. The sheer destructive intensity of it was immobilising and I can well understand that Rabbi's experience. When I began to open to the feminine energy that I now consider to be my wisdom mother, it was deeply confronting. The negative emotions that surfaced from my unconscious were intense and disturbing.

Later I experienced a luminous and joyful vitality in connection to the feminine, but at first, there was resistance, distaste and rage. During that time, I supported myself spiritually by doing a lot of work with wrathful deities like Kali from the Hindu tradition and Sekhmet from the Egyptian tradition. I share my experiences and teachings on both those divine feminine badasses in my book *Crystal Goddesses 888.* (If you want to work with such divine goddesses, I have also recorded separate meditations CDs and downloads for Sekhmet and Kali. You can find the Sekhmet meditations on my *Meditations with Sekhmet and Narasimha — Supreme Spiritual Protection with the Lion Headed Deities* album and the Kali meditations on my *Black Madonna — Healing Meditations through the Power of the Dark Feminine* album, as well as *The Kuan Yin Transmission*™ *— Music, Mantra and Meditation with the Universal Mother* album.)

I also turned to nature as my sanctuary, to Gaia as my high priestess, and was shown the path to wisdom. She held me and let me be in the truth of my experience with a sense that the pain would pass and become a source of wisdom in my heart. Before I was ready to leap out of my corporate life and was still struggling with depression and confusion, my time in nature was my only real soul time. How I felt when I was with her, was how I wanted to feel all the time. I wanted to feel that things were right, were true, were beautiful and were alive. I understood there would be winter, but as it served a greater purpose and helped promote life, I could accept the lessening of the light during that season. Time with nature brought me comfort.

Emboldened by the healing and support I received from nature, I began to seek a connection with the feminine in new ways. I went from always wearing black to exploring colour. I still wear black when in the mood, but it's no longer a staple in my wardrobe — which now looks like a cosmic circus exploded and transformed itself into kaftans. I fell in love with colour and how it made me feel. It was like a creative fire was alight within me. I loved exploring colour therapy and channelling in meditation. I can always tell when there is another sacred uprising of the feminine within my soul — because I invariably experience an increased desire to create music, to sing and to dance, accompanied by a renewed obsession with colour.

When I first explored a deeper communion with this feminine aliveness, I began journaling my dreams. At first, they seemed downright weird. I worked with a therapist who taught me to stop and sit with the imagery to reflect on what the symbols could mean using my intuition and inner knowing. A new world of feminine mystery opened to me. Dreams became teachings in the mystery school of the Divine Mother. I discovered the work of Jungian analyst and advocate of the sacred feminine and the sacred masculine, Marion Woodman. I relished her offbeat wisdom. I began to understand the workings of the unconscious through dream images and how they could heal us. I loved that I had no conscious idea what a dream was about at first and could discover so much by unpacking the imagery and reflecting on the messages. I learned that within the unconscious we all have a powerful non-rational, non-linear and completely honest healing intelligence that knew how to be real, whole and alive. I just had to learn how to listen to her and hear her messages through the strange sacred communions that took place each night.

I also learned that to benefit from the blessings of the feminine, we must go through a type of initiation. I had no idea what that meant before I went through it. It was only through that personal process, and then seeing several of my clients and students (both men and women) go through their own version of it that I began to see the common threads and realised what was happening.

Feminine initiation always entails challenge or failure through which there is the promise of eventual wisdom and greater aliveness. However, before wisdom is realised there is disorientation. The way one used to navigate the world (especially if it was based on power, intellect, an external identity or inherited belief system) would no longer work. The failure of the old system meant that one had to reach within to find a connection to something beyond the old ways that could act as a guide. One also had to learn patience and have a willingness to accept that this inner guidance would show what it wanted to show, when it wanted to reveal it and no amount of begging or demanding would bring immediate answers! We must become willing to bear not knowing and develop enough trust that we no longer needed answers to feel everything was going to be alright. We could then take the journey, without any certainty as to how it would unfold. We were willing to take the path, blindfolded in a sense, guided by our feelings rather than outer circumstances. It was a complete reorientation out of the ego and into the heart wisdom of the soul.

We don't consciously decide to go through initiation. It is something we are called to when the divine timing is right. It happens when there is something we are meant to become and the only way to fulfil that something is to be initiated into surrender to a greater wisdom than our own personal will and mind. We must be willing to be *grown* by the spiritual powers of life to undertake initiation. We don't know what the divine feminine is going to ask of us, but we do know it will be for the greater good on all levels. She shares her many gifts with her initiates. Some of those gifts are emotional fulfilment, love and respect for our bodies, vibrant energy, strong intuition, a sense of purpose, the birthing of talents and the ability to manifest from the heart.

Michelle Raffin, author and founder of a bird sanctuary in the United States, shares a touching story of a rescued finch she named Oscar. He could only get off the ground an inch or two and was unable to fly like the other finches in the aviary. He wanted to join the other birds at night time and tried flying up to roost at the top of the aviary, but he just couldn't manage it. Michelle improvised a small perch for him using bamboo stakes, so he wouldn't be on the ground at night. She realised that he would hop onto the stake and then focus his eyes on where he wanted the next stake to be. So, she would place it there and the process continued until he had 'instructed' Michelle to build a ladder for him so that he could hop along to reach the other birds at the top of the aviary each evening. She described herself as the carpenter and Oscar as the architect. She describes this precious interaction as her first experience of a two-way communication with a bird. Michelle's take on the interaction was that cross-species communication is not only possible but desirable, in this case, especially from the bird's point of view.

Allowing nature to interact with us awakens the recognition of what tribal peoples have long known — that Gaia is a soulful intelligent divine being expressing herself in many forms including, not separate from, our human bodies and our feathered friends. Having this sense of her opens the possibility of feeling nurtured and loved by her and of interacting with her as soul mother and guide for us all. We can cross the threshold of feminine initiation and allow our souls to be birthed and to blossom.

HEALING PROCESS

If you can, perform this healing process in nature or with a natural item on your altar such as a crystal, plant, piece of fruit or glass of water that can support your healing process. When you are ready, say the following invocation aloud:

> *I call upon the Earth Mother Gaia, high priestess of the soul, upon the luminous star goddess Alcyone, Cosmic Madonna of synthesis, and the Crystal Angel of Menalite, guardian of the priestesses. Through unconditional love, I choose to trust in your guiding grace. I open my body, mind and soul to restoration and to real and loving connection to my own authentic nature. I place my trust in the unfolding journey of my life, with respect for the inner growth provided by the sacred feminine at play within me always. I surrender the need to know and I embrace the gift of aliveness.*
>
> *I open my heart to the possibility of sacred relationships that benefit all beings. May karma be softened by grace for all beings so that we may reach out to lift each other with unconditional love. May all thresholds and transitions be blessed with the protection and guiding grace of the Divine Mother. Through the highest wisdom for the greatest good, so be it.*

Give yourself some time to express your sacred feminine spirit. You may do this through playfully creating art or shapes with your body through yoga or making some free sounds, hugging your body, connecting with nature or saying some prayers over your altar if you have set one up. Watering a plant or otherwise helping nurture the process of growth in another living being, can also be an expression of your sacred communion. If your body needs to release some energy or emotion, then you may like to dance or journal or both. You may like to sit with your awareness on your breath as you give your body, mind and soul a chance to rest in connection with each other. Take as long as you wish to complete this portion of the healing process.

When it is time, place your hands in prayer at your heart for several moments to complete your healing process.

CHAPTER TWELVE

THE UNIVERSE IS CONSPIRING FOR YOUR SUCCESS

STAR GUIDE: SKAT

Star teacher Skat is positioned on the right leg of the water bearer in the constellation of Aquarius but is actually in the sign of Pisces. The star, and its constellation, are considered to be favourable influencers in the human realm, and bringers of good fortune. There is some debate over the origins of the name Skat. My favourite theory is based on Arab maps that referred to the star as ši'at which translates as *wish*. This makes sense as Skat is known as having wish-fulfilling properties. Skat is said to increase one's personal charm, contribute to lasting happiness, open the mind to psychic ability, increase our sensitivity to spiritual wisdom and subtle energies, and provide us with an abundance of friendship.

Skat illuminates the ample blessings that can flow through Piscean energy. It is said that Pisces holds a little of everything within it. So, whatever you may need to wish for, Skat in Pisces can answer your prayers and help your soul evoke what is desired. As with all white magic, it is wise to be careful what you wish for, as we really are setting the Universe in motion with our dreams and desires. This is true for all wish craft — including wishing on a star.

One of the wisest ways to manifest is to focus on the inner aspects of what we would like to experience and leave the outer details to the Universe. The moment we start telling the Universe which people should be involved, what time it should happen and how, is the moment we create obstacles and potentially generate negative karma by trying to override the free will of all beings. Manipulating circumstances or people into the way we think they should be rarely ends well. When it comes to deep and powerful soul-level practices for wish fulfilment, it's best to put it out to the Universe with a mind open to as yet unseen possibilities and trust that the Universe will manifest our wish according to a higher wisdom, for the greatest good. When we ask for something from the heart and allow the Universe to deliver in accord with higher wisdom, it comes with the bonus of creating positive karma for all involved. Thus, we are helping all beings fulfil their heart's desires.

Said to emanate the qualities of Saturn and Jupiter, Skat is about enduring rather than temporary wish fulfilment. Jupiter is a friendly, generous, planetary big brother that increases luck, good fortune and blessings in our lives. Saturn, whom we met when we talked about initiations of earth school—such as commitment, manifestation and embodiment—in Chapter Eight, helps us prepare to receive Jupiter's blessings.

Saturn and Jupiter can seem like opposites and even their astrological sigils look like each other in reverse. However, they work very well in harmony with each other to allow blessings to become enduring sources of happiness. Winning the lottery, spending it all and ending up in the same, or poorer, financial state than before the win, is an example of a Jupiter blessing without the Saturn grounding that would help it last.

In Skat, these two planetary players can unite energies to help us experience the unconditional love of the Divine and to sustain that experience. It is not about flash-in-the-pan moments so much as becoming permanently engaged in a more rarefied field of consciousness from whence our lives will shift accordingly. It can take a surprising amount of strength to let go of the past, to gracefully surrender grief, fear or anger and step into a gentler, happier and more trusting way to live. Skat helps us do this. Put simply, Skat helps us take the steps necessary to creating a happier life.

The Delta Aquariid meteor shower occurs from July to August each year. This shower radiates from a source quite closely aligned with and named in Skat's honour (Skat's astronomical name is Delta Aquarii). When warmed by the sun, a comet sheds pieces that spread out into its orbital stream. Meteor showers occur when Earth crosses the orbital path of a comet. Curiously, the parent body of the Delta Aquariid meteor shower is not certain. It could be from several comets.

Skat teaches us to detach from how we think the Universe needs to deliver our blessings. When we fix our minds on only being able to receive certain things from certain people or certain life situations, we make it harder for the Universe to give to us. Blessings can come to us from many sources, including those we don't know about at the time! When Skat connects with the soul there are blessings headed your way. It is likely that they will come from unexpected or even unknown sources. The Universe invites you to receive those blessings as a gift.

Skat can also bring healing where there has been some sort of mystery or confusion over your lineage. This may relate to your parentage or family tree. It might be on a spiritual level in terms of the traditions or teachings that would best suit you this lifetime. If you have broken with an ancestral line—by stepping away from family or disconnecting from a spiritual tradition or school—Skat reassures you that the nourishment which was not able to sustain you in those places can come to you from other sources.

Skat supports our healing process even when we cannot know all the details of a situation or feel as though pieces of the puzzle are missing or unclear. Sometimes an issue can be traced to a childhood wounding, but at other times, the origin may stem from further back in your family line. The unresolved wounding of a parent or grandparent can be unconsciously handed down to the generations that follow. The descendants don't know all the details, but still have the wounding to deal with. Also, the origin of an issue in this lifetime may be due to past-life karma. At a soul level it is authentic and needs your attention, but you may not be able to make sense of it by referencing your current life circumstances and this can create confusion.

For those issues that we struggle to heal because they seem like a mystery or don't have clear origins, Skat is helpful. We don't have to solve the mystery to resolve the problem. Skat helps us to be in the present moment where we can work on healing what we can in the here and now. We learn to focus on what we can do and leave the rest up to the Universe. In the healing process some clarity may come, or not, but we can know freedom regardless.

When there is a relationship issue you would like to heal, and the other people involved are not willing or able to communicate with you to work on healing together, Skat can help you to heal your part of the story. You can be karmically clear and free to move on with your life, whilst allowing the other parties to move on in their own time.

A quirky trait of this star is its reputation for providing safety in a deluge. A psychic or emotional deluge could come as an inner eruption from the unconscious or an outpouring or uprising of emotion triggered by some external event. It could manifest as feeling overwhelmed and anxious. The deluge could be physical circumstances such as a natural disaster or a tragedy that creates challenge and distress for yourself and others. A lightworker, healer or psychic may need to contend with a deluge of negativity that originates, for example, in another person's pain. Skat offers a field of protection during all sorts of challenging situations. It teaches the soul how to keep the lightness and brightness of our being stable under any conditions. Now you may have an even deeper realisation as to why you'd contemplate Skat when singing, "Catch a falling star and put it in your pocket, save it for a rainy day."

THE CRYSTAL ANGEL OF GALAXITE

It is found right here on Earth, but galaxite can open the soul to our greater galactic home. Also known as galaxyite, this stone has micro specimens of iridescent labradorite within it, so it sparkles just like the Milky Way. The profound feeling of love that our galaxy emanates should be enough to conquer any fear of what's out there. To look at pictures of the Milky Way taken from space is like seeing the Divine made flesh, on a grand scale.

It is safe to connect to the Universe and to trust in its goodness and love in our lives. When we need reassurance of this, galaxite can help us get out of mental rumination or the fear of mass consciousness and into the emotional wisdom of the heart. Galaxite helps us find peace and optimism when facing the unknown.

This stone can facilitate a connection with galactic energies which brings numerous practical benefits to our life on Earth. We can become more intuitively aware of our soul purpose and spiritual mission for this lifetime. This helps us make more meaningful choices and set our priorities, so we can live a happier, more authentic and fulfilling life. We cannot fulfil our divine destiny if we are stuck in a lifestyle that resonates with the choices and priorities of others. It is important that we are aligned with our own soul values.

There is a healing grace in galactic awareness that understands every piece of the greater creative expression has its place, purpose and value. It encourages us to be true to who we are, so we attract the matching pieces of our soul puzzle such as meaningful opportunities, relationships, situations and more, to fulfil our divine mission. We learn how to feel part of life, supported by it and supporting it, through our authentic expression of soul. If you have felt alone on your soul journey, galaxite can help you find your tribe and feel more connected. If there is some waiting time before that happens, it can enhance your sense of spiritual connection to the galactic goddess of the Milky Way who supports and nurtures you.

This stone can help anyone who is feeling lost, uncertain of who they are or why they are here on this planet. It helps souls find their unique and perfect place within the greater scheme of things. It can also help us develop a more unconditionally trusting nature by putting our problems into perspective. If the Universe can create a galaxy, then it can create a solution to our problems, too. Galaxite helps us connect to the love that our galaxy emanates, so we can more readily believe that the Universe is kind, generous and willing to use its tremendous creative power to care for all beings, including you and me.

SPIRITUAL GUIDANCE: TAPPING IN TO THE GENEROSITY OF THE UNIVERSE

Abundance includes, but is not limited to, financial prosperity. I have known many financially wealthy people who were not abundant, but demonstrated a poverty of spirit through greed, fear and stress. This destroyed the happiness and peace which many people assume comes with an increase in money.

Many years ago, I taught spiritual wellbeing classes and offered psychic healing at a high-end health retreat. Due to the cost of staying at that resort, only the fiscally blessed could afford to attend the retreat. It was an interesting experience for me. I had worked with a range of people, from all sorts of backgrounds and with a variety of income, but this was the first time I was working with a concentrated group of people who were very wealthy. I was curious to see if their problems were different to those expressed by people from other socioeconomic groups. Their problems were much the same as everyone else's irrespective of wealth.

I do want to acknowledge the particular emotional strain and mental anguish that can accompany financial pressures. It is my profound wish that all beings have the support they need on all levels, including financial abundance, to manifest their divine destiny. It is my wish that all beings come to rest in the abundance and grace that emanates throughout our Universe. I also want to acknowledge that money and happiness are not always bedfellows.

For those that have financial security yet feel chronically insecure and fear losing what they have, there is a poverty mentality at work. Some may say it is better to be rich and miserable than poor and miserable, but I say they aren't our only choices! Personally, I'd rather be at peace. I prefer to trust in abundance, gratitude and love, no matter what ups and downs may be happening in my life, financial or otherwise.

Learning to manifest abundance and prosperity can help us to fulfil our spiritual mission. It can be hard to focus on creative endeavours when we are worried about how to pay bills, for example. Yet, spiritual practice is about tuning in to a deeper place of peace where we can respond to the inevitable fluctuations of circumstance with grace and trust. We can learn to lean in to the Universe and tap into its generosity. We don't put our faith in the outer world as much as the healing power of the inner world to restore, correct and protect, so we can move forward, supported from within, for the greatest good.

Opening to abundance is not about how much we have or what we can get, but more about our attitude to what we have, what comes our way and what we share with others. Abundance is a generosity of heart. It doesn't thrive when we give from a sense of duty or obligation or when we give so we receive. I remember one spiritual teacher saying that when she needed more money, and her funds were dwindling, she would give some away. She believed the Universe would mirror her action by returning those funds to her. There's an element of truth in this—the Universe is a cosmic mirror—but the intention behind that action that could render it contrived or manipulative.

Generosity is not about what we can get in return. In a way, it is not even about giving. It is about living fearless and free — not as though there is a karmic chequebook to balance. Although I earn my living and help support the income of other people through my work there are some occasions when I feel spiritually guided to work with others at no cost. It's not something that I plan and it's not something that tends to happen in response to someone asking for free sessions or 'scholarships' for something or other. It comes as an unpredictable directive from Spirit and I just go with it, trusting that there is a reason for it whether it seems obvious to me or not. I don't think about it beyond that.

I remember receiving this directive from Spirit on several occasions for a young woman I was mentoring. I never thought anything of it, but for one session it didn't quite feel right. I went against that subtle feeling based on history. Spirit had asked me to work for free for that person on so many occasions, so surely one more would be okay. It was a misguided approach on my part. The session was heavy and difficult, but that wasn't really the issue for me.

Afterwards, I felt like I was stuck in karmic bond with that person. I realised I had been giving from a place of unconscious duty and obligation rather than spiritual direction. It is not that Spirit didn't want that young woman to have help, but there was a higher understanding that she wasn't in the space for the grace to be able to flow. Perhaps if I had refused her request, things may have been different a week or month later. I cannot know the details of why it wasn't quite right or what would have happened if I had trusted that gentle inner no, but I do recognise it wasn't the highest choice I could have made at the time.

The karmic bond took some time to clear in meditation. It was a good learning for me. Charity is helpful. Paying forward a kindness can be an expression of much-needed divine mercy in this world. Yet, the generosity that allows spiritual grace to pour through has its own wisdom and timing. When we are in that flow, the gift is effortless not burdensome. That is why we need to be unscripted, spontaneous and free. When we try to contrive generosity, we are not surrendering ourselves as willing vessels to the higher wisdom of grace. When we are in a place of abundance it is easier to trust in the workings of divine timing understanding that for all things there is a season.

People on the spiritual path sometimes have guilt around receiving financially, as though it would somehow undermine their progress or distract them from more meaningful ways of living. I have heard vicious criticisms of well-known spiritual teachers who seem business oriented. It doesn't make them less spiritual. If their soul journey is to develop a business and integrate spiritual helpfulness into it, then they need to work toward those aims. It works to a higher purpose, no matter what anyone else may think about it.

I don't really approach my work as a business per se. The whole field of business is not really that interesting to me, yet I do need to put financial mechanisms in place to generate income through my work, so I can continue to share it with those who can benefit from it. A friend of mine who runs a spiritual business, from a place of authenticity and integrity, absolutely loves the business side of marketing and so forth. That more people find her work and are helped by it, through her passion for growing her business places it in alignment with her soul purpose. Marketing is not something I am particularly interested in, but I do like to share messages with people in a way that feels genuine and helpful.

Sometimes we need to move into areas we would not otherwise feel comfortable in, so we can accomplish our higher purpose. And, sometimes that means I need to give my lovely social media angel more videos to share on Instagram! I don't believe we have to become experts in marketing, websites or business to share our work with the world, but we are likely to need practical skills that can help us further our reach. Asking the Universe to help us succeed in our soul mission and being willing to explore and experiment with this on a practical level, increases your sense of financial abundance, but even more importantly (I feel), it fosters a loving fulfilment as you reach people you can genuinely empower with your message.

When we ask for help to grow our financial prosperity, a business, an income, loving relationships or our level of peace and trust in the goodness of life supporting us, we are going to be guided deeper into our spiritual journey. For most people, this usually means reprogramming our survival fears so that we can rest in a more trusting and relaxed state. Parts of the brain are wired for survival. It seeks out the herd for protection as it thinks *there is safety in numbers.* This in-built mechanism can help some species survive, but it can create more problems for human beings than it solves.

We can struggle to shift out of that survival state when we don't recognise the potential of our evolving species … if we don't realise that we are creatively empowered. We can make choices that can lead us into a fresh experience of life. We can use the 11.11 frequency to shift our reality. We may need to remind ourselves regularly of the power human beings have to choose our responses and thus choose the reality we evolve into. We don't need to act like a species that shelters themselves in the crowd, for fear that something might happen if we were to stand up. Actually, something does happen when we stand apart from the herd, so to speak. Life happens! But this doesn't have to be scary. It can be amazing.

Our society is predominantly fear-based, and attitudes based in trust tend to run against the control-and-dominate-to-feel-safe mindset that is usually taught as the way to financial and emotional security. If you want to learn to trust more, feel happier and have faith that the Universe supports you on all levels, then you will be challenged to go through two spiritual initiations.

The first initiation is daring to unplug from mainstream consciousness and challenge the idea that it is safer to believe what everyone else does. If you, like myself, have felt utterly depressed at the negative beliefs of people around you and felt that the only way you could be yourself was to thwart the system and choose your own way to live, then you've already shown you have enough courage for this step. You would not be reading this book—the content of which is hardly in line with mass consciousness—if you hadn't already begun this journey.

The second initiation is the shift from the survival mentality of *kill or be killed* and *any means to an end,* to a belief system that recognises your character and integrity are powerful enough to create healing change within you and in the world around you. This means recognising humanity as a divinely blessed species with the ability to have an effect in the world through consciousness. It isn't about trying to control life, but taking part with willingness, courage and joy, even when there is no longer the illusion of certainty within the crowd that buoyed a false sense of security. You can start to live by the truth that your inner world affects your outer experience, and you have creative license to play with that as you wish.

I concluded long ago that the only real certainty and security in life is divine connection. It will always be there for us, supporting us to grow, evolve and fulfil the divine purpose for which we were born. Everything else is just scenery along the way — some beautiful, some confronting, but all of it changeable and just part of the journey. The more we put our minds to the higher truth of the Divine, the more our ability to shift into abundance unfolds and our experience of life relaxes.

Given how much tension almost everyone carries in their minds and bodies, trying to hold on and not collapse, it is important that we give ourselves permission to take this journey into abundance. When we let go of the old ways of thinking about money and ask Spirit to show us a path with more love, trust and peace, it can benefit us on so many levels. That shift in attitude is often enough for us to relax so the Universe can step in and do what it does so well — sort things out so that all beings fulfil their life purpose! That includes you. The more relaxed and trusting we learn to be, the more we are able to stop chasing what we think we need and become open to receiving what the Universe wants to offer us.

The transition from habitually worrying about a perceived problem to being so relaxed you don't think about it, can be awkward and strange. As I learned to stop obsessing about what I thought my problems were, and emotionally and mentally let go, I would suddenly think, "Is this bad? Shouldn't I be worried about something?" It was like I had internalised the belief that worry was a way of being realistic and responsible. It was only when I noticed that my problems tended to evaporate when I stopped obsessing about them and life continued to work out beautifully even when I wasn't anxious, that I realised it was far more productive and helpful to practice relaxing rather than tiring myself out with worry. My life worked better that way, on all levels.

When we genuinely believe that we are on this planet for a reason and that the Universe is benevolent and wants to grow us into fulfilment, then we must also believe that it is safe to trust what life wants for us. It is in the space between what our minds fear and what our hearts know that Spirit enters our lives and makes its presence, its plan, its purpose and its generosity felt. It is also the space where we discover a sense of being led and guided which can bring such relief. We must be willing to create that space … even if we do so as a kind of spiritual experiment. We can, at the very least, cultivate a positive sense of "maybe this can work out if I just let it go" and see what happens. That can be enough to begin with. If we can free ourselves from the stress of striving to be in control of things that we do not have the power to control, even for a moment, we can experience relief and enough breathing space for life to take over. And, anxiety departs. Then, we can experience for ourselves that there is a higher or greater power working for the benefit and evolution of all beings, including you and me. It becomes our reality.

When we stop projecting our childhood wounds and experiences (such as believing we will be abandoned or disappointed if we reach out and ask for help in living the most fulfilling life for ourselves) onto the Universe, we can expect life to respond. The Universe may not always respond predictably, but it will always lovingly provide us with what we need. We may even become so willing to trust that the spaces where we don't know what will happen become the ones that we are most excited for. This can happen when we believe in the goodness of what is meant for us. We can choose to create space where we stop grasping and chasing and are open with readiness to receive, trusting that life will deliver experiences and blessings of great and precious value that we will enjoy.

Nature photographer, Konsta Punkka, takes the most extraordinary pictures of animals in the wild and captures moments of vulnerability, curiosity, beauty and humour. He shared a story about one of his all-time favourite images which happens to depict one of my favourite medicine totems. The image is of a young fox gazing intently into the lens of the camera. It feels as if the fox is coming toward the camera to explore what is happening with no sense that the photographer is intruding in the fox's realm in any way. This is typical of Punkka's photography. He somehow graces us with images of the natural world and its creatures that are completely undisturbed by his presence. His photography puts us right in the midst of the sacred natural world. I believe this is possible because his creative process is so open and trusting.

Punkka found a path near a railway bridge and noted that a fox went that way to hunt several times a day. For several hours each day, Pukka laid down near the path. He was showing up and waiting for the moment, not trying to forcibly create it. He didn't interfere with or feed the fox or any other animal during the process. He just put himself in the place where the action was and had patience. After several days of this, the fox sought him out — and the emotion on that beautiful creature's face! Curious, intense, real, vital and wild. It translated into a beautiful photograph that gave the world a glimpse into the raw undistorted beauty of nature. It's incredibly healing just to look at this man's work, and even more so to discover the sacredness and receptivity inherent in his creative process. With patience, respect and observation, we can notice when the Universe presents the right opportunity to us. This mindfulness is a spiritual practice.

We can become confused around matters of abundance when we try to control circumstances with our consciousness, rather than develop our consciousness through our circumstances. A man once asked me about a card he consistently received from my *Lightworker Oracle* deck. It was *Spiritual Decree* which is about trusting your voice, the power of your intention, that you have a say in what you want to create in your life and that the Universe is listening to you. He couldn't understand why this card consistently turned up in his personal readings. When I told him to trust in himself and his voice, his response was to 'decree' that a challenging time in his life was over. It was an affirmation of sorts.

I am a fan of working with affirmations to cultivate a positive mental attitude as it improves our health and our ability to creatively move through the curveballs that life sends our way sometimes. However, we can unintentionally misuse them by trying to change the reality around us, rather than within us. This is like wanting to move the ocean to our backyard because our view would be better. If we want to be closer to the ocean, we need to do the work to get there — by taking a walk or moving to a new house, for example. We may need to work on our beliefs and practices around exercise or finances to get there. The desires of our heart can motivate us to grow. That's great. Affirmations can help us do that by changing our mindset, so we are more willing and committed to taking the necessary journey. Using affirmations to change the external situation—like the location of the ocean—would be a wasted and misplaced effort.

This man was missing the message that there is blessing in circumstance — even in karmic circumstances that seem challenging at the time. Many things happen in our lives that are not part of expected, ideal or preferred reality. There will be times when things flow beautifully, and we feel connected to the Universe, in harmony with the world and in love with life. We may see the Divine as the generous mother who only offers benevolence, beauty and bounty.

Then there are days when we feel as though the dark mother is showing her face — and she's mad. We may be denied something we want, an obstacle may appear, we might hear 'no' when we wish for a 'yes'. It is a more advanced spiritual practice to retain equanimity and the willingness to move through the challenges. It is often the advanced spiritual practitioner that is prepared to say: "Okay, part of me doesn't like this. I am struggling with it. However, I know the Divine loves me and divine love is unconditional, so there must be something good that can come out of this. I am willing to go through the process and be open to what is currently a hidden blessing, with trust that it will eventually reveal itself as something beautiful and worthy."

In all situations where I have been 'held back' from having what I wanted, there has been a sense of growth and goodness that I eventually experienced from it. It wasn't always easy — even with that awareness. Sometimes it was very painful. I felt crushed, disappointed, a lack of support from the Universe and fear that nothing would ever turn itself around and work itself out. I felt alone and very insecure. It was amazing to me that given some time, and some more information, that the very thing I once found so hard to accept became something I fervently thanked the Universe for sending to me! When some situation or other did eventually happen, I realised I would not have been ready for it a moment sooner. Patience was something I once considered to be a necessary evil — something I had to put up with because everything and everyone seemed to move slower than I did. As I matured (a bit), I came to realise that patience was a way of accepting the wisdom and protection of the Universe that was taking care of me.

I began to realise just how much we can unconsciously push away the help that is constantly flowing our way with our expectations. We can believe that things must be hard, that we must struggle or that if we don't receive something now, we never will. We can forget the basic premise that the Divine is more powerful than anything else and put our faith in lesser gods, so to speak, such as fear or doubt.

When we work on cultivating the mindset of abundance, we are really being open to receive — not what our ego wants, but what life is offering. This is easier when we believe the Universe is generous, and that life is not something we have to fight against to survive, but something to lean into to thrive. In playing with these viewpoints, we can begin to decondition the mind, methodically undoing the painful experiences of lack, abandonment, betrayal and disappointment of childhood (and past lives) and begin to experience abundance as a real and reliable grace of a Universe that is always with us and within us.

HEALING PROCESS

It will be helpful to have a pen and journal, or a note-taking device, for this exercise. Begin your healing process by reflecting on the beliefs you have about abundance. You could home in on these beliefs by reflecting on any areas where you feel you are holding on tightly, rather than relaxing your grip and trusting that whatever is meant to be and remain in your life, or flow into your life, will do so. Make some notes about any fear-based beliefs you can identify. You can then have a prayer conversation with the Universe where you ask for help letting go of those beliefs. Writing them down helps us become aware of the programming we are carrying and can be enough to trigger a shift. This transition may begin with questions such as, *"Is this actually true? Does it need to be this way? Is this just something that I have experienced in the past and can change now?"*

When you are ready, say:

> *I call upon the Crystal Angel of Galaxite and the star teacher Skat. I open myself to your healing grace and abundant blessings. May I be assisted, through unconditional love and merciful compassion, to recognise and release the conditioning that has kept me in fear, scarcity, lack and distrust. I choose to believe in the generosity and grace of the Universe, and that*

many good things are on their way to me now. I choose to feel gratitude for the many blessings I already have, expanding my heart, with trust in all that life wishes for me to experience, receive and share. Through the highest wisdom, for the greatest good, so be it.

It is now time for an abundance practice. List five things you are grateful for today, donate some money to a worthy charity, say a prayer on behalf of another or imagine the generosity of the Universe pouring into your heart and washing away your painful beliefs from the past. You might also imagine someone receiving something they really want and need, and their heart opening with gratitude. You may wish to practice a combination of these things.

When you have completed your abundance practice, simply say thank you to the Universe and imagine you are acknowledging all blessings received and all blessings soon to manifest. You have completed your healing process.

CHAPTER THIRTEEN

LIVING ACCORDING TO A HIGHER KNOWING, UNCONDITIONALLY

STAR GUIDE: SIRIUS

FOUND IN THE SIGN OF CANCER, the astrological sign of the Divine Mother and the feminine capacity for birth, Sirius has been revered for its powerful energies by cultures around the world for thousands of years. Associated with ambition, pride, fame, wealth, leadership, fire and impetuous behaviour, Sirius is a star of the raw and powerful Shakti. In the Hindu tradition, Shakti or the divine feminine, is power. It is the energy that generates action and manifestation in the world. Sirius is associated with Jupiter and Mars. It combines the benevolent optimism and divine power of Jupiter with the fierce, warrior-like energy of Mars and is a protector of light akin to a wild warrior or fierce mother goddess. Sirius is a generative, activating energy in the soul.

One of Earth's closer star neighbours, the Sirius system is 200 to 300 million years old. It is a binary star system, so what looks like a single beacon in the sky to the naked eye is two stars, Sirius A and Sirius B. There is conjecture that a third star, Sirius C also exists. At the time of writing it is not scientifically proven, but some occultists believe it exists nonetheless, if only in another dimension. Intuitively I feel this to be true. When I sat down to write this chapter the words *Sirius C* popped straight into my mind and I sensed its presence, even though I had never heard of it prior to that moment.

If it currently exists on either the etheric or physical level, the presence of Sirius C will reveal itself when we are ready to receive those frequencies as a collective. At present, humanity still seems to be learning how to handle the voltage of the binary system! Spiritually speaking, sometimes we need to walk before we can run.

So, the mystery of Sirius C may need to remain just that for a time. As Sirius brings through the divine feminine who often appears in triple form, I will say that I do love the notion that we could eventually be recipients of her wisdom to a greater degree. And, then, the C might stand for crone, the third aspect and powerful dark face of the feminine that masterfully liberates the soul from attachment.

As for the binary system that we can currently access energetically, Sirius A is about twice as massive as the Sun. Sirius B transformed from a main sequence star, to a red giant before collapsing into its current state as a powerful, dense white dwarf star around 124 million years ago. The Sirius system supports the soul in shedding old identities and surrendering to transformation. Sirius B holds a legacy of light and creative influence and shows us our contribution continues on, even if we feel our more energetic and youthful days are drawing to a close.

It also helps us understand that there is a time and a place for birth. Sometimes there needs to be a shield or veil of mystery placed over what is yet to be, so we can complete the tasks that need to be done in the here and now, without becoming overly excited (and distracted) by our delicious prospects. That is the teaching of the tantalising mystery of the occulted or *psychically veiled* Sirius C.

During a deep meditation with a spiritual group, my soul took me on an unexpected journey to Sirius. It was before I really knew anything about the astronomical reality of Sirius, so I was surprised to see two stars in relationship with each other. Then, I heard sounds unlike anything I had heard with my physical ears before. I realised these were the *notes* of the two stars — the sound their frequencies created in harmony with each other. It sounded like these two divine beings were singing to each other, in some heavenly lullaby.

Tears poured down my face as somewhere very deep within myself, I recognised their tones as familiar. It was like hearing a mother's voice after being away from home for an exceptionally long time. It was deeply comforting, but its sweetness also broke my heart open and I sobbed with joy and recognition. When the meditation ended, the people around me asked what had happened. When I explained they asked if I could sing what I had heard. To my amazement and theirs, notes poured out of me — although I could never completely and faithfully reproduce what I had heard in that sacred celestial song. I also recognised that at some level my soul related to that star as a spiritual nursery where it could connect with the Divine Mother. A loving relationship with the divine feminine is just one of the astrological blessings of the sign of Cancer, which Sirius radiates.

Astrologically, Cancer bears the ability to generate and create. Interestingly, Hippocrates is said to have named the disease that bears the name of cancer for the Greek word *Karkinos*, which means crab, the animal associated with the constellation of Cancer. One of the hallmarks of cancer the disease is that its cells multiply quickly, their generation process outstrips the natural rhythms of the body and causes imbalance. The sky wisdom of Cancer, with its connection to the divine feminine, cycles and natural rhythms, can help us slow down when the super-fast frequencies of the mind throw us off balance. This type of rebalancing can contribute to the eradication of many problems on our planet.

In esoteric astrology, Cancer is the soul's gateway into a new cycle of lifetimes, signifying a new chapter of spiritual potential and development. Sirius heralds a comparable cycle of rebirth and renewal. In ancient Egypt, the star was worshipped as Sopdet, the goddess of abundance, divine timing, blessings and fertility. The ancient Egyptians recognised the heliacal rising of Sirius— the first sighting of Sirius on the eastern horizon after a period of being occulted by the sun's light—as a sign the Nile river would soon flood. This annual event was key to the wealth and fertility of ancient Egyptian culture and marked their New Year. The presence of Sirius is a blessing of abundance, fertility and fresh starts. It is a star teacher of hope and promise. If you have felt disconnected from spirit, your guides or parts of your own self, Sirius can indicate reunion — a drawing together after a period of separation.

Sirius has long been a guiding light for Earth. Sirius was acknowledged by the Dogon Tribes in Mali, Africa as a home for extra-terrestrial beings that visited the Earth. Many powerful star teachers have come to Earth to aid humanity and those who were considered to have come from Sirius were often revered as gods. Isis is an example from ancient Egypt. One may also postulate that Tara, a divine being in the Hindu and Buddhist traditions, heralds from Sirius. I see her as the same being as Mary and Isis and feel those divinely feminine emanations have a special relationship with this star, whether as a birthplace or a cosmic portal through which they can transmit their energies. If you would like to learn more about the sacred connection that links Isis, Tara and Mary (and also Kuan Yin and Kali), *The Kuan Yin Transmission*™ goes into this goddess unity consciousness in greater depth and is accessible in a book, card set, four-disc album of music, mantra and meditation and my in-person training program for invoking the goddess frequencies of the sacred feminine.

The themes of renewal and resurrection brought through in the mystery teachings of Isis and Osiris are said to have helped humanity restore itself after the disaster of Atlantis where technological power caused destruction because there wasn't enough soul presence to handle it with wisdom. Sirius is often connected to souls who have been through great darkness but through an astonishing series of gracious blessings are able to find and radiate peace and spiritual light for the benefit of all beings.

In esoteric astrology, Sirius is known as a spiritual sun that holds knowledge and wisdom from higher worlds. When our Sun and Sirius rise together each year, we have the spiritual rising of two suns. It is a powerful activation of light and higher consciousness for humanity. This can be a beautiful affirmation of unity between otherworldly realms and the earthly world — particularly for star seeds.

In ancient Chaldea (modern-day Iraq), Sirius was known as the Star of the Dog, or the Dog Star that leads. Still referred to as the Dog Star in present-day astronomy, it is located in the constellation of Canis Major or *Greater Dog*. I like to see this as support for a crone star, Sirius C, as the crone goddess Hecate is associated with a dog, and with gateways, crossroads and transitions into new cycles, all of which are also associated with Sirius. (You can find out more about Hecate in my book dedicated to the divine feminine, *Crystal Goddesses 888.*) In Chinese astronomy, Sirius is the *celestial wolf.* Wolf medicine helps the soul teach and embody unity consciousness. When Sirius connects with our souls, there is a higher-level transmission taking place and a connection with spiritually evolved consciousness is unfolding. It comes as a sign of forthcoming renewal, support for our path, teachings that are coming through for our soul journey, abundance and blessings. With Sirius, we can put our faith in the revival of the light.

THE CRYSTAL ANGEL OF CAVANSITE

A naturally brilliant azure blue, cavansite works on the upper chakras of the throat and the third eye. Those who have or need the energy of the pure blue ray in their soul are attracted to this stone. As a frequency, blue is profoundly spiritual, healing and peaceful. It opens us to higher wisdom, inner understanding, truth and the healing of the mental body. It strengthens the throat chakra and our innate ability to organise information and priorities based on our soul values.

Modern society exposes us to a lot of information. Even if we don't think that much about the information going in, the barrage of incoming *noise* that we need to filter through is far beyond what it was in the past. Thus, healing for the mental body has become increasingly important. Time out to *empty* through meditation or the contemplation of nature is helpful for present-day humans as is exposure to supportive cleansing and restorative frequencies. Being energetically cleared by the blue ray that emanates through cavansite can be especially helpful to those who work with the mind, ideas, consciousness, information, invention or any activity that involves intense mental focus and discipline over extended periods. This stone can help restore the mind after periods of prolonged and intense focus.

Cavansite also helps with the art of prioritising so we can accomplish what we desire through a strategic approach, rather than trying to do everything at once and ending up overcommitted and non-productive. One of the higher abilities of the throat chakra is to intuitively discern what needs to happen now and what we can put aside until later. If you have a lot on your plate, creatively speaking, spending the right amount of time on the right project at the right time is essential if you ever want to complete anything! When we trust our throat chakras, our intuitive sense of timing is excellent, as is our ability to set and commit to the priorities that honour our soul calling.

Cavansite speaks an energetic language all its own. You may have seen other blue crystals, but none will feel quite the same as this. Cavansite supports any work connected to language, especially the inspirational, channelled, creative and healing use of words. Powerful spoken word art like rap, trance mediumship with higher intelligent beings, and inspired poetic expressions are a few examples where cavansite would allow the inner artist to tap into unusual creative sources, translating inspirations into communications that others can receive. This is particularly useful when one wishes to tune into higher guidance, because it can be difficult to put spiritual knowing or feeling-based experience into words. Cavansite facilitates an effective, meaningful translation of intuitive impression into verbal expression.

When we feel a connection to cavansite, there will be a breakthrough in understanding. A mystery might be penetrated, or a truth will finally be revealed. It also fuels the ability to apply learning in our lives in creative and practical ways. It is a beautiful support for living a creative, inspired and practical life based on inner truth.

SPIRITUAL GUIDANCE: LEARNING TO READ THE SIGNS

Many years ago, I was in a relationship with a loving and kind man. He had grown up in an abusive environment where his father misused anger. As a result, he had internalised the belief that anger was bad and had repressed it altogether. He had become one of those people who said things like, "I just never get angry." Whenever I hear such words, I think there is something amiss. If anger isn't felt from time to time, it is more than likely being suppressed.

Suppression is not conscious, so we don't realise we are doing it. We might believe, for example, that we never feel angry and not realise that our depression is anger trying to release itself. We may believe that anger is unhelpful, unspiritual or unkind. Yet, when we do some work to reclaim our anger, we also reclaim its potential gifts — clarity, boundaries, energy and drive. We must use it wisely as it is easy to misuse such a fiery energy to burn ourselves and others but opting out of learning how to consciously relate to anger is opting out of being truly alive and vital.

As for my lovely former boyfriend, there was not much of a place for any sort of anger in his emotional vocabulary — even for healthy anger. On the one hand I adored his gentleness, but on the other I struggled with not being able to use the wisdom of anger in a conscious way, such as expressing concern about setting healthier boundaries in our relationship. Over the years, although I loved this man very deeply, I began to feel submerged in the relationship. It was as though there was no acceptance for a need for space and separateness to balance out our intense closeness. It was all emotional inhale with no exhale.

When I did listen to my healthy anger and asserted my need to occasionally socialise without him, for example, on my return I would find him in a state of emotional breakdown and addictive acting out. My need to balance independence and connection were greater than our relationship could sustain. Yet, I couldn't imagine walking away from such a pure-hearted love. To keep the relationship going, I also began to suppress my anger. It was like putting a cork on a rumbling volcano. Eventually the Universe decided I had been trying to coast along in this state for long enough.

I was picking up my boyfriend, waiting in the car for him to sign off from work for the day, when I noticed a group of his colleagues standing outside talking to each other. As I gazed at the group, to see if my boyfriend was amongst them, my glance felt magnetically drawn to one of the men. He was smoking, which I disliked as a habit. Nonetheless, I energetically connected with this man, and felt struck by lightning. I blinked a few times to try and clear my vision, but all I could see for a good five seconds or so, was a luminous golden light around him! It was like he existed in another dimension of reality altogether. I had never experienced anything like it before. I felt ignited from the inside and whatever cork had been in that psychological volcano was well and truly consumed. I felt a passionate energy that had been suppressed along with my anger for some time. I tore my gaze away from that man, reeling from the intensity and unexpectedness of the experience, and feeling simultaneously confused and vitalised.

When my boyfriend came out of work, he slapped his arms around this man's shoulders and introduced him as his mate. The Universe was not going to let me avoid dealing with what I felt! In the weeks that followed, this man, my boyfriend and myself ended up socialising together, often. It was hell dealing with my feelings for this man, my love for my boyfriend and the growing realisation that this was bigger than my ability to control. The more I saw this man, the more I realised how much the suppression of anger had been taking its toll on me. I felt alive around him. I felt my passionate nature rising again. I realised I had not been fully living. The sacrifice I had made so the relationship could continue was not so wise.

Eventually I recognised that I had been acting co-dependently, that it wasn't healthy for me or my boyfriend at the time, and that I needed to end my relationship.

It was not about that man, but I could not ignore what he unleashed in me either. My painful and intense crush began to fade as I came to understand that my intense desire for that man was not about any real bond between us. The intensity I was feeling was that of my own emotions breaking free. I realised I *needed* this huge, overpowering push from the Universe to break me out of the relationship I was in. Anything less than that I would have been able to ignore.

Whilst my love for my boyfriend would never fade completely, I came to see that our relationship was already over in a way. My soul growth had broken right through it. I would always feel affection and hope for the best for him but breaking up was the right thing to do. It set us both free. Even though it took courage and brought up a lot of growing pain and the grief of loss for both of us in the years ahead, I never regretted that decision. To this day, my heart feels compassion, goodwill and hopefulness for that beautiful man. I hope his soul journey has led him to a place of much-deserved happiness, freedom and love.

I share this story here because before I came to understand what was going on, I almost felt harassed by signs from the Universe. I hear a lot of people talking about similar experiences with signs. Don't get me wrong, I am a firm believer in signs. I have taken massive leaps and put financial, emotional and spiritual security on the line to follow them and they have faithfully led me to greener pastures, again and again. However, before I could trust in such signs, I had to learn how to distinguish between the signs the ego created and the legitimate signs of divine guidance.

The man I had a crush on, let's call him Tom, drove a red truck. All I seemed to notice on the road during that psychologically torturous time, was the shockingly abundant appearance of red trucks. Suddenly they were everywhere! Now, I am pretty certain a million red trucks were not suddenly sold in the greater Sydney area, but it sure seemed like it. Six months earlier they could have surrounded me, and I would not have noticed because red trucks had no personal meaning to me. The part of me that was in pain and attempting to make what was happening about Tom, rather than my personal growth, wanted so much for all those red trucks to mean something. But all they showed was that I was thinking far too much about Tom and not enough about what was going on in my soul.

One of the quickest ways to distinguish between an ego-generated sign and true divine guidance is to see if it leads anywhere meaningful. If it just creates more confusion and distraction and keeps you in pain, it is a false sign. Seeing an abundance of red trucks didn't lead me anywhere or generate anything new. It simply continued the charade of emotional connection that was little more than a fantasy, covering up the wild inner woman that was going to move me on in life whether I expected it or not. Eventually I had to recognise it was fantasy at work, not higher guidance. I'm happy to report that I can see a truck of any colour on the road now, even red, and not think twice about it. Show me a numberplate with the name MARY on it (I adore Mother Mary) or 888 or some other number pattern however, and it's another story!

Rather than avoiding signs altogether, I learned to embrace them with more awareness. As a child I always assumed, without question, that the Universe was listening to us and responding. From shooting star and white feathers in my path to more specific and astonishing signs, I knew the Universe was speaking to us daily.

As I deepened my exploration of divine signs, I realised that although our prayers are always being answered, the Universe knows what it is like to be human. If we receive a sign too quickly or easily, we might think it is just a coincidence and dismiss it. It's happened to me before! Genuine signs not only lead somewhere good, but they have a habit of startling us into paying attention. They often come unexpectedly. They often have a sense of humour to them as well as a feeling of kindness and reassurance. And, shortly after the first sign, some further confirmation would pop up.

A formation of birds circling above when I happen to look up has opened my heart to sense connection and trust in divine timing. A ladybird landing on my arm while I wondered if I had broken a bone comforted me with the knowledge that it would be alright (it was just a sprain and healed in a few days). A more intricate series of signs helped me find a beautiful home when I had to move on more than one occasion. In whatever way they come to us, real signs have a goodness and peaceful reassurance at their heart. They are like breadcrumbs from the Universe, leading us along the right path. Genuine spiritual communication evokes peace, encouragement and love, even when the guidance suggests there is work for us to do that we would rather not do (like moving to a new house!). Often that guidance will still the fears in our minds and show us we are supported and don't need to be afraid.

Some years ago, I was living in a place that I quite liked. It was in a beautiful part of the greater Sydney area, deep in nature and surrounded by ocean views which I found very soothing. It had been my sanctuary in many ways. One afternoon, while in a session with my mentor, I noticed a small statue of Kuan Yin on a bookshelf in her office. It had no doubt been there for a long time, but I had never noticed her before. In response, my mentor spoke about the statue, telling me that Kuan Yin would normally be holding prayer beads something like rosary beads. We then began discussing Mother Mary and the intense devotion so many people feel toward her. The conversation helped trigger an awareness in me. Mother Mary had been popping up unexpectedly and more strongly than usual in my meditations over the previous weeks, though I couldn't explain why that was the case.

On the drive home from my mentoring session that evening, I noticed a bird trapped on the freeway. He was unharmed, but the cars were driving so fast that he didn't seem to have a chance to take flight. My heart broke at his plight, so I called the local wildlife protection service and asked if they could help. They assured me they would send someone to see if the bird could be helped.

When I got home, the owner of the house showed up on my doorstep. It wasn't out of the ordinary, we were on friendly terms and he often popped by to chat about something or other. That evening I took one look at him and before he said anything I suddenly blurted out, "You are going to throw me out!" We were both shocked by my sudden outburst. He then confirmed that he was selling the house. I would need to move.

I felt a deep sadness. This was where I had spent the last years with my beautiful cat Leo before he died, although my intuition had guided me not to bury his body on that property, but to scatter his ashes in a bushland area nearby (where my guides showed me that he had liked to prowl at night and gave me a glimpse into his secret feline night-time antics and an explanation of what he got up to on those nights when I called for him to come inside but he stayed out like an unruly teen until 2am). I sat down that evening, felt the grief and loss, and moved through my fear and helplessness about needing to move. A chapter in my life was ending. However, I soon decided to trust there was a greater purpose for this unexpected twist of fate.

A few moments later, the wildlife volunteer who had ventured out to the trapped bird on the freeway phoned me. She was happy to report that he had flown away to safety. I thanked her for the wonderful work she did and asked her name. "Mary," she replied. Something clicked in my heart. Mary was looking out for the little ones who felt like they were not safe. I felt comforted about the bird and my own situation.

The next day when I was arranging real-estate viewings, I found a place that felt like it was built just for me — something I had never felt before. As I walked around this little 'tree house' noticing the light, the quiet and the abundance of beloved tree friends, I imagined myself writing and living there and was overcome with peace and happiness. I walked up the stairs toward the road and saw an expensive, sleek black car cruising down the street. A young couple got out of the car and headed down to view the apartment. They oozed money, confidence and power. There was something about that shiny black car that left me feeling disconcerted. I couldn't quite explain it, but I knew it was up to the Earth Mother as to what she wanted to happen in this little cul-de-sac. If that young couple moved in, it would generate a different energy than if I did. As I returned to my little red Fiat, I told Mother Earth that I was willing to accept her decision. I wanted to live in that place, but only if my presence was the right frequency for that area and the sort of energy it needed at this time. The response I heard was instant, "You can live here if you wish to."

Then it was just a matter of waiting to hear whether my application was accepted. I was teaching a workshop, which just happened to focus on working with Mother Mary energy. As always seems to be the case when Mother Mary is with me, I was unexpectedly gifted roses. In this case, the roses were pink, yellow and white. I ended up using them in a rose blessing in her honour for the participants. Soon afterwards, I noticed her on the cover of *National Geographic*. She was certainly making her presence felt.

I then found out that what I had heard psychically was correct. My tenancy application had been accepted. When I moved in a few days later—it all happened very quickly—I opened the front door to take the first steps into my new home and there resting on the counter was a welcome gift from the owners. It was a large bucket filled with white, yellow and pink roses. I stopped in my tracks as I recognised Mother Mary's signature yet again. I felt that Mary was saying this place was my rose blessing, that everything was going to be okay. That was several years ago, I am still living here, and this place has been a sanctuary for me. I am loving my time here and open to whatever the future holds too, with trust in Mary's sense of timing, grace and humour.

I know that divine signs can help us immensely. I also know that we must be careful about how we interpret or misinterpret them. A man on Facebook wrote about a decision he had made. He spent time and energy writing posts on matters that meant something to him. However, he noticed that the posts that got the most responses were photographs of people's lunches! The written posts he poured his heart and soul into seemed to gain so little feedback by comparison and he was frustrated by this. He concluded that his efforts weren't creating an impact and he decided not to bother writing deeper posts anymore.

To me, this was an inaccurate interpretation of events and far from being a sign from the Universe. Allowing the ridiculousness that happens on social media, where more excitement is generated by a salad than an incredible insight about the state of the world, to determine our actions is not wisdom. If a 'sign' evokes apathy or despair or shuts down your voice, it's not a divine sign. It could be the work of an ego in pain. In this instance, it was seeing invalidation and reinforcing a wound about not being heard or valued. It would be better to work on that wound. Yes, the priorities of mass culture as reflected in social media are often superficial but working on his ego pain would allow him to continue to do something about that, rather than be silenced by it. What if his mate's salad got a hundred responses and his wonderful post on the situation in North Korea got ten responses? Those ten people may be able to bring more light and wisdom into our world than a hundred hungry foodies. His voice still mattered. Comparing the reactions to the two types of post was meaningless, and yet also destructive to his confidence.

Theodore Roosevelt is quoted as saying, "Comparison is the thief of joy." We need to be careful when comparing ourselves to anyone or anything, including our ideas about how things should be. It is better to get out of the comparison habit altogether if possible. I felt like I was watching darkness extinguish a light when I read his frustrated words. I hope at least that in sharing this tale, others can avoid falling into the same trap as this bright and intelligent man who was using the often-vapid world of social media to generate awareness.

There will be times when we feel unheard or that we are not making a difference. I have been there myself. In these moments, a message saying quite the opposite will often come through out of the blue. I remember a man my chiropractor had referred to me. He wasn't on a conscious spiritual path per se, and I didn't really know why he had come to see me, a spiritual mentor, at all. Nonetheless we chatted, and I just spoke generally to him about his life and Spirit. At the end of the session I wondered if it had been of any use. A year or so later my chiropractor told me that something I had idly said during that session made the man decide not to kill himself. I nearly fell off the chiropractic table when she told me that! His suicidal thoughts had been spiritually veiled in the session and nothing of the sort had been shown to me.

I trust that there was a higher wisdom in this, and that what he needed was what came through, but I was surprised because I am generally shown a fairly in-depth picture of the people I work with. I was also surprised because I had no idea that something which seemed so lacking in impact to me had created such a depth of response in him. We never can tell just how much our voice, or our way of being can assist others. It is best to be who we are, to embrace our light and shine, trusting that the Universe will work through us even when we don't realise.

I'll finish this discussion by sharing a quirky little tale with you. I was driving along the streets of Sydney behind a truck. There is nothing unusual about that, except the huge sign on the back had the unusual surname of one of my online students emblazoned on it. It had nothing to do with the student, who lives in the United States, but it did make me think of him. "That's a big sign!" I thought and then snort chuckled as I realised that it was literally and possibly symbolically a big sign indeed.

The following day that student posted in the online healer training group that he was feeling so amazing. He had been to his local metaphysical bookstore to buy one of my oracle decks and the women who worked there had gone into an appreciative frenzy about my work. Swept up by their warmth and enthusiasm, he piped up with glee, "She's my teacher! She's my teacher!" As he shared this funny little moment with us in the training group, he remarked that the US was ready to receive a visit from me. This was something I was wondering about at the time. A short time later, I was invited to be a keynote speaker at a US trade show. I took this as confirmation that it was time for me to take that step and venture from Australia to the United States. I felt that the Universe, via a truck (not red) and a supportive online trainee (who has since become a valued member in our online graduate community), was encouraging me and confirming that the timing was right. My time in the United

States that followed soon after was a beautiful, rewarding series of experiences through which I could share my work, and for which I was profoundly grateful.

May the signs that come to you from the generous and wise heart of life be recognised for what they are. And, may the fearful or confused workings of the ego—which are sometimes part of our soul journey—be recognised for what they are and responded to with compassion and wisdom. May the true signs always show you the way.

HEALING PROCESS

Say aloud:

> *I call upon the Crystal Angel of Cavansite and the star teacher Sirius. I open myself to the loving and truthful signs of the Universe, to receive blessings of hope and renewal that create clarity and generate higher wisdom. I ask that the loving hand of the Universe graciously guide all beings onto their true and authentic life path with protection and perfect timing. So be it.*

Imagine, see or intend that there is a luminous sphere of brilliant blue light before you now. It feels angelic and radiant with love. Allow it to wrap itself around your energy field, as though bright-blue wings of light are holding you. This is the auric field of the Crystal Angel of Cavansite. It is a translation field through which you can clearly receive divine guidance and understand it in your heart. See, sense, visualise, imagine or intend that a heart connection is gently forming between your heart and that loving, blue, angelic presence. Relax into this.

Now become aware of a brilliant white star system. You may see these stars as two spinning spheres of light. You may sense their spiritual energies, their loving awareness of you, their sounds, their grace. A light shines from these stars and filters through the blue energy field of the crystal angel around you and into your heart. Allow this stream of light from Sirius to come gently, steadily and for as long as is necessary according to the wisdom of this star teacher. The transmission may be quite quick, or it may need some time to complete. Focus on your breathing and allow this to take place.

You may see, sense or feel guidance, or you may simply be open to the blessing in complete trust that it will manifest as a divine sign at the perfect time and in the perfect way.

Rest for as long as feels good for you. You have completed your healing process.

CHAPTER FOURTEEN

THE LUCKY COSMIC LOVE BOMB

STAR GUIDE: SADALSUUD

SADALSUUD IS A HIGHLY LUMINOUS supergiant star and the brightest star in the constellation of Aquarius. Estimated to be around 60 million years of age, this ancient star friend derives its name from an Arabic expression (saʻd al-suʻūd) which translates as the *luck of lucks*. To me, the emanation of this star teacher feels like a cosmic love bomb of good fortune, alignment and truth.

As an Aquarian luminary, Sadalsuud manifests the transmission for the Age of Aquarius. Aquarian ideals are very much the embodiment of sacred rebels, earth warriors, priestesses of the sacred feminine and spiritual visionaries. It is a creative, idealistic, community-oriented, and yet individualistic energy that straddles the divide between respecting ancestral wisdom and honouring the radical creativity required to birth a new social consciousness with love as its primary principle.

There is much debate around when this new age shall begin. The truth is no-one really knows. Astrologers and astronomers have differing points of view, even amongst themselves. Dates for the onset of the Aquarian age range from the mid-1400s to 3500 CE. Consciousness is somewhat akin to an ocean. The conceptual divisions placed on the earth's seas act as maritime boundaries for various human purposes. However, the blending that happens in the waters of the earth, such as where a river meets the sea, is less linear and more organic. There's a zone in the middle—the transition zone—where the water is neither river nor the sea. We might call this creative and interesting place of much biodiversity an estuary.

We could consider humanity to be in a spiritual estuary of sorts. We might say those in a state of consciousness that relates to lower frequencies are denser, like salt water. They are heavy with the ways that are established on this planet. Then there are those bringing in a way of being that holds less density and are more like fresh water sourced from the rains that fall from heavenly skies. The fresh water begins a new cycle. As it flows toward the sea, it carries the frequency of higher consciousness to the ocean. The salt crystals of the sea absorb the new frequencies and through their recalibrated state, an upgraded evolutionary consciousness resounds through the oceans. This process is a continuous and cumulative one. We bring through the consciousness of the new age in our own spiritual waters. As we grow our consciousness, we bring fresh frequencies into the consciousness of the greater human collective as the richness of our blood carries the frequencies of our hearts through our bodies. The purpose of the new age is to anchor the guiding principle of love. Love will be grounded into the crystalline layers of creation, including the oceans of consciousness, to purify, nourish and protect all the creatures of Mother Earth, including humans. Sadalsuud, the cosmic Aquarian, supports this process.

Sadalsuud is more than 611 million light-years from Earth, but it is bright enough to be a stable anchor point by which other stars are found. Its extraordinarily bright light can help the soul see clearly and be discerning, which is so helpful when we are dealing with the pretty poisons we explored in Chapter Five. These are behaviours or situations that seem harmless or even helpful on the surface but are actually quite dangerous to our self-esteem and authenticity. Like a Venus flytrap, they can lure us in and it is only once we've suffered that we realise they aren't what they appeared to be! Sadalsuud helps us see through convincing, yet false, appearances. We can learn how to feel the inner vibration, to discern the wheat from the chaff, by strengthening the intuition that allows us to see beyond appearances and deeper into the true nature of people, places and things.

Sadalsuud helps us be discerning by guiding us to use the brightest point we can imagine as a reference point. We connect to the feeling of that highest frequency—it may feel like love, peace, compassion and detachment—then we compare how our choices feel. Which one feels closest to that high vibrational state? Which one feels as though it takes us away from that state? If we want to experience the happiness of a higher vibrational existence, then we make choices that align with it. When we make decisions based on what will improve the situation at hand, we are basing them on a painful state of being. That thinking moves us in the right direction, but Sadalsuud encourages us to aim higher. If we make the reference point for weighing up our decisions the most joyful, spiritually connected and switched-on state we have ever known (in the present, the past or as an aspiration for the future), we can manifest dramatically positive shifts in our lives.

In Chinese astronomy, Sadalsuud represents emptiness. For the typical Western mind, that concept will be quite different to what it means to an eastern mind more familiar with Buddhist philosophy. In that context, emptiness is the infinite potential of our true nature. It is the endless creative ability to manifest projections, be they terrifying or tantalising. We tend to see our mind's creations and believe they are real. We can be terrified by our projected fears as we do not recognise them for what they are in truth.

I'll give you a silly and slightly embarrassing example. I was walking toward the changing room at my local gym, when I was startled by what I thought was someone walking awfully close to me and trying to get past. I stood aside to let this interloper through only to realise I had seen my own shadow out of the corner of my eye and mistaken it for another human!

Rather than clinging to the creations of the mind, and making ourselves unduly afraid, we can work with Sadalsuud to understand that those creations are expressions (usually based on unresolved childhood wounding) rather than realities. As the mind heals, the projections it creates for us can make life so much gentler and feel so much safer. When we are dealing with reality, we can help others on their paths to healing, so they can use their minds with more wisdom and kindness, too. As a collective we can dream a more beautiful manifestation for the benefit of all. We can recognise the power our minds have to create horror or healing for ourselves and for each other.

Sadalsuud is also an expression of the feminine Yin or great void which is the cosmic mother's spiritual womb and the source from which all birth emanates. This Yin energy holds the qualities of emptiness and helps us understand another of its wisdoms, which is the magnetic nature of space. When we want to be attractive to blessings, to love, to abundance or whatever other frequencies we choose to infuse into our minds, creating space is the trip switch that draws such forms into our experience. Sadalsuud can help us re-orient our approach to manifestation so that it becomes a more relaxed and trusted natural process. I have experienced this star as one of destiny and blessing coming together in spirit and the flesh. It brings a kind of wish fulfilment that can happen right before our eyes. A love relationship may appear after a difficult romantic history or some other form of divine healing and loving blessing will enter our lives.

Sadalsuud is referenced in the ancient Indian astrological teachings, associated with the deities of earthly abundance. On the Euphrates, Sadalsuud was known as the *Star of Mighty Destiny*. In Egyptian, Persian and Islamic mythology, Sadalsuud was a herald of spring. When it connects with our souls, it indicates a time of new life, a release from struggle, loss, suffering or contraction into an easier and more graceful time of expansion, manifestation, abundance and expression. Sadalsuud invites us to check in with the quality of our choices and ask whether we are consistently aligning ourselves to the brightest source of inner light. This star also amplifies our ability to manifest. By aligning ourselves with higher-frequency thoughts and behaviours (forgiveness, unconditional love and trust are a few examples) we can open ourselves to some extraordinary blessings. It facilitates our experience of the ultimate kindness, benevolence and generosity of our Universe.

THE CRYSTAL ANGEL OF BARITE

Barite manifests with startling variety. Formations vary from rosettes to rhomboids and fan-like clusters and its colours range from pink, clear, white, brown and pale green. It is almost impossible to recognise what makes them the one genus of crystal. Barite reminds us that truly being ourselves does not mean locking into one identity or one way of being, living or defining ourselves. If you thought you weren't a fit person, for example, you might create an entire lifestyle that supports that belief and prevents you from discovering what your body can do. Barite encourages you to discover that there is much more to you than you realise. There are many ways that you can be yourself to the point that you, and others, may be surprised. When I launched my dance music project, *Divine Circus*, some of the clients I had been doing spiritual readings for were surprised to see their gentle-spirited psychic in wild attire dancing and singing on stage. One client who had known me for over ten years asked if I was still doing readings. I was. The wild child and peace-loving healer live quite happily alongside each other within my soul. This is a barite quality.

Some people like the idea of broadening the inner horizons of the self. They are willing to go through the awkwardness of awakening a new aspect of the personality, and maybe feel a bit clumsy with it until it becomes integrated and strong. If they feel silly or vulnerable in the growth process—which is natural—they don't judge themselves for those feelings or allow them to become an obstacle to continuing their journey. Some people will be more frightened of this process. Loosening up one's identity to find disowned aspects of oneself may feel destabilising or even threatening when we have relied upon a very fixed sense of identity to feel secure. A woman who strongly identifies as a mother could struggle to find her artist self, for example. Barite can help even the wary soul to realise they will still be themselves as they explore who they are beyond what they have defined themselves to be. In fact, they will be *more* of themselves.

They say that change is as good as a holiday. Barite helps us remember the value and the sheer mischievous joy of mixing things up, of embracing the unexpected, of breaking with patterning and stepping outside of what we have always done. If you've been thinking about pursuing a new activity or exploring different behaviours, Barite supports you. Barite encourages you to trust your potential and take the steps. This can be very freeing and may lead to a rebirth of sorts by transforming the way we see ourselves and experience our lives.

SPIRITUAL GUIDANCE: THE UNIVERSE IS ALWAYS UP TO SOMETHING (GOOD)

Pronoia is the belief that the Universe is conspiring for your success. It is my belief that the Universe is a benevolent place. I see challenge as tough love at worst, and at best, a hidden blessing waiting to reveal itself. Challenge is most certainly *not* a punishment or some type of spiritual payback. I believe karma is a spiritual curriculum for the soul, a way for us to learn from experience, sometimes in graceful flow and at other times through overcoming obstacles. It's my experience that we are given what we need to find our fulfilment when the time is right according to a higher wisdom that knows and loves us with great tenderness and intimacy.

When we need to learn through some type of overcoming, it's because there is a higher and loving purpose in it. It could be the development of a character trait that is going to be necessary for us to continue our journey. That trait might be equanimity, patience, trust, endurance, detachment or the ability to let go. A challenge may be the Universe giving us a sign that we are capable of more than and it is time to step up. This is a vote of confidence from the Universe, in our favour, in our potential and in our spiritual success. When challenge shows up in our lives, we are meant to move through it and will have what we need within to do so. To find what is needed, we may have to go searching for greater inner resources and thus develop emotionally, psychologically or spiritually through that process. As we go through it, we grow through it.

I *do not* believe that the Universe just sits back and watches us bumble through life, perhaps cheering when we get something right and moaning when we make a mistake. It's my sense that the Universe is actively engaged, knows what's coming next, and from that place of insight, is helping us in every moment. It is preparing us and guiding us to grow the qualities and abilities that we will need in future. Have you ever realised that the only way you were able to handle something was because of something you went through previously? Our lessons are opportunities to heal and find more peace in the present as well preparation for what lies ahead.

I believe the Universe dynamically champions our spiritual fulfilment on all levels. Switching our mindset to this sort of belief makes it easier to trust and be open to life, even when it pushes our buttons and feels difficult. In doing so, we can commit to being here on this planet with courage.

Many religious and spiritual traditions claim there are beings, even deities, clamouring for a chance to have a human life. The Tibetan tradition expresses this as *precious human existence — incidentally this is* the Tibetan script I have tattooed on the back of my neck. Tibetan Buddhism places tremendous emphasis on the value of the body as the spiritual possibilities that can come out of a human lifetime are so rare and powerful.

I don't think I really understood what that meant until I was getting my tattoo on my fortieth birthday, which I wrote about in the second chapter. Even with all my soul passion and awareness of Spirit, I still needed forty years of earthly experience to gain some understanding of the courage needed to commit to human life and embrace it as a sacred gift rather than something to be endured as a kind of sacrifice to a higher purpose.

I remember what I felt the moment before I committed to my human existence. It was a wave of sheer terror! Being alive, awake and aware on this planet, and not hiding or distracting myself from whatever life brings, felt like a decision to trust unconditionally with no safety-measures. Eventually the fear faded, and I was left with the realisation that when we make such a commitment, we are making it easier for the Universe to help us in a myriad of unexpected ways. The decision can be so hard to make, yet after doing so, the way does become easier.

When we are learning how to trust life, unresolved childhood traumas tend to arise. They typically centre around unmet needs, be it the need for safety, protection, guidance or the sense of inner certainty and presence that can help us feel supported no matter how unpredictable life may be. Childhood trauma can happen irrespective of whether a parent loved a child. For example, a parent who is stressed due to issues beyond their control may not be able to be emotionally available for their child for a time. For the child, that disconnection may trigger feelings of distrust around being received, cared for, listened to and so on. Any form of neglect, including abandonment and emotional and physical abuse, can create great distress in the mind, body and soul of a child. When we fear that our needs will not be met and have pain around why we think that is the case (such as feeling worthless, irrelevant, unimportant, valueless and so on), those are the feelings we need to work through as we practice trusting the Universe.

It is so important to do inner-child healing work, to resolve the trauma and begin to repattern the mind, body and soul. An effective way to do this is through working with a skilful therapist who can role model a new way of relating to give you the experience you were missing in childhood through your therapeutic relationship. This may include things like unconditional regard, non-judgement, reinforcing positive self-image, kindness, caring, stability and consistency as they are reliably present for you in each session. Even if you have done work with a therapist before, when the time is right, the progress can be astonishing. However, the same issues around trusting the Universe may arise in therapy as well.

During a mentoring session, I suggested that my client may like to consult a therapist to help her dislodge a painful pattern of abandonment and distrust that was keeping her stuck in unhelpful behaviours. The client didn't like this suggestion, or more accurately, absolutely hated it! Being sensitive and aware of her feelings, she instantly noted that she didn't want to have to rely on anyone for anything! This was exactly the problem. This stubborn pattern was the reason she wasn't making progress in her life, despite all her efforts. Until she confronted the original pain of abandonment, that ran very deep in her sensitive soul, she would not be able to risk reaching out. Any form of reliance was strenuously avoided, so she could continue to avoid any possibility of repeated abandonment. As a result, her desire for a relationship was thwarted. While she blocked her ability to allow others to help her, she wasn't allowing herself to accept the opportunities that came her way. She had been unable to build a network of connections that would allow her to attract and help others as a professional healer, which is what she wanted. She was learning to trust in less threatening ways, such as having a session with me. Her ability to trust would grow, as she was ready, and her healing and transformation could grow, too.

If you are not quite ready for a therapist but want to explore some inner-child healing on your own, I have created a downloadable mini-program, *Healing the Inner Child*. This is available on my website, along with many other healing resources that can support you. As you become ready to take the step, I do encourage you to ask the Universe to help you find a great therapist or other healer with a temperament and capacity that suits you. Do some research for practitioners in your area, reach out and have some conversations until you find one that feels like a good fit and then take the journey.

I find it intriguing that working on inner-child experiences doesn't only relate to the child within. When we reconnect to childhood experience it tells us a story about what was happening in the family at that time. As we process the pain of our experiences, we can begin to see things in a broader way. We often understand more about our parents, and their parents. We gain compassion and awareness about the legacies and wounding of our ancestral lines.

Soul groups incarnate to work through these enduring karmic patterns. Each soul takes part of the journey, hopefully making some progress, before handing it on to the next soul—who usually incarnates as their child—to continue to work through. It is like handing on a baton in a relay race. When we do our inner work, we can save future generations from the same issues we are working on. When a soul is unable to confront ancestral wounding, it simply continues until someone, somewhere down the line, takes up the karmic gauntlet. Examples of continuing ancestral wounding can be seen in repeated patterns of abuse or disease that manifests from generation to generation often with unnerving precision around the age it appears. Sometimes the patterns of wounding are subtler and don't show up as exact replicas from one generation to the next. You can nonetheless see how the issues of your grandparents, flowed to your parents, and are relevant in your life, too. These struggles may have to do with speaking up, claiming your voice, setting boundaries or freeing yourself from repressive beliefs so you can pursue a meaningful life purpose.

Of course, our ancestral legacies also hold innate abilities and talents. We may descend from a long line of healers, psychics, musicians or strong-minded and pioneering individuals. Inner-child healing helps us uncover and integrate our supportive family legacies, too.

I have found that star seeds, priestesses and lightworkers are often the generation where these ancestral karmas are most fully confronted. They have enough spiritual awareness to recognise what needs to take place to break the patterns. Some people say inner-child work is childish, selfish or indulgent, but it can unravel and release generations of unresolved trauma thus freeing future generations from continuing the karmic burden. It brings resolution and relief to generations of our ancestors. The people that decry inner-child work are often the ones most in need of it. The souls that do embrace their inner-child healing journey are offering healing to many more souls than they may realise.

Patterns of distrust can be hard to break. However, they can and will shift especially when one realises they are patterns and not true reflections of the nature of the Universe. When we begin to trust, a positive loop begins to form. The more we trust, the more things can work out according to a higher wisdom. When we see this unfolding, we trust more readily the next time, and so on. Our life and the resolution of its various difficulties takes on a feeling of increasing grace. We become willing to be open about matters we might previously have avoided. We become bolder and more spiritually confident.

Then a new understanding starts to emerge. We realise our problems are not about what is happening (or not happening) in our lives. Problems are created by ego (mis) interpretation. Ego is founded on the false belief that we are separate from life, so its every creation is fundamentally flawed. This belief in separateness is one reason the spiritual path assails the ego and is both liberating and, at times, downright painful. When we go through the challenges and knocks to the ego, we gain something so beautiful. We can recognise our precious nature and our belonging. We see that we are not above life, but part of it. This can be very calming to the mind afflicted by the fear and anxiety that arise when we are in the nightmare of believing we are the separate, perhaps forgotten and alone.

One night I was tossing and turning in bed, worrying about something or other. Suddenly, I opened my eyes at the exact moment a shooting star passed by the window. A second earlier or later and I would have missed it. I giggled because I remembered a childhood song about catching a falling star and putting it in your pocket to save it for a rainy day. I figured it was a good sign. Then suddenly there was another shooting star! I thought for a moment about a teaching my astrology teacher had given me, to look for three points in a chart that say the same thing. She believes that when the Universe wants to tell you something, it will say it three times. I don't test the Universe, but in that cheeky moment I did have the passing thought that if the Universe was really letting me know everything would be okay, there would be one more shooting star. Then—of course—a third shooting star passed by my little window and that was enough to help me remember that it was safe to trust. I slept peacefully.

It is often only in retrospect that we know the truth of how much the Universe is working in our favour and for the liberation of all beings. Much of what happens between the Universe and us occurs in the depths of our being where our everyday consciousness may not be able to penetrate. Divine grace is at play in our lives in a way that is completely unfathomable to the conscious mind most of the time. Yet, as we let go of the ego need to have the Universe perform according to our likes and dislikes, and connect to the heart with curiosity, trust and openness, we can recognise the grace weaving its way through our lives.

An American television series called *Joan of Arcadia* was based around the relationship between a not particularly religious teenage girl and God. The latter kept appearing and giving the girl tasks. He would show up in various guises, as a gangly newspaper seller, a curvaceous African American woman who was serving lunch at her school, a construction worker outside her home, and so forth. Joan wouldn't always recognise God straight away. As soon as she did, she tended to ask a lot of questions, including why things needed to be as they were. Any time he asked her to do something, her first response was, "Why?" God was patient with her, but he never actually responded to her questions with an explanation. I had the sense that the explanation would not really be possible for her to understand. In one episode he responded to her question with the following reassurance, "I gave a lot of thought to the Universe prior to creating it. I've designed it carefully and specifically. You'll just have to trust that."

Our creative mind power is such that our projections can be very compelling. Our mental machinations can make the inaccurate or false seem real. When we forget that interpretation is not truth, we get ourselves into confusion, distress and suffering. In my experience, finding more peace and happiness in our lives begins with simple, kind and open acknowledgement of when our ego is at work. It tends to be a restless and easily bored character, so it will often be at work, darting around here and there, jumping on things that feel good and judging those (things, people, places, situations) that don't. This is just what it does. We might say it is its nature, like a dog's nature is to sniff and chase cats, and a child's nature is to be curious and explore and undoubtedly end up in some trouble at various times. It makes no sense to get angry or try to shame the child, the dog, or the ego, for its nature. We can recognise it and respond in a helpful way. We put the dog on a leash when walking past the neighbour's cats, child-proof the house from dangerous items, and when we witness the judgements of the ego and we respond with compassion.

One ego trap that can cause distress is the notion of timelines. This is the idea that certain experiences have a *proper age* during which they should occur and anything other than that is abnormal. Cultural trends can influence these timelines. Living longer and having children later undermines the notion of being *on the shelf* if you aren't married with children by 25. However, the notion of it being too late to do certain things can be internalised unconsciously and cause unnecessary pain.

I specifically want to mention this because certain soul types, and that can include star seeds, tend to be late bloomers. Even though they are old souls, and often considered wise beyond their years, they often grow into their fullness later in life. When others may be declining from the peak of their career or retiring, the star seed may feel like they are suddenly stepping into their power. For star seeds in particular, this can mean love comes later in life or that one feels lost professionally for a time before the true nature of your life purpose really becomes apparent. You may have to do a lot of time in the trenches in your chosen field before you get your time in the sun, and so on. It is not always like this, but it can be, and it is important that you don't allow ego interpretations to shame you or create doubt.

I would like to add that being a late bloomer doesn't mean nothing happens until you are 80. Admittedly, I have seen many divinely gifted souls really step into joyful fulfilment in their later years, completely defying the stereotypes of winding down for age and loving the rebellious freedom of just being themselves in harmony with their own soul timing. However, being a late bloomer is less about age and more about getting out of your head and into soul trust of the timing of your own unfoldment.

The need for trust and patience is greater for these extraordinary souls. You may be familiar with those movie characters who are popular in high school where everything comes so easily to them, and then it's downhill. They wistfully reminisce about the past and nothing else exciting really happens in their lives. The life of a star seed tends to be the opposite. Typically, it starts with a profound initiation of sorts. This is some challenge that causes pain and in doing so, opens the star seed to a path of inner healing which is part of their spiritual training at a soul level. This can start at a young age. My initiations began in early childhood, and this is not unusual for old souls who just want to get on with the spiritual job that they have come here to do. Those early initiations lead to the development of certain traits, awareness and insights that are essential for the fulfilment of their divine destiny.

It is so important for star seeds to give themselves permission to take a healing journey this lifetime, no matter how long it takes or how much help they need through that process. Allowing themselves to be supported and to focus on their healing without guilt or shame, frees their soul to process the trauma and gain wisdom and whatever other abilities and character traits are meant to emerge from it and successfully pass the initiation. In passing the initiation, the star seed has happiness, wisdom, empowerment and have also received training in how to heal in an earthly reality. What they have learned to do for themselves they become able to do for others. The spiritual skills that come from processing childhood trauma can be some of the most powerful spiritual talents that we have at our disposal to fulfil our greater life purpose.

Don't give up. Trust in the perfection of the divine timing of your spiritual trajectory. There is goodness and genius in it and there is always kindness in that timing, no matter whether it fits with your initial expectations or the expectations of anyone else. Genuinely trusting in the goodness of the workings of the Universe, is a hallmark of spiritual maturity and an ability to function as a guide for others on the spiritual path. This can be especially true when the workings seem mysterious to us.

The nudge from the Universe that encourages us to fulfil our destiny doesn't always begin in childhood. All might seem fine for these souls until a disaster of some sort sends their world into a tail spin and what seemed to provide support no longer does. A career might fail or a relationship and all its comfort and identity and lifestyle may no longer be available. There may be a breach in a relationship with a child, a death, a redundancy, a disappointment, a health crisis or a loss. Some event or inner crisis arises to mark the entry into the sacred territory of initiation.

Josh Oswald Sanders, a Christian writer, describes this process through the metaphor of the eagle. The eagle builds her nest high in the mountain crag, first lining it with sticks and then carefully lining it with soft fur, feathers and grass. When it is time for her eaglets to hatch, they do so into a world of plush comfort, with regular meals and all needs provided. Then to their astonishment, the eagle mother begins to tear away the soft comforting fur lining, leaving the uncomfortable layer of sticks exposed. The nest becomes so uncomfortable that the young birds climb up to the edge, to see if they can escape it, only to meet with an intimidating view of endless sky and rocks below. Mamma eagle gives one of the eaglets a push and it begins to plummet out of the nest. Swifter than its fall is the eagle mother's flight. She swoops beneath it and catches it on her wing, bringing it back to the known world of the nest. This process is repeated until that little eaglet discovers its own innate capacity for flight, develops it and becomes able to fulfil its destiny in the process.

If the eagle cannot learn to fly, it cannot thrive nor become what it is destined to be. Life supports our divine fulfilment even when it may seem to be indifferent or mean spirited. It nudges, encourages, comforts and it nurtures. Sometimes it does this in ways that we don't understand at the time. Yet they are always serving our growth. To accept and flourish through this, we need to have faith not only in life, but in each other and in ourselves.

HEALING PROCESS

Place your hands at your heart and feel connected to the love that is within you. You may feel a subtle warmth within. You may see, sense, feel or intend to connect with a colour, mantra or image that resonates with unconditional love for you in this moment. Just rest in that heart connection.

When you are ready, say aloud:

> *I call upon the star teacher Sadalsuud, and invite your brightest light of good fortune, abundance, love and prosperity into my body, mind and soul. I call upon the Crystal Angel of Barite and welcome your support as I discover an authentic me that is so much more than the limited identities through which I have defined and known myself. With trust I open myself to the Universe, to be blessed with all the resources needed to fulfil*

my potential, to live my authentic being and to successfully carry out my divine life mission. I graciously accept the higher wisdom inherent in divine timing. Patience and peace are twin lights shining in my heart. I trust myself and my ability for spiritual growth. I invite unconditionally loving divine wisdom to help me manifest my life experiences in resonance with the highest vibrational realities available to me. Through the highest wisdom, for the greatest good, so be it.

Reflect on any prayers you wish to say regarding your personal journey, particularly if there are any issues that are especially painful and persistent for you. It doesn't matter whether you can see a connection to childhood experiences. Just speak to the Universe, from your heart. If there are others that you wish to pray for, to request blessings and help on their behalf, feel free to do so.

When you have finished your conversation with the Universe, place your hands in prayer at your heart. Can you imagine, intend or feel a sense of trust that the heart of the Universe is one with your own? In the beating of your heart, there is reassurance that the Universe is already responding to your healing process with love, protection, grace and divine intervention. Relax. Be grateful. Smile.

You have completed your healing process.

CHAPTER FIFTEEN

EXPANDING YOUR SPIRITUAL CONNECTIONS AND INFLUENCE

STAR GUIDE: BETELGEUSE

BETELGEUSE HAS INSPIRED FASCINATION, awe and debate over the correct way to pronounce his name! Generally, *Bettlejuice* or *Betelgez* (my preferred pronunciation) are considered acceptable, though I doubt this star teacher is unduly bothered. When your heart reaches out for him, he will respond.

This red supergiant is one of the largest stars known to astronomers with a radius about 1400 times larger than our Sun. This star being generates extraordinary amounts of energy. High mass stars like Betelgeuse burn their fuel quickly and as a result only exist for a few million years. For comparison, stars like our Sun exist for billions of years. At around only eight million years old, which is quite youthful for a star, this star being is already on the verge of the final stage in a massive star's life which is becoming a supernova. You could say that Betelgeuse is on a fast path of evolution.

When we feel a soul connection to Betelgeuse, a quickening of the spiritual life is taking place and we can make fast progress. We are encouraged to go for our path with gusto, not to hesitate but to act. There is a fast track to success, to promotion, and growth and we will be able to grow to fit the new demands or challenges. We may not realise it, but there is brilliant potential within us.

A classic Betelgeuse soul type considers themselves to be a beginner on the spiritual journey and yet makes rapid progress. You have probably met people like this in meditation groups. They show up to their first ever class and have a powerful experience! I have met many of these souls. I see them as bringing through soul wisdom that has always been within them. Their minds don't realise what their souls already know! From an outsider's perspective, they might seem like super-fast learners with a particularly strong natural talent for the spiritual path. And, perhaps they are that, too.

A connection with Betelgeuse can also be a reminder that we can do a lot in a relatively small time frame. Betelgeuse encourages us to shine unapologetically bold and bright, to show up without hesitation and to embrace big tasks with courage. Patience and a respect for process are aspects of wisdom, so too is the understanding that sometimes we just need to have confidence and go for it. Betelgeuse's energy is like a rocket launcher for the soul and supports it to shine fearlessly and say yes to bigger challenges. He can help the soul to overcome procrastination, fear of being *too much* or a desire to hold oneself back so others don't feel bad. This star teacher encourages the soul to shine with the understanding that in doing so it lights the way for others.

This star teacher is destined to support future generations of stars. Through its life journey it creates and stores many of the raw elements needed to build the next generations of stars. When it eventually explodes as a supernova, it will blast its inner storehouse of life-forming elements into the galaxy and new stars will be born. In that sense, it is highly creative and will leave a positive, life-affirming legacy in its wake.

For our souls, this is analogous to a positive contribution that will outlive us in this world. At a deeper level, our soul is capable of a kind of spiritual fertilisation that benefits those yet to be born. The spiritual work, the creative expression and the energy that we generate through our life journey is not lost at the end of our earthly incarnation. Anything we choose to cultivate within our souls will become nourishment for future generations. Our wisdom, light and offerings can live on, and will have more impact than we may realise. When Betelgeuse connects to the soul it has a deep and powerful reserve of creative energy, which can bring much benefit to the world when it is unleashed into expression.

This star guide also teaches the soul how to work with light. The light that we learn to create in our bodies through spiritual practices like meditation and prayer can become powerful enough to reach beings we may not even realise are in existence. Our inner light can grow strong enough to permeate other levels of reality to assist souls through dreams and even those who are taking a spiritual journey on the inner planes, without bodies, and need support to take the next steps on their journey. Much as the sun shines and beings can gravitate toward it for warmth and light, the inner light of our soul can bring comfort to many. By working with the power of light in our soul healing journey, we are also lighting the way for other souls to become free. Like Betelgeuse our spiritual growth can become a fertiliser for the birth of future generations of light-bearing beings.

Betelgeuse has an ultrafast rotation, over a hundred times faster than astronomers predicted for a star of its huge size. Scientists have postulated that Betelgeuse may have consumed a star with the mass of our Sun about 100,000 years ago. For the soul, this speaks of an ability to take in manifestations of light—such as spiritual teachings and transmissions—and to digest them so they become part of one's own being and increase one's vibrational frequency. Betelgeuse helps the soul understand that spiritual teachings can become part of who we are, transforming us from the inside and allowing us to accomplish tasks that would not otherwise be possible for us to attain. It teaches the soul that with spirit, certain things are possible even if the mind—or the beliefs of the scientific community, for example—may not be able to explain it.

Betelgeuse teaches the soul how to become ready, willing and able to absorb spiritual teachings. There can be great teachings provided to us, truly valuable and potentially life-changing, and yet if we are not paying attention, they are like precious seeds that we step on or over on our busy way. It's happened to me when I've heard a teaching and vaguely wondered if it could be useful for someone else, dismissing it as being irrelevant to me, only to realise some hours later that it is astonishingly useful and on point! Being able to recognise a gem of spiritual teaching and truly take it in and be transformed by it, benefits ourselves and all beings. Betelgeuse reminds us that we are never too advanced to learn something new. He can also help us learn how to take in information and process it thus becoming the sort of listeners that can be wonderful parents, friends, healers and partners by really receiving communications from those in our care.

In *Esoteric Astrology*, Alice Bailey channels a mysterious Tibetan ascended master who communicates that our cosmos is the body of a great being. Seven different star systems make up the chakras of this great being. The name accorded to this divine being is God, although obviously many of us will have different ideas conjured up by that name. In the Tibetan master's teachings, Sirius is the third eye of God, the Pleiades are the throat chakra and our Sun is the heart centre. The teachings reveal that what the soul is to the human being, Betelgeuse is to this great being. Betelgeuse is a cosmic soul.

Whether or not that teaching resonates for you, we can take from it that Betelgeuse has a far-reaching influence in our cosmos and is a stellar manifestation of the quality we know on Earth as soul. This star being filters the energies of many great luminary beings, processing them and shining them forth for the benefit of other beings. It teaches our souls how to be receptive, magnetic, giving and dynamic.

As Betelgeuse demonstrates the magnificence of the soul, we may become readier to trust our own soul. I'll share a little prayer that I used to speak to my soul at a time in my journey when I was first learning about that part of myself. I was learning to trust my soul and realise that even when I might have felt out of control, impatient, doubting or anxious about my life, that she knew what she was doing and was working with higher spiritual guidance to showing me the way forward one step at a time. That prayer was:

I don't know what you are doing or how this is all going to work itself out, but I know that you know, and if I need to understand something, I also know that you'll tell me. So, thank you!

THE CRYSTAL ANGEL OF NEBULA STONE

When I first gazed at a little piece of this stone, black with its subtle green markings, I felt like I was peering into the Universe itself. It has a quality I can only describe as infinite, as though it opens the gateway to a more expansive experience of our being. It was like gazing into a tiny nebula. Nebulae are clouds of dust, hydrogen, plasma and helium. They are the nurseries of the Universe, where stars are born. It is significant that this little stone bears that name.

Nebula stone can help us tap into our potential, to go back to our spiritual roots and discover our lineages. Those could be ancestral lineages but could equally be the various star systems that hold a deep connection with our soul. Those lineages can also be a way to access an original wounding point without being caught in the chain of events that followed. It can help us get to the core issue; deal with it, and not become confused or distracted.

Discovering true lineages can help us better understand what we are here to accomplish, the issues we are working through and the gifts we have to work with. It can help us understand ourselves and claim our place in the Universe.

If you feel like a spiritual orphan cast out of your family of origin or that you don't belong to society because you feel so different to others, nebula stone can help you remember that you are a child of the stars. It acts as a reminder that you belong to the Universe and the earth (where nebula stone is found no matter how cosmic it appears to be) and that you are beautiful and valuable just as you are. When someone is going through issues around adoption or family secrets that make understanding one's heritage quite difficult, nebula stone can bring deep insight and comfort.

Not only does nebula stone help us reach the point of origination, it helps us create new forms. This could be new responses to old wounds or fresh ways of living and being. It can help us discover our creative potential, to nurture light and to birth awareness of the soul in ourselves and in others. Nebula stone soul types tend to stimulate others to grow on their soul journey, especially through deep inner work and connecting to higher energies such as the stars.

As nebula stone contains quartz it can be programmed according to the intention of the custodian of the crystal. It is wise to clear and reprogram any quartz piece that comes into your possession according to a loving desire to access higher wisdom.

SPIRITUAL GUIDANCE: THE UNIVERSE IS ALWAYS LISTENING (SO WHAT ARE YOU SAYING?)

When we don't recognise the interrelationship between our energetic projections and our experience of life, the world can seem like a very random and even frightening place. The monsters of the mind appear to be *out there* and able to harm us. When we realise they are projections, and we consciously heal the foundation of that content in our minds, they disappear. It is simple but not always easy to remember or put into practice.

Carl Jung, the founder of analytical psychology, described it this way: that which we do not bring to consciousness appears in our lives as fate. The teachings of Jesus Christ in the Nag Hammadi scriptures hold that what we bring out from within us will save us, what we do not bring out will destroy us. A New Age version of this teaching might make the connection between unresolved emotional trauma and the manifestation of disease, an understanding which is now becoming more acceptable to the mainstream, too.

So, when life happens, we may try to assert control over externals without realising all the action is taking place in our inner world. When we try to work on the externals rather than our inner realm of consciousness, it's like using a magnifying glass to find the issue, but having it concentrate the sun's light and create unwanted fires in our yard. We cannot control the heat of the sun, but we can angle the magnifying glass, so we aren't causing more fires. If we don't attempt to prevent the fires that we *can* control—by shifting the magnifying glass—but instead tell the sun to stop shining, we are not going to get great results. The results that we do obtain will be hard won, as we'll spend a lot of time and energy putting out our fires! We might decide we can't do anything about it and try to practise detachment as our beloved yard goes up in flames. There's a lesson in that to be sure, but there is a less painful choice. If we shift the position of the glass, the situation will resolve naturally, and so much unnecessary struggle, pain and suffering will be avoided.

When we make the connection between our consciousness and how we can meet life, we begin to relate more peacefully and productively with the Universe. We can choose to stop trying to control the flow and greater movements of life. Instead we recognise that we can engage with that flowing power in any way that we choose: reluctantly, enthusiastically, cautiously and/or boldly. We can greet life as a warrior who fights against what is, or as an artist who is willing to be moved and inspired … the choices are as unlimited as our imaginations.

It is not as though one choice is particularly superior to another, but some are more peace inducing. Having free will means we get to choose how we respond to events, and through that response, we can learn and grow spiritually. We might choose to be the warrior, we might recognise that it has served a much-needed purpose, and then we might realise that there could be another way. When we soften our approach to life, to our own journey, and melt the pain that may have driven the warrior energy within us (for example, an abandonment wound may mean we always had to fight for ourselves because no-one else would) we can try new ways of being. We may need to work with a healer, a therapist or both for a time to accomplish that. Such a process would eventually require us to let the warrior take some much-needed time out. We can then allow new energies to rise from within and take over the role of guiding our journey. Our consciousness is something like soul art. Infused with spiritual inspiration, it is an authentic expression of our soul views, which can change and evolve over time.

When we recognise our consciousness as a creative soul expression, rather than a fixed reality that we have no power to influence, it opens many possibilities. We suddenly realise that we get to choose how we want to live and as we grow, the choices we make are most likely to become kinder and wiser. Every choice holds potential for spiritual growth and development, whether it be via a rough road or smooth sailing. By being aware that we are constantly making choices, we can recognise how empowered we are to create our life experience.

These ideas are not particularly new to metaphysics, the New Age or self-help fields. They have been around for a long time. They also exist in spiritual traditions that are thousands of years old. However, knowing of something and personally experiencing it are rather different. For example, hearing or reading about what it is like to have a broken heart, does not fully convey what it is like when you go through an experience of heartbreak. When we really begin to *get* these ideas and *live* them, something very potent begins to happen for us spiritually. Rather than feeling carelessly tossed about on the wild waves of life, we can feel more like we are free, empowered and creative. We may not always enjoy what we are creating, but when we recognise that, we can have a sense of humour about it, perhaps, and maybe embrace an inner healing process so we can start to change it. This is how we can shift the magnifying glass that I mentioned in the example above. We can direct the glass using our minds to focus on what we want to amplify in our own consciousness. We change the outcome without having to change the external forces that are beyond our control.

It's my unwavering belief that the Universe is always listening and always saying yes to us. The issue is not whether our prayers are being heard and responded to, because they always are, but what it is we are putting out into the cosmic void with our consciousness. What are we using the magnifying glass to amplify? Whatever we declare with our energy, our thought, our attitude and our expectations, positive or negative, the Universe lovingly mirrors back to us. We have been given free will, so we can make that choice.

Sometimes we only realise the content of our consciousness, especially the psychological and emotional content that exists beneath our everyday awareness and intentions, through the life that is mirrored back to us. If we look, we can see the hidden truth manifesting in our bodies and our circumstances. For example, on one level we may believe in abundance, but at another level always feel that we are struggling. There may be a deeper issue of self-worth, self-respect, trust or unresolved abandonment that we need to work on so that our head and heart are in connection. Inner conflict around the possibility of experiencing both spiritual purity and material wealth, or spiritual devotion and romantic relationship, may be subconsciously holding us back from being more receptive. We may need to clear a past-life vow of poverty or chastity and adjust our present-life attitudes. As we do our inner work and spiritual practice to become consistent in the new way of thinking, being and emanating certain frequencies, the changes in our inner world will be reflected in outer world manifestations.

I want to say something that I feel is important to include in any discussion around creating our own reality, as it can so often become a cause for unnecessary distress. When I was a teenager, I discussed these ideas with a family member. I was so excited because I could see a way out of her suffering and struggle, a way for her to feel empowered, to change her life and become happier. I thought I was sharing this amazing key to freedom with her. I was so excited by the prospect that there was something I could do about the bleakness, despair and overwhelm that I often felt as a teen, that I could turn it around without waiting for external circumstances to change, that I assumed (most naively) that all others would feel the same.

I was surprised at the time to realise that she was deeply offended by what I was saying. She interpreted what I felt was a beautiful soul empowerment as an attack against her. She thought I was blaming her for the problems in her life. I thought I was talking about responsibility and empowerment, and she thought I was talking about criticism and blame. Although I was trying to help her, I had to learn another valuable lesson: there is little wisdom, or kindness, in attempting to impose our beliefs upon another, no matter how much we may feel it could benefit them.

That is quite different to sharing our views in an appropriate context, especially when someone asks for information. In such cases, we can speak up and be as vibrant and visible in our truth as we dare to (playfully? boldly? gently?) be. Dzongsar Jamyang Khyentse Rinpoche, one of the Tibetan Buddhist teachers that I love to learn from, says it's quite stupid not to talk about your beliefs at all, but to do so only with respect. If you feel someone is open to it, then share with sensitivity. When we try to convince, which is what teenage me was doing with the missionary zeal of a New Age convert, we come across as if we know better than the person's soul as to exactly where they are at on their path. That is arrogant, and where there is arrogance there cannot also be wisdom and compassion. As healers, whether undercover or advertised, it is our job to be in the light. The sun doesn't try to make the moon into its own image. If it did, life could not thrive. Each being has a right to fulfilment in accord with the wisdom path that best suits its nature.

This applies to ourselves as well as others. Remember, a threat to the ego often liberates the soul. We have great ability to create the quality our life, but if this knowledge is used to suggest that having a rough time of things means your consciousness is somehow failing and you feel guilt, fear, anxiety, self-criticism or shame, then your ego is using this teaching as a weapon against you. If you are thinking, "I create my own reality, and it's not all sweetness and light, so I'm obviously screwing up here," give yourself some credit.

Our consciousness is an ocean, a soulful, divinely human ecosystem, a deep and layered realm that relates to us as individuals and to a larger collective. It is not a case of flipping a switch and suddenly having a new consciousness and the life of our dreams unfolding before our very eyes. Purification and healing of consciousness requires skill, patience, persistence, and a good sense of humour doesn't go astray. It is a process. We will have improvements along the way, often quite dramatic and astonishing results that are very positive. There will also be times when we are dealing with the rise of wounded aspects of self. These aspects are still not fully conscious, and when they project outwards, we experience them as less than desirable events or circumstances. We are not messing something up when this happens. We are in a healing process and our inner being is trying to tell us something. The healing involves pulling back the projection as we figure out what is really being said at a deeper level. This can be painful but can eventually bring relief, freedom and a new way. So, it is not a sign that we are screwing up at all. There is always something of great value that can emerge from our darker experiences of life.

The ego knows how to use otherwise helpful spiritual teachings as weapons against us and against others. It can do so quite convincingly. The words may sound sweet, but the effect feels vicious or *off* somehow. The moment a spiritual teaching creates any sort of judgement about the nature of our lives (or each other) and what is happening in our lives (or our bodies, minds, finances, work, relationships, etc.) then ego has taken over. We must disentangle the teaching from such misuse and put it back where it belongs, which is in the hands of our soul. When a spiritual teaching is in the hands of our soul, it empowers us and feels loving. Even if a teaching is helping us realise that we need to leave behind the familiarity of what we know, when it is in the hands of the soul, it brings relief and optimism.

When we open our hearts to life with such beliefs, we aren't denying problems. Optimism breeds confidence and this is important. We are telling the Universe that we are ready to find a solution outside of the current paradigm of suffering. You are saying, "I want to be inspired, energised and uplifted to conquer the darkness in the world with love and creativity. Show me how to live in a way that can help the world as I courageously use my gifts and talents. Let's transform what isn't working for all into a solution infused with divine grace."

We can live as a valiant affirmation or we can disconnect from gratitude. Either way, the Universe loves us unconditionally and will say, "Yes, okay, if that's what you choose, let's create that together."

When the mirror of the Universe is showing us something we need to heal, optimism allows us to acknowledge it, so we can go after it with grace and courage. The Universe will help us find whatever information we need, and it is amazing how pieces of the puzzle fall into place. We can heal if we wish to do so and the

Universe will assist. Our job is to let go of expectations and take the journey.

Sometimes what you are healing is about a far broader matter. This kind of healing is a contribution to a greater collective wound. This is often the case for star seeds, priestesses and lightworkers who typically have some type of global significance for their work this lifetime. Even the issues they are working through personally can relate to broader problems in the human collective. It might be about learning how to be more open and less fearful, something most human beings could benefit from at times. It could also be about healing a wounded ancestral lineage. Sometimes the karmic inheritance you are healing goes back a long way and has become *stuck*. An issue might not seem to relate to you personally and yet you feel you need to do some work on it.

An example of this happened for me. The issue arose some years ago through a series of very disturbing dreams where I had an intense fear that I was going insane. I searched through my own life, through childhood memories, even past lives, and yet couldn't find a connection to the dream content. The closest thing I could find from my own life journey was the moment when I realised I was seeing things differently to (apparently) every single person in my life. When others tell you that you are crazy, you may start to believe it and falter a few times before you gain self-confidence and embrace your new awareness with trust. This wasn't like that however, it was something far more violent and disturbed.

I worked on the feelings as though my own unconscious was trying to tell me something, but it seemed like something foreign had floated into my dream life. It caused me distress and I was having trouble processing it because it didn't really feel like it belonged to me on a personal level at all. Yet it had come into view through my dreams, so I knew there was something that I needed to work through.

I eventually decided to have compassion for it and let it be part of the mystery, at which time the Universe helped me unravel the confusion. I wouldn't normally talk to my mother about my dream life, but one day we were having an unusually candid discussion and I shared one of those insanity dreams with her. She instantly, and very openly, responded by telling me stories about the near-mental breakdown my grandmother had experienced when her husband had died and her mother, my great grandmother, had been relentless in her psychological domination over her — no doubt out of her own fear of death and abandonment. In my grandmother's vulnerability and all-consuming grief, she was almost cracking under the pressure. She was terrified that she was going insane and there was talk of checking her into a mental institution. Although neither of those fears ever eventuated, and I grew up with a psychologically-sound grandmother until she passed away when I was in my twenties, the fear of it remained unresolved in our collective family soul field and it was showing up in my dreams.

As I heard this story for the first time, something clicked into place. I recognised there was some kind of psychological violence at work in the emotional lives of the last three generations of my matriarchal line. Given that I was receptive and willing to work with whatever was needed, it had found its way into my unconscious where it was being processed in my dream state. I had a sudden insight about the psychological violence I had inherited, and how it was the inner wound that allowed me to dominate my body into ill health some years prior. This startling realisation helped me have more compassion for the ways I had been relentlessly dominating of my own being, always pushing and never resting. I began to heal this tendency as I became more conscious of the psychological inheritance that had imprinted it in my field.

It was a valuable healing insight that began shifting experiences I had been attracting into my life. This included some abusive personalities with controlling and dominating attitudes, which I was most willing to put an end to in favour of more wise, compassionate and loving people who had no desire to control or use me as their emotional dumping ground. One of the most precious gifts from those difficult times was that I learned the value of kindness and how essential it is in any kind of relationship — including the one we have with ourselves.

As it turned out, of course, the issue I was working on for others was also one that I was working on for myself. It was just so deeply unconscious that I couldn't see the connection. At a spiritual level this makes perfect sense. After all, we are all connected, none of us is ever truly separate from the other. Together we are building a world for all. Star seeds, lightworkers, healers, priestesses, spiritual practitioners, white magicians, creative artists and so on play a special role in this process. We can approach the co-creative task with fear in our hearts (and we have daily evidence of where that leads us) or we can try a different way.

Being willing to engage with what is showing up in our inner and outer life, with this sense that there is a deeper guiding wisdom at work, opens the heart. When the heart is open, it can create and empower the path to clarity and resolution (often with joy and humour). We become able to pray with conviction and surrender, rather than pleading and doubt. That in itself brings inner peace and allows us to stop getting in our own way. We can let the Universe do what it needs to do to guide us. Remember, the ego loves to imagine that one can become a butterfly by wishing it to be. The soul knows it is necessary to go through the caterpillar stage and our transformation happens naturally. It does not need to be controlled, but rather allowed and experienced — in all its strangeness and miraculousness.

The unexpected delight that can take place in that process is an experience of the sacred feminine. She can only be experienced. She is the bite of the apple. The description of it, the theoretical understanding of its nutritional value or chemistry may be helpful but cannot come close to the actual tasting. We can get to a place where we can appreciate the power of our creative nature whether our mental creations are fearful or fabulous. Of course, we likely want to minimise the fearful and bling up the fabulous, so we have an easier way of things and can help others break free from the psychological ties that have them bound in fear and hesitation.

While we are redecorating our inner mental realm, we can begin to understand that even if it is much less fearful, sassier and more spirited, it is still mental projection — but one that can be put to better use, for the greater good. There is a greater freedom in this, too. At one level, we stop believing that our stories are more than stories. Tibetan teacher Dzongsar Jamyang Khyentse Rinpoche described it so beautifully. When engrossed in a movie, we may feel emotions and go through the journey with the characters in the film. They feel real to us, but we can press pause on the movie and go to the toilet knowing the story will still be there when we return. We know what is real (a full bladder) and what is a story. We enjoy the story. We may share the story. We may even dream about the story. We can value it, learn from it, grow as a person through it, but we understand that it is not an ultimate reality. It is a story — as amazing as it might be. Playing with this idea in relation to our own mental creations (especially to terrifying stories based on unresolved past traumas that can keep us locked in pain, doubt and negativity) is a path that leads to relief and to freedom.

You may wonder whether not believing in 'stories' means not caring about anything in this world. That would be a bit like Christmas losing its potential to affect people's lives because you decided Santa Claus wasn't real. Through the sacred feminine journey of *experience,* we know that those stories sure feel real, even if we ultimately know that they are not. A sensitive child may be so frightened of a scary film that they become afraid to go to sleep at night. You may have experienced this, even as an adult. You know how convincing storytelling can be, whether in a film or what happens in your own mind. With compassion and wisdom, we realise it doesn't matter that they are stories rather than a higher reality. They are relative truths, apparent realities to each person creating their story. We understand that we can all need help finding our way through our story, whatever it may be, and a learning can come through that story which would not have manifested otherwise. We walk our path, learning through our stories, and more often come to rest in higher understanding and spiritual freedom which is the ultimate destiny awaiting all beings.

HEALING PROCESS

You will need a pen and journal, or other note-taking implements for this process. Take a moment to connect with your heart. Let the external world go as you turn within and give yourself time to reflect. When you are ready, write a list of the matters you would like to hand over to the Universe for healing. These are matters you are willing to grow and work through. This may mean you need to be open to the grace of a higher power for healing and protection. Maybe you can even think of them as stories that you would like to evolve and see from a more loving and wise perspective. Say aloud:

> *I call upon the star teacher Betelgeuse and the Crystal Angel of Nebula Stone. I call upon my own soul, the higher self, which is connected to the Universe in harmony, love and grace. I am willing to receive all resources and unconditionally loving assistance so that the karmic legacies of my ancestral inheritance can be resolved through merciful compassion, divine grace and the highest wisdom for the greatest good. I open myself to all true sources of spiritual light that will help in this process. I trust in my soul's ability to process, create and align me with a higher frequency of unconditional love in all aspects of my life. I ask to be gently guided with mercy and compassion, so that I may recognise and consciously evolve the mental projections that help shape my experience of reality. May divine love bless, protect and guide all beings to spiritual freedom. So be it.*

If you have some items on your list that you would like to specifically add into this healing process, say:

> *I now specifically ask for help from the Universe in resolving the following matters with unconditional love and higher wisdom.*

Read your list. Then say:

> *I give thanks for the grace, compassion, mercy and protection that helps me into a new, healed reality from this moment on. May all beings be happy and free.*

Bow your head to your hands in prayer. You have completed your healing process.

CHAPTER SIXTEEN

THE REORGANISING POWER OF YOUR HEART

STAR GUIDE: REGULUS

ONE OF THE ROYAL STARS of ancient Persia, Regulus is known as the *Watcher of the North*. This guardian star being is said to emanate the presence of Archangel Raphael. It is 85 light-years from Earth, so when we see Regulus now, we are viewing light that emanated from the star 85 years ago. That is quite amazing to think about. Fortunately, as we contemplated in the introduction, spiritual energy is not restricted by time and space, so we can connect to Regulus spiritually and share the same moment, together, in the here and now.

Regulus is the brightest star in the constellation of Leo which is the astrological ruler of the heart. Leo is depicted by a lion in the zodiac. In many ancient cultures, the lion was recognised as a symbol of power, dignity, integrity, strength, and the archetype of the king. In Arabia, Regulus was referred to as *The Kingly One* and sometimes as the *Heart of the Royal Lion*. Regulus derives from the Latin word for king, Greek astronomers called it the *Little King Star* and it was similarly referenced in ancient Babylon. In Hindu astrology, it is called the *Mighty One* or the *Great One*. An association between lions and kingship are common to African tribes and Turkish culture, also.

The transmission of Regulus helps us realise that the heart is the king of the soul. When we allow it to be our guide, our lives are ruled by the higher principles of courage, compassion, wisdom and forgiveness. We step into our royal or divine nature and as we honour our heart, we assume a role of spiritual leadership on this planet, even if we don't think of ourselves as typical leaders. Genuine spiritual leadership is not about gaining power, dominating people or controlling situations. It is about service, devotion and the protection of those in your care.

Perhaps you can imagine what kind of world this would be if such an energy was the dominant guiding wisdom in the hearts of all those in authority? Fortunately, as we discussed in Chapter Ten, when even some of us live in higher consciousness it is enough to tip the scales. As we take our spiritual journey, learning to serve a greater and more inclusive purpose, we become part of a transformational alchemy that shifts how power expresses itself on this planet.

Discerning, reframing and living in a way that goes against the grain of mainstream conditioning takes spiritual intelligence. The reorganising power of the heart holds all the creative spiritual intelligence we could ever need. When we have different people and factors to consider and we are willing to give up the idea that our limited opinions are good enough for making the best decisions, heart wisdom can show us the way. The heart works in a way that is beyond mental understanding and that is okay. We don't always need to understand something to trust in and benefit from it. The heart holds the key to becoming a vessel for the compassion and wisdom of our Universe, a channel for a greater intelligence that understands how to meet the needs of all beings. It is not possible for human intellect to fathom such an extraordinary feat. However, with the guidance of our hearts, it is possible for us to become part of the divine solution.

Imagine that we are all pieces in a cosmic clock, each with our unique role. In fulfilling our role, the other parts of the clock can fulfil theirs and together the clock can keep time. If one of those pieces tried to become responsible for the entire clock, by stepping out of its place and checking on other pieces, the entire system would fall apart. Kingship and divine leadership are not about leading in an ego-defined sense of the term. It is not about being *the boss*, so to speak.

The genuine ability for conscious (or kingly) leadership comes from being true to our place and purpose. From that fulfilment, others are also empowered. It is about shifting from fixed opinions to more neutral intuition as often as we can (and not about controlling or choosing anything other than our own alignment). My first spiritual teacher would say, "How can Spirit guide a mind that is already decided?"

Sometimes we need to consciously undo our opinions about how we think things (or people) should be and become more open-minded. It is not always easy, but opinion is not higher truth, it's a viewpoint based on past experiences that have conditioned our emotional and mental energies into certain patterns. If we want to serve the higher principles of the heart, sometimes our opinions must go! We may have to drop judgements we held in the past, perhaps even some moral judgements that we lived by. A greater spiritual intelligence is at play and needs to flow through us, into the world, unimpeded by our limited views. We cannot really know what another person is learning at a deeper level. So instead of trying to convert, we create. We aim to be the light for those in our world and as our heart grows its ability to love unconditionally that will eventually include those we once would have judged.

There are many stories of wise kings assuming a disguise and going amongst their subjects to gain information and better understand the plight of those in their care, so they can be better guardians. As their charges don't recognise their authority, they speak freely and behave without moderating their behaviour. This exercise makes it possible for the king to gain a more honest and realistic assessment of what needs to be done. This is often the case for the emanation of the king in our souls. Others do not always recognise us for our guiding light. It will sometimes feel like you are leading from the inside, invisibly, without recognition for the subtle but helpful influence of your energy. Is this not how Spirit so often leads? It is not something to dismiss or feel is 'less than' in any way.

Regulus is also known as a law giver for humanity. It upholds the spiritual principles of a higher justice. The spiritual laws are natural limits or boundaries for the soul. Those of us who are free spirits might not be so comfortable with the idea of limitation, but we need it for growth. Lattice woodwork can hold up a plant and help it grow strong until it is no longer needed. A playpen can keep a child safe from harm until it is ready to navigate more of the world. Limits help us by giving us a safe space where we can test reality. Spiritual laws are limits for the soul. They allow for growth and give our experiences context, meaning and higher purpose.

Regulus helps us develop an intuitive understanding of how to live by the spiritual laws of the Universe. Whether we are talking about the law of economy or efficiency (which suggests the Universe knows the best way to manifest so it's wise to trust it!) or the law of attraction (which helps us understand the magnetic relationship between our inner world and our outer experiences), Regulus can help us recognise how these laws operate and apply that knowledge to benefit the soul.

The association with Archangel Raphael means this star teacher is a healer who is balancing and centring. Regulus can renew us into wholeness through the inner guiding wisdom of love, which emanates from the heart chakra. As one of the Royal Stars, considered to have far-reaching global and cosmic influence, Regulus is a celestial healer in service to many beings in many worlds. When he connects with our soul essence, we can be sure that a wonderful experience of healing and of our own awakening as a healer and heart-centred guiding light is taking place in whatever way resonates with our soul purpose.

THE CRYSTAL ANGEL OF PHENACITE

This crystal is typically available in small sizes and can be quite expensive. It is usually clear, sometimes with a soft tint. Glassy in appearance, phenacite has highly reflective, small faces and looks like light in form. Phenacite is a master teacher on the power of consciousness. It can bring reassurance when our outer circumstances seem out of our control. When we continue to put faith in our inner self, and take our inner healing journey, things can and will change in our lives.

There is a movie called *Patti Cake$* about a young woman who dreams of becoming a rapper. Patti's great passion is to find a way to express a powerful and authentic voice through rap, a creative genre in which she has tremendous talent. Yet she faces obstacles at every turn. She is under financial strain and lives with her alcoholic mother who suffers from her own unfulfilled dreams of being a singer and doesn't hesitate to ridicule Patti's dreams. Her encouraging badass of a grandmother is very unwell and relies on Patti for support. Patti is subject to shaming and judgement about her weight and her desirability as a woman. There are scenes in the film where the struggle not to be silenced is made visible. Those looking to oppress her, usually in the form of criticising her weight, her skin colour or whatever other means they can think of to steal her power away from her, seem to be winning. But she fights back to claim her worth and her value and refuses to give up. The power of her self-belief eventually overcomes so much of the hate and fear around her.

Phenacite can help us remember that we have this power within. It is more than willpower. It is the invisible strength of the authentic self that knows who we are and what we are here to be and will not allow anyone or anything to get in the way of our true expression. That is the power of our heart. Our spirit can literally change our world.

Phenacite emanates wisdom from far beyond the earthly realm. This lovely little crystal that is born of the Earth Mother functions as a cosmic transducer that can plug into and relay non-earthly higher frequencies from various star systems. The energy can seem strange or even a little disorienting upon first exposure, but once the mind adapts to the frequency you will discover that so much love radiates from this crystal. If you tend to float off into higher frequencies and find it difficult to ground during and after meditation, then you may like to combine your work with this stone with one or more of the grounding stones in this book such as elestial quartz, rutilated quartz or zebra stone. That way you'll keep your feet on the earth whilst your head is in the clouds (of star dust).

SPIRITUAL GUIDANCE: THE PHYSICAL REALITY OF THE SOUL

Many years ago, when I ran a weekly meditation circle for beginners, a regular student brought a friend of hers along to join us. We sank into our guided visualisation and called in divine energy and the students had their unique and varied experiences, which we shared together after the process. Our new classmate shared her beautiful heartfelt experience of the Divine. She was new to this sort of thing and the experience blew her away. She was keen to return for more.

The following week the regular students returned to class, but the new student was not amongst them. It turned out that some hours after the previous class, she was rushed to hospital believing that she was having a heart attack! However, when she was examined at the hospital, she showed no physical problems at all. In a sudden intuition it occurred to me that what this woman had believed was a physical heart condition was the release of stored pain from her heart chakra. Thankfully not every person is affected this way, but for whatever reason this was her experience. Her body and soul obviously wanted to release something—perhaps to avoid an actual heart attack in future—and so they drank generously from the divine offering of the meditation circle and purged as was needed afterwards.

This woman is not alone. The flow of energy often has a physical effect on the body. I have seen many people so struck by the flow of spiritual energy that they have not been able to control what is happening in their bodies. This can be rapturous and joyful. At other times, if the person is unsure of what is taking place and that it is safe to allow it, they may become frightened and uneasy that their body is shaking or moving in odd ways that they cannot consciously control. It can be disconcerting, but it can help to understand that the cause is not spirit, but the body's release of stored pain. As for the student who didn't have a heart attack, she returned for further meditation classes and sessions and in the years that followed her path continued to blossom somewhat less dramatically (for which she was grateful).

There were times in my journey of self-healing where my body has purged emotional and psychic pain that was stuck in various place. I was stunned by how physically powerful and visceral such emotional energy could feel. In the same way that anger may heat us up and have us needing to move or do something, repressed emotion can need a way out. It can be released through dance, making sound, creating art, crying or writing in a journal.

I vividly remember an experience that happened decades ago, when I was dealing with some pain I felt around the absence of my father in the early part of my life. As I wrote about that experience in my journal, the pain that erupted was so strong that it felt like a sledgehammer was pounding straight onto the centre of my chest! My body was bravely letting go of old grief and pain, but my goodness, the sheer physical intensity of it literally took my breath away. I wasn't afraid because I understood what was happening and I trusted the wisdom of my own body and soul. I trusted that if something was releasing so powerfully, it must be the right time for it and I could surrender into the process. However, I had no idea that emotion could cause so much physical pain. At least, unlike a physical injury that may take a long time to heal, when emotional pain releases, we quickly feel normal again (well, as normal as we may ever feel).

There are also subtler experiences of energy affecting the body. If you have a meditation practice you might have similar experiences to my own. While sitting still in meditation, the flow of energy can be strong enough to realign my spine, causing little cracks and shifts as though I was having a (divine) chiropractic adjustment. Even my eyesight, which is good anyway, can improve after a genuine spiritual cleansing or blessing. Colours become more vibrant and the world appears hyper-real with such detail and clarity, not unlike focusing a camera lens to bring something into sharp and perfect focus.

There are also affects we may not be able to consciously recognise. I have had several acupuncture sessions from a wonderfully gifted traditional Chinese medicine practitioner who migrated from China. He loved it when I came for sessions as he soon realised that I was one of the people who could feel the movement of chi or vital life energies which the acupuncture process helps to rebalance (he estimated about 10 percent of his clients can feel it). I would share what I felt, often noting that he could place a needle in one place and I would feel the flow elsewhere, invariably at some point on the meridian line triggered by the acupuncture.

After several sessions, he pushed a tiny acupuncture needle deep into a point at my lower belly. It was deeper than he would usually do. Just when I wondered if he would ever stop pushing that needle in, I felt it *touch* something. An image of what the needle had tapped into instantly formed in my mind. I could see and feel what seemed like a large internal egg deep in my lower belly. I told him it was oval and lying horizontally and asked him what it was. He replied that it was the Dan Tian centre, a type of chakra or power centre in Chinese healing. I don't know which one of us was more excited that I had felt it! It was fascinating to feel this energy centre that I had heard about from Chi Gung practitioners over the years, and to have it feel just as real as my arm or leg.

I have never needed proof of energy healing, because I have always felt it as such in my body. If someone needs to know that acupuncture and meridians are genuine, I'd be happy to vouch for it! The interesting point here is that the same things would happen in the body of someone who doesn't have the energy-reading traits I have. They just wouldn't recognise it at the subtle level. They may feel more relaxed, that they have more energy, or they may not notice much at all. Yet the same process would have occurred for them as it did for me. This could be why acupuncture has been practiced for thousands of years.

Then, there are the exchanges of energy that happen between spiritual beings and humans without anyone acting as an intermediary. This might include sensations of pleasure, love, chills, tickling, spaciousness, the heart opening or of the bliss one feels when praying, meditating, channelling or doing some form of healing. Often enough, participants in my classes report that when I lightly touch their bodies for an energy transmission and then take my hand away, that they feel another hand touching and think it is me again. It is only when they hear me singing or speaking from the other side of the room that they realise it's not a human touch at all, but loving and gentle energy flowing from their spiritual guide.

One of my favourite examples of a direct energy encounter between spirit being and human being happened to my first boyfriend. We awoke one morning to find that he had a handprint on his torso. It was softly red in tone, as though there had been a lot of energy transferred from the hand that left the imprint on my boyfriend's skin. He placed his hand over it, but the print was smaller than his hand. He asked me if I had done healing on him during my sleep. I didn't think I had, but it could have happened unconsciously, so I placed my hand on the imprint to see if it matched. The imprint was larger than the size of my hand! We were both amazed! We felt that he had received spiritual healing during the night, likely for the organ underneath the site of the imprint. We assumed it was from a spiritual being of a human shape that was slightly larger than me and slightly smaller than him. Being quite cosmic in nature, my first boyfriend attracted several unusual experiences on his spiritual journey, all of which were loving, if not a little strange at times.

Physical energy is just that — energy. It seems physical and therefore separate from our energetic field of chakras, meridians, chi and the like as it vibrates more slowly and therefore appears to be still and solid. This is so that life can happen. One day I was parking my car at the gym parking lot, when I randomly thought about how glad I was that the energy was dense enough to appear still as it would be difficult to park my car between two 'moving' vehicles.

Energy is most subtle in the higher or more ethereal realms and therefore the least likely to be perceived by the five main human senses. Those who have learned to sense energy using more refined versions of those senses such as clairvoyance, clairsentience and clairaudience, will be able to recognise subtle energies in a way others may not. From time to time, we may see or feel the spiritual presence of higher beings or loved ones that have passed away. We may see flashes of light around people, colourful energies in meditation or have feelings of heat and warmth flow through our hands to bring healing to others when we give them a hug. We may recognise that the words that come out of our mouths to comfort another are sometimes not from us at all but from a greater wisdom for which we are a willing (if not surprised) channel. Psychics and healers often learn how to read these subtle energies to support their work, although I know some excellent healers who simply use their techniques according to their training, don't tend to sense much at an energetic level at all, and yet carry out great work.

As energy becomes increasingly dense, it is experienced as heavier, more substantial, and is able to be grasped by the senses and experienced by the body. It drops from the etheric realms of spirit, ideas and feelings, into the physical world as cars, our bodies, Mother Nature, our loved ones and so on. An emotional issue in this life may have begun in the subtle realms as a karmic wound from a past life. If we are not willing or able to deal with that emotional pain, then it will continue to gain density until it concretises as early phases of an illness (which we can hopefully correct before it needs to go further and become a fully-fledged disease). Healing that wound can happen at any phase in this process, although it can be difficult to see there is something we need to deal with until it shows up in our lives in a way we can no longer avoid.

When dealing with circumstances that need healing—whether as financial, health or psychological issues—I feel that a dual approach is best. I find that working with an energetic and a physical world approach, through an inclusive, wholistic strategy works best for most people. Two heads are better than one, as the saying goes, and we can often benefit from an additional perspective.

There are instances where apparently emotional issues, that we might assume need an emotional approach for healing, improve through skilful medical testing and supplementation that redresses imbalances in the body's biochemistry. For example, overly high copper levels can manifest as unnecessarily volatile emotional sensitivity and fluctuations. With the right zinc supplement, the person's ability to sustain emotional balance can improve remarkably. This won't always be the case. Sometimes it really is more about therapy, dealing with unresolved childhood issues and healing at a psychological level, but in such instances working with the body to improve health and wellbeing will support the process.

Being into spiritual healing and energy work is great, but it can also be good to look at where that approach can be enhanced through medical wisdom (and in my experience, that refers to practitioners who have a functional, integrative and wholistic approach to medicine and are willing to work with lifestyle and natural supplementation rather than going straight to medication). The same principle applies in reverse. When we think an issue is mostly physical and needs physical treatment to correct, emotional healing can help us unravel the patterning that created the emotional environment where the physical problem manifested.

I also think it's helpful to remember that healing and recovery are not always the same thing. A client of mine who is a talented spiritual healer was speaking to me of a woman she was working with who was in the final stages of a terminal illness. Through the process of spiritual healing she was finding peace around the ending of her life. She wanted to leave her body, she had lived a good life and at one level she felt she was ready for death. At another level, she was unable to let herself surrender. As she connected more and more with spirit, she found a gentleness and peacefulness within her that was new. She became more open to connecting with people, where previously she had cut herself off from life, become depressed and developed anxiety due to disengaging from those around her. In her case, the healing was the blessing of a peaceful dying process that happened as she finally experienced what it was to be more fearlessly alive. She was not cured of the disease that had manifested in her body, but she was most certainly healed.

For others, spiritual healing may be enough to evoke a full recovery. Sometimes a conventional medical process can result in a physical recovery *and a* spiritual healing. There are cases where the removal of a cancer or other diseased tissue can remove the painful patterning so that the person becomes freed from it. I noticed this with a client who had cancer and chose to endure the arduous treatment process. Through that process she became more willing to recognise that if she kept placing her needs second to the needs of others, her illness would return. So, she stopped allowing people to take advantage of her, one of the major contributors to the development of her breast cancer (to be clear, I do not advocate the notion that everyone with breast cancer has the same underlying issues and would benefit from taking the same journey this woman did). After her physical recovery, she was emotionally tougher and able to say no to people who placed inappropriate demands on her time and energy and she took better care of herself. She changed and grew through the journey. There was recovery, but there was also healing.

I know of two men—of different ages, ethnic backgrounds and lifestyles—that both had heart attacks and nearly died. Neither was changed by the experience or the treatment. After the surgery they were informed of lifestyle changes they could make, but they resisted and returned to their past ways. As they had not addressed the underlying issues, they were unable to make the needed adjustments. There was a temporary recovery but no actual healing. The same issues would arise again.

True healing is not a temporary pausing of symptoms but a multilevel and multidimensional phenomenon. The healing path is different for everyone. Some may start spiritually and progress to the physical, which is the way my journey happened to go in this lifetime. Others begin with the physical and move into the spiritual.

If you work with an aware and conscious doctor (I have found the number of such practitioners is rapidly growing and it is worth the time and the process of elimination it can take to find them), you will find that allopathic medicine can be immensely helpful and support your spiritual journey when administered carefully and with a wholistic approach. I really don't like the idea that some people have that conventional medicine is only for unconscious people who aren't doing their spiritual work or that spiritual work should negate the need for conventional medicine. Sometimes spiritual healing can indeed eradicate the need for medical treatment, but medical treatment can still play an essential role. I understand that modern medicine, as a system, is very much wounded. It has the potential to dehumanise and frighten people and lead them away from an experience of true healing. Medicine is rather like religion as it was described by Hindu wild child and saint, Ramakrishna, "... like a cow; it kicks, but it also gives milk."

I remember something quite startling that the Dalai Lama mentioned in a talk some twenty years ago. He said that at one stage he had needed to eat meat because his body had become sick and a vegetarian diet was not enough for him at that time, even though it was his preference. Going off a vegetarian diet would have great spiritual significance to him. This was a profound statement about the love he had for his body as a vehicle through which he was serving so many on this planet. His body deserved care. It also highlighted that no matter how enlightened we may be, we do our spiritual work to become wiser about how to work with physical healing approaches, not necessarily to transcend them.

I do caution you not to allow yourself to be intimidated by doctors of conventional medicine. Some doctors freely admit that many of their patients know more about their illnesses—through dedicated research and the information available these days—than they do. And so, the doctor is willing to work with the patient rather than dictate to them from a place of assumed superiority. Some are open to spiritual healing. Even when you have a great doctor, you can still assume responsibility for your healing and empowerment and your spiritual work is part of this. We want to honour the power of our spiritual practice, but we don't want to ignore a helping hand and the benefits it can bring simply because we'd like to heal the situation spiritually. As the example of the Dalai Lama shows, sometimes to heal physically we must also grow spiritually. This can mean dropping judgements and trusting what life brings us.

The pieces of the puzzle for our wellbeing will come as we take our journey. I will confess that I've had to wait many years for some answers because they weren't yet discovered. I believe that my need, and the need of others, for those answers were part of the magnetic power that helped pull them from the universal mind into human knowledge. That's why I believe we need to be stubborn when it comes to healing. We need to ask the Universe for what we want and need. Doing this can contribute to the greater good. The right healer will often come at the right time but being a stubborn divine detective who keeps looking until something really resonates as right for us is important.

Some years ago, I had a recurring pain in my shoulder blade where I had pulled it when I was a teenager. The pain only seemed to arise during meditation. It would throb throughout the meditation and at the close of the session it would go away. This happened for years and then eventually stopped. Years later I had a skin condition on that same part of that body. Even though it was mild, it was irritating, and I wanted to sort it out. I saw a healing professional about it, but his diagnosis didn't seem right as the treatment prescribed wasn't doing anything to heal it. I was frustrated, so I prayed to the Divine for healing.

Then I dreamed of an incredibly happy surgeon. He was smiling as he removed something from the back of my body, in the exact location of my shoulder blade. I remember the sensation of whatever he had been pulling out, a feeling of it being drawn out of me and the slight pull of the spiritual stitches, that half woke me. I felt that I was having issues in that part of my body—the injury when I was a teen and the pain and the skin irritation later—because of a karmic weakness. Something was amok in my energy field in that spot. I remembered that my first boyfriend, who was a natural psychic healer with notable talent, had once laid his hand on my shoulder and told me he sensed a memory of my father leaving and my great pain around it. So, it is likely that the karmic imprint that kept manifesting as problems in that part of my body had to do with unresolved pain around the absence of my father. I felt that the celestial surgeon had happily removed the karmic seed.

The morning after my dream, I felt different. I went to a dermatologist who correctly prescribed the situation and it rapidly healed and disappeared completely. The dermatologist was quite shocked and kept saying: "If I hadn't taken a photo of the condition that was there, I wouldn't believe you ever had it. It's like it never existed."

Grace for the dream healing was granted following my prayer. Something also shifted for me emotionally. I realised I had internalised a painful situation from my parents' divorce and believed a man couldn't ever really commit to being there for me in a way I could rely on. Following this dream, I no longer held that belief. Healing at the spiritual level allowed for healing at the other levels to naturally unfold.

HEALING PROCESS

The colour green is often associated with Archangel Raphael and the heart chakra. It is often a rich emerald green, but I have seen many different shades of green light in the auric field around the heart chakras of those I work with. Green is the colour of healing, transitions and crossroads (which are thresholds of healing where we leave the past behind and open to a new way). You may like to create an altar with green as a colour theme or allow your eyes to rest on something green in your environment such as a tree. You could even look at some pictures of nature to nourish your heart with the green frequency. When you are ready, place one hand on your heart and say aloud:

> *I call upon star teacher and cosmic healer Regulus, and Archangel Raphael, guardian of the healing ray. I call upon the Crystal Angel of Phenacite, transducer of higher frequencies and master teacher of the creative power of consciousness. I call upon the spiritual strength of my authentic self. I align myself with the healing wisdom of the Universe and ask for help in healing of all facets of my being to support the fulfilment of my divine potential and the free and complete expression*

of my authentic self in wellbeing and peace. I surrender to the reorganising power of the heart and allow new insights, understanding and behaviours to emerge from my healed consciousness. I trust myself to live in a way that honours and respects the soul. Through the highest wisdom for the greatest good, so be it.

You may like to imagine, feel or visualise a beautiful green healing light is shining in the heart of a cosmic lion with brilliant, white angelic wings. This is Regulus, a beautiful star guide who is watching over you and offering healing, protection and assistance to resolve the challenges in your life according to higher spiritual laws.

Within the heart light of this great star being, a tiny crystal seed shines clearly and brightly with sacred messages your soul can understand. This is the Crystal Angel of Phenacite. The light of these two angels can flow into your own heart, connecting you to the healing intelligence of the Universe. Now rest for as long as you wish.

You have completed your healing process.

CHAPTER SEVENTEEN

SPIRITUAL FREEDOM TO OVERCOME TOXIC SYSTEMS OF POWER

STAR GUIDE: ANTARES

ANOTHER OF THE ROYAL STARS of ancient Persia, Antares is the guardian or *Watcher of the West* and said to house the frequencies of Archangel Uriel. Some say it is Archangel Oriel. In angelology, it is generally accepted that these are names for the same being. One refers to this being as divine light, the other as the holder of the divine fire. Uriel is a powerful archangel and in the form of Antares, watches over many beings including humanity and provides the spiritual light needed to make successful transitions, be they from one world to the next or from one chapter in our lives to another.

In ancient China, the constellation where Antares is found was known as the *Azure Dragon* or *Dragon of the East*. Antares was the *Fire Star*, which thematically links it to the angelic associations mentioned above, and the spiritual properties of fire which include its ability to give light, warmth and, if used wisely, to nourish life. The dragon symbolism includes access to secret knowledge, supernatural power and physical vitality, which can be used for protection or for destruction.

These metaphysical powers mirror those associated with the wisdom of Scorpio, the Western constellation where Antares is the brightest star. This star teacher is a red supergiant that marks the scorpion's heart. For a sense of its enormous size, if Antares was at the centre of our solar system it would consume all the inner planets and extend into the asteroid belt of the Milky Way. Antares teaches us to recognise the possible effects of our energies—especially if they were overwhelming to another—and how to create healthy space and boundaries, so we can remain as powerful as we wish without our interactions becoming intrusive.

In astrology, the sign of Scorpio gets some confusing press. It is a powerful and charismatic energy, which unfolds over three degrees or levels of evolution, each represented by an animal symbol. The first level of Scorpionic teaching is symbolised by the scorpion itself and represents unyielding fortitude and a noble refusal to be dominated by another. There is an old myth that a scorpion would sting itself and end its life rather than be captured. This is questionable as the scorpion is immune to its own venom, but the symbolism is considered relevant in astrological wisdom where Scorpio energy represents the instinct for self-defence even if that involves self-destructive behaviours. My grandmother used to refer to actions that were supposed to protect us, but just ended up hurting us as, "Cutting off your nose to spite your face." Any person who has experienced an addictive behaviour or tried to protect themselves from the possibility of harm or rejection through self-sabotage has experienced this very human trait firsthand.

Antares helps us honour a healthy instinct for self-sovereignty, dignity and freedom with compassion and wisdom. Instead of destroying ourselves so another cannot destroy us, rejecting ourselves so that the rejection of another has no sting, and so on, we can channel that instinct for self-protection and powerful will in more conscious and constructive ways. We can learn to love ourselves and set boundaries so the rejections that inevitably come along do not disturb our innate sense of value as a human being.

The second wisdom level of Scorpio is symbolised by the snake. Serpent medicine has various mythologies from various traditions, but wisdom and transformation are the most universal and enduring of its correspondences. In Hinduism, the serpent symbolises rising inner energies, our Kundalini Shakti, that awaken the chakras to higher understanding, insight and wisdom. The ancient image of a serpent eating its own tail found its way from the *Egyptian Book of the Dead* into modern mystery traditions as the Ouroboros. Sometimes depicted as a dragon rather than a snake, which ties into the dual symbolism of Antares, this powerful totem speaks of continuity, evolution and transformation. The symbol encompasses an understanding of destruction/creation and death/life as repeating cycle. Snake is transformational intelligence. The ability to shed its skin and emerge renewed, freed from the layers of the past, symbolises the rebirths we go through as we grow on our healing journey. We can use the destructive power of any life situation as an impetus to shed what isn't working and create a new sense of self in the process.

This leads into the third and final evolution of Scorpio's wisdom, the eagle, a symbol of tremendous insight and perspective. Those born in the sign of Scorpio or with strong Scorpio energy in their natal charts are the seers of the zodiac. They can recognise the light and the dark in human nature without judgement and therefore have great clarity. The eagle can fly high, nests above the rest of the world and is able to cover a vast territory with its massive wingspan. The vision of Scorpio, and Antares, can help us see things from a much higher and broader perspective. At this refined level of stellar transmission, Antares leads us into the realm of the visionary who has a wide-ranging perspective and can see the microcosmic workings of the macrocosmic wisdom. It helps us see the divine plan unfolding and to tune in to divine timing, so we know when to rest and when to act.

Antares translates as *Rival of Ares*. Ares is the Greek god of war, known as Mars in the Roman tradition. The red colour of the star means it has a similar appearance to the red planet, Mars. Every two years the planet and the star are conjunct or appear to be sitting one atop the other from our perspective. Antares shows us another of this star teacher's mysteries as a rival or force against Ares. It helps us shift from being a warrior in an earthly sense (always fighting against life, ourselves, others or the world) and into the role of spiritual warrior. The spiritual warrior never battles against other humans but fights against his or her own ego as they learn to live as a light on this planet.

Antares helps us to stop using our ego to fight our battles. We can instead learn to live with the courage of the warrior from the soul. When this star connects with our soul, we can be learning to let go of ego defensiveness and place our trust in the deeper wisdom and protective grace of our souls. It can also suggest that a time frame of two years is in some way significant for the soul. Two years of growth or struggle may be coming to an end. You may be entering a spiritual growth phase of two years during which many things will bring more light, joy and wisdom to your life.

Some astrologers associate Antares with negative energies, even with evil. I do not believe this is the case. As with some of the negative associations made with Polaris, these come from an ego perspective. When Scorpio's transformative powers are working through the soul there is a destructive component, but it is not evil. Some destabilisation is necessary for growth. The more the ego holds onto a way of being that is not in harmony with the authentic soul journey, the stronger that destructive force will feel. It is not malicious. Its intent is to liberate. The target of Antares' destructive divine fire is the ego. As an Archangel, Uriel aids in the transmission of divine light and divine fire. Light reveals truth and fire fuels purification and transformation. When we feel a strong connection to Antares in our souls, we are likely going through a process of spiritual cleansing and transformation. That may relate to our ego or to the negative effects of the ego at large in the world around us. Antares has a far-reaching influence in our Universe, so the emergence and protection of the light and wisdom provided by this star being will have a wide impact in our world and beyond.

THE CRYSTAL ANGEL OF SPHALERITE

I was very drawn to this unassuming, spiky grey stone before I had any notion of its name let alone its properties. I discovered it was especially helpful for those in the public eye wanting to avoid unconsciously taking on the projections of others. Belief in one's own press is the number one enemy within when it comes to being authentic. As that was a fate I wished to avoid, a large piece of sphalerite has rested on the sideboard in my home ever since. It is a loving reminder to keep it real no matter what others may have to say about me and how I choose to live, either in praise or in judgement.

Reinforcing our connection to our authentic selves is always useful, especially when people in your life want you to behave a certain way to meet their ideals or their negative projections. This is particularly relevant to those souls who feel they are moving a group of people along with them on their journey. I see souls like this in my practice sometimes. They are like the black (or rainbow!) sheep of their tribe — be it family, school, industry or other type of community. They often stick out like a bird of paradise in a field full of daises! Their tribe may never go as deep, but these heart-centred souls stimulate their spiritual growth. Sphalerite can help these souls stay true to themselves, even when they are under pressure to be more like the group and less like themselves. When they give themselves full permission to be themselves within the group, everyone benefits at a spiritual level.

A connection to authentic self comes with a connection to genuine instinct and intuition; i.e. the neutral, truth-speaking parts of our being that help us answer a question that I am so often asked, "How do I tell the difference between genuine guidance and wishful (or fearful) thinking?" When we are in our heads or our ego pain, it is hard to tell the difference. When we are in our bodies, we can feel the effect of guidance and that is how we discern its quality. The proof of the pudding is in the tasting, as the expression goes. Genuine guidance, whether it is what we want to hear or not, has a neutral quality that simply resonates as truth. If you are someone who deals with a lot of opinions, information or energy and must somehow sort through it to find your own truth and feel grounded and integrated enough to act on it, then sphalerite will be helpful for you.

This crystal angel can help undo cycles of bullying. Bullying comes from a place of fear that masquerades as dominating power. It is an attempt to impose a painful ego reality upon another. Sphalerite can help break the cycle by protecting would-be targets from feeling like victims. It supports the soul in standing true to its own sense of value and recognising the other's actions for what they are — an expression of pain.

SPIRITUAL GUIDANCE: AUTHENTICITY TO FREE YOURSELF FROM CULTIC SYSTEMS

Human beings are social animals designed to need each other. As the saying goes, "No man is an island." This is not weakness, but part of our spiritual physiology and how we grow and prosper on all levels. Even though some of us are more hermit-like than others or more comfortable in solitude than others, our need for connection and belonging is just as compelling. Although, we might express it in more subtle or unusual ways. To meet our in-built need for connection we seek out various tribes, be they family, friends, spiritual groups, common interest groups or cultural groups. These groups can provide us with energy, bonding and belonging. Of course, group energies can be problematic. A bunch of unique individuals relating to each other is not necessarily going to be a simple and harmonious matter, even when the intentions are pure.

There are tribes that are about honouring the individual and based in love. These are rarer, perhaps because a reasonably enlightened group of individuals is needed to maintain a balance between personal freedom and personal responsibility, so the group feels bonded and can function as a greater organism but doesn't consume the uniqueness of the individual in the process. Those groups are about fusion and synergy rather than enmeshment and control. Belonging to a conscious and loving tribe where we can be ourselves and serve a purpose beyond ourselves is a deep and nourishing human need.

A cultic system is a way of relating within a group that does not meet that need, often while promising to deliver something far more enlightened than it is able to. A cultic system can be present within any type of group. I have seen it manifest in families, spiritual schools, workplaces and religious groups, just to give a few examples. The basic problem with a cultic system is that it is crazymaking. It needs you to adopt the ideology of the group at the expense of your own authenticity. At the same time, you aren't allowed to acknowledge that this is what is happening (unless you want to be banished from the community or punished in some other way).

Cultic systems are energetically vampiric. They steal the life force from the authentic self and use it to feed the energy fields of the authority figure(s) in the group. As the vital energies of the members are drained and they are disempowered, a growing sense of insecurity and fear creates a greater dependency on the group's authority figures. The worse the vampirism, the stronger the toxic bond that develops. It can get to the point where an individual no longer seems to exist outside of that group or even within it. They become completely submerged in the destructive system. It is quite astonishing and disturbing to see. Examples of this are not as rare as one might think and less extreme (but still profoundly damaging) examples of cultic groups are easy to find in modern society.

The hallmark of a cultic group is that membership (that bestows a sense of acceptance and belonging) is conditional upon certain rules. The main rule of a cultic system is that you obey their rules. Their rules can include social mores, beliefs and behaviours. There may be rules around dress, speech and relationships. Now this could apply to almost any group. All tribes have mores and conditions for membership. The difference with a cultic group is the degree of obedience needed—which is generally absolute—and the consequences of breaking the rules. The threat of a severe and terrible outcome will be attached to non-compliance. This may be expulsion, ex-communication, going straight to hell, falling foul of the guru, incurring divine wrath or confrontation. Being abandoned or rejected by a group that felt like family can be an incredibly painful experience. This all aims to violate and eventually annihilate the individuals' authentic sense of self along with their spiritual dignity and freedom.

I once read the blog of a woman who claimed to be a guru who wrote that any disciples who left her would forgo the blessings she had given them. This is a classic example of cultic manipulation. Spirit gives freely and generously to all those who are ready and willing to receive. It never takes away blessings. Spirit never judges our use of free will but is always guiding, supporting and encouraging us to take our journey according to our own strength, courage and wisdom. The threat in cultic families is that love is withdrawn if you don't obey. A parent may become cold or emotionally punishing if a child expresses a feeling or view that conflicts with the parent's idea of how the child should be. Only parents who have narcissistic traits will inflict this upon a child. These parents do not allow the child to be who they are but instead need them to perform according to the parent's wishes.

Cultic systems gain strength through the darkest aspects of the human ego — fear, vengeance, obsession with power at any cost and virulent hatred of the feminine in her various forms including the freedom-loving soul and the unique, creative expression of the body. The fact that cultic systems may claim to worship the feminine or are spiritual in some other way only adds to the crazymaking qualities of such groups. We may not recognise the cultic qualities of a group at first. We may be drawn to the beautiful ideals that they represent well before we realise that we are caught up in a unhealthy tribe and need to find a way to be healthy within the group (perhaps beginning to heal it from the inside) or where there is too great a resistance (and cultic consciousness is extremely fixed and resistant) we need to find a way out, so we can heal and repair our sense of self and seek out healthier groups.

Cultic groups can be unconsciously attractive to those looking to belong. Cultic groups can promise an intense sense of belonging. It is true in a sense as the members go very deep into bonding, but as I described above, it is of a toxic nature. Healthy belonging enhances your individuality. It doesn't demand that you march to a beat that is not your own. Yet, sacred rebels and other black sheep are often drawn to these groups. One reason for this is cultic groups often position themselves as being special or unique in some way and present as a safe place for other special and unique people. For someone who was rejected for being different early in life, this might seem like a haven where that original wounding can be resolved. It can look like a chance to be loved for who you are, but the reality of the experience is quite the opposite.

Such groups can also appeal to those at a crossroads who are suffering from insecurity or doubt. They might unconsciously be seeking the sense of certainty that arises from a confident and demanding leader. Hitching your wagon to another's view of the world and allowing someone else to take responsibility for your reality can soothe any anxiousness you have about the unknown. These groups may feel like a place of refuge to someone who is familiar or comfortable with strong rules, until they are ready to grow. At that point, that very same culture may seem like a prison.

I have found myself in cultic spiritual groups on a few occasions. I always managed to learn something and extricate myself from them, but it was a painful journey and it took a few experiences to understand why I kept being drawn into them. For me, there was a sense of the familiar. Authoritarian energy was in my childhood, in my schooling and I recognised it in the world around me. I was accustomed to having demands placed on how I performed academically, athletically and even creatively. I believe a culture of obedient performance is entrenched in our school system and in the corporate world where living bodies are forced to sit for extended periods as brain machines performing like well-trained animals rather than moving, breathing, taking in natural light and learning in ways that are more open and connected to life. Most modern people will find cultic conditioning familiar at some level. For me, that familiarity combined with the desire to meet people who would recognise and acknowledge my inner light as something appealing because I didn't experience a lot of that early in life. Yes, I was loved. Truly seen and understood, not so much.

So, when I met a teacher who saw and valued my spiritual abilities, I wanted to move closer to them and their group. However, just because someone saw something in me, it didn't mean their motivations were altruistic. This was a painful lesson. I felt that I was used for the group purpose, paraded about as prize unicorn to attract other members and milked for energy to serve the group agenda. It was just as invalidating to my essence as the original wounding I was unconsciously trying to heal.

For some reason, I never fully dropped into the cultic systems that I found my way into. This may have been due to my sheer stubbornness which has been a saving grace in my life many a time, and the rebellious tendencies of my maternal family line, which I had inherited. However, I had one experience where I felt perilously close to losing connection to those saving anchors. During a meeting with a teacher, I sensed the pull of the group energy and suddenly became aware of what seemed to be a great, dark abyss opening beneath me with a gravity that wanted to suck me in. I hovered at the brink of this and still remember my thought process at the time. Was this a surrender into spirit? Was my ego holding me back? Despite the confusion in my mind, my heart would not let me fall. I feel as though a protective being was holding the back of my shirt preventing me from going forth into something I sense would not have been kind, loving or generous.

Typically, members of cultic groups are sensitive as to whether other group members are 'in' the group as deeply as they are, whether they are committed at any cost, or not. The premise being that the more 'in' you are, the more important, powerful, evolved and worthy of respect you are. As I was involved in the group, but hadn't fully committed, I was considered something of a wild card. I tended to stand out because of this and this attracted attention that I didn't really want. I was viewed with pity by those who were in the group the furthest, as though I didn't get what it was all about. Others regarded me with suspicion as if my free thinking was contagious and could disrupt the entire community. This did occur from time to time, although I never tried to be a liberator as such. For those who were unsure about the authenticity of the various groups I found my way into over the years, I was treated as something of a hero. Those who were thinking of leaving the group and needed to talk to someone who would not judge, nor try to convince them either way, often seemed to find their way to me. I was confided in and leaned upon as others sought to make their exit from the group. This of course fuelled the suspicion of certain others even more!

I have compassion about it all now, and I also find it a little funny in a way, but I also know just how confusing and painful these groups can be. My feeling for those struggling in cultic groups is prompting me to write about this topic. As I do, I am imagining the reactions of some of the key figures from a couple of the spiritual groups I was part of for a time. I suspect they would laugh, be dismissive and suggest that these were all my own issues. Although my issues led me into those situations, that does not mean the issues of the group were all in my head. This is what the crazymaking nature of a cultic system would have one believe.

This leads me to a key point about cultic groups and how to identify them. A spiritual group may claim to be about love and light, but we must look to the reality of the experience not the outer images, words or company policies. Cultic groups are interested first and foremost in power. They want to control the people in their group. It may be money that they want, but it might also be their skills, minds, bodies, or in some cases, the energy, power and talent of their souls. They are believers in any means to an end. They achieve their means through standard cultic tactics. They manipulate, they dominate, they control, they exploit, and they may tell you that it is for your own good, for the good of the planet, to clear your karma or any convincing sounding reason.

Spiritual abuse is not something I hear people talk about, yet I have experienced it and seen it at work countless times. To me, this type of abuse is a violation of your freedom and your responsibility to choose your life journey and be true to yourself. It strikes at the legitimacy of your essence. To honour your essence, you need the space and freedom to find your own way and to have a direct experience of your life journey without having to contort your truth to suit that of another. I also see that pressuring someone to remain in a group, whether it be a family, a gang, a religious order or spiritual group, is a form of spiritual abuse. To break free of spiritual abuse, we need to lay claim to our personal freedom to choose how we live and to respect ourselves, regardless of whether others support, oppose or doubt our choices and wisdom.

Spiritual abuse can also manifest as consciously intended manipulation during guided group meditations. This is a fine line. If we are using words to guide others, we want to do our best to ensure they are inspired by a greater wisdom. The moment our words become about what we think someone should or should not do, we are getting into toxic territory. I have been in meditation sessions where blessings were given to those who were going to donate to the school. This willingness to open people through meditation and then plant thoughts in their minds that served the financial agenda of the organisation shocked me. The notion that a financial contribution would secure greater blessing reminded me of the Catholic Church's disturbing practice of selling indulgences to mitigate the punishment for sins. As far as I could tell, the belief underpinning this tactic was that this teacher's divine mission was so important that any means of gaining support was divinely acceptable. I find this notion to be dangerous, not divine.

This kind of mental manipulation happened in subtler ways, which I imagine would go unnoticed by most people. This school claimed to run completely on donations. This term never seemed quite right to me given how manipulated and pressured I felt to 'donate' certain amounts. These practices seemed to fly in the face of the concept of donation in the first place.

One day, as I considered how much I would like to 'donate' for a workshop, an amount jumped into my mind that was about three times what I would consider a reasonable amount to pay. I paused, startled for a moment at why I would think such a thought. I became still and gazed at the thought, realising that it was not my thought at all, but a thought form purposefully created by some members of that school. Using intention and energy techniques, they set up thought forms on the lower levels of the astral plane, so that when people began to think of workshops, they would connect with this idea of how much the school wanted them to pay. Unless they stopped to see what was going on, people would simply consider the amount was their own thought.

Before that experience, if I had heard someone say such a thing to me, I would have wondered if they were paranoid and delusional. Yet there it was, clearly visible on the psychic level. I could even see the group building the thought form. I was stunned. That this psychic manipulation was happening in a school that claimed to be about Spirit was even more startling. In advertising or business such things are more expected, but when a spiritual group condones the use of occult techniques to surreptitiously manipulate the free will of their community members … let's just say that I had a full-on Kali moment of protective divine rage welling up within my heart. I have never ever had Spirit justify a lack of compassion or respect by claiming it was a means to a greater end. In fact, I believe Spirit would say that you cannot reach a greater purpose if it involves such behaviours.

I am not sharing these experiences here to make you feel fearful or suspicious, but to help you become discerning and aware. We need to acknowledge that when human beings get together, even for spiritual pursuits, shadow material can arise. It is not whether it is there but how we deal with it that matters. If we aim for an open, conscious response, with a sense of humour, we'll generally be on good ground to work through it, so the group can bond in a healthy way and grow. In cultic groups the shadow stuff is said to be the student's material to work on and the group leaders, or more 'in' members are absolved of responsibility. It is like the parent that demands certain behaviours from a child and then blames the child for failing. That is a cultic dynamic. It is not interested in authentic relating and mutual responsibility. It focuses on blame and power.

When it comes to spiritual abuse, the problem for most people is that they don't realise it is happening. You may think that it mustn't be so bad or that it doesn't really matter, but like people who suffer from the rare genetic disorder that prevents them from feeling pain, it doesn't stop them from being harmed. In fact, failure to recognise when something is damaging to us increases the possibility of harm because of the absence of healthy recoil. The damage accumulates until we have an even more complicated situation to resolve.

Our free will is fundamental to our experience as human beings and I would define any attempt to violate it as spiritual abuse. Freedom begins and ends within us not in our outer circumstances. When someone tries to control you, your life, the way you think, your right to choose your own path and develop your own consciousness, they are trying to violate your spiritual rights to freedom, integrity and sovereignty. Your choice to continue to honour yourself prevents that abuse from taking place. To overcome it, lay claim to your freedom to live your life and be yourself. There is the freedom to grow and become wiser even in making mistakes (which from the soul perspective are learning experiences rather than mistakes).

I've been booted out of more groups than I can count for thinking outside the square of what was considered acceptable for that group. I've lost friendships due to the evolution of my thinking where I suddenly saw the unhealthy behaviours that sustained the friendship and stopped allowing them. It wasn't a question of love. It was just a question of whether the group or friendship was strong enough to grow into a new way of being. In those cases, it was not. In other cases where there was less rigidity and more trust, the insights that I (or the other parties involved) gained were well received and the relationships flourished because we shared them.

Sometimes we need to have the courage to let go. It doesn't invalidate our past. What was relevant for the caterpillar was important then. Even if the butterfly doesn't need it anymore, there is no butterfly without a caterpillar past. Yet sometimes we can feel guilty about leaving others behind. It's almost like the familiar but misery-inducing beliefs are a sort of psychic slum, and to leave our loved ones behind there can feel like an abandonment or betrayal. I have had moments with my loved ones where I was so moved by their suffering and so deeply wanted to alleviate it that I would unconsciously lower my frequency from peace and happiness into worry and despair, as though this would bring them comfort. It did absolutely nothing to help that person and just left me feeling anxious because I was not in the truth of my being. I needed to have faith in my goodness and compassion, without punishing myself with unnecessary pain out of some misguided idea that I could help someone who was drowning in their suffering by diving in and drowning with them. It is better to hold a higher frequency that could help raise their energy, if they are willing.

When we find ourselves crossing the line of another's freedom, we can recognise it and apologise. This can be an internal apology from soul to soul if you feel the person wouldn't know what you are talking about or that it would confuse them. Even if someone wants us to tell them what to do, we don't have to agree with their belief in their perceived inabilities. We just step back. We reaffirm that every person we meet is a powerful soul having an experience. We may never understand that experience and nor do we have to for us to have compassion and respect. You can set your own boundaries, live your own truth and allow others to do the same. As Spirit often says to me, "There is more than one type of flower in the divine garden."

Sometimes they also say, "There are more foods than cheese!" Which is odd and often evokes laughter but is straight to the point. Not all people, paths or foods are meant to be the same. Allowing for creativity, diversity and our ability to find our own way in life is where the full experience of being human has a chance to unfold.

HEALING PROCESS

Take a moment to make a conscious connection to your own heart. You may like to do this by resting your hands at your heart or thinking about things that generate a feeling of love, gratitude and happiness in you.

Visualise, feel or intend that you can connect to the inner child within your heart. You may see, sense, feel or intend that this is a spirit of yourself as a child this lifetime. He or she may appear in any form, in any age. The child within is highly creative and it is good to allow that creative part of us to express itself honestly and authentically, even when we are surprised at what arises. Even if you cannot consciously feel that child self in your heart, trust that he or she is there.

You may like to place your hands on your heart with an intention to recognise, soothe and protect this part of you. You can speak to this part of you to give affirmation, recognition and love. If this part of you has unresolved pain around judgement, neglect, abuse or betrayal, then allow that part of you to speak of that without fear. He or she may tell you about feelings or stories or desires. Receive whatever is expressed with love and open-mindedness. It does not need to be assessed as true or false, bad or good. It is simply an expression which you are receiving.

It is then your turn to respond with love, encouragement, acknowledgement and validation. You may wish to express your intention and ability to protect this part of you. You may like to affirm that even with what you have experienced, you are here, in the present moment as a beautiful divine being. This is not to invalidate the impact of your past experiences but to encourage you to recognise your courage and strength. Say aloud:

I call upon the star teacher Antares who mirrors the divine strength within, to look into the shadow of my being and bring light, love and compassion to what is found there. I call upon the Crystal Angel of Sphalerite. I give thanks for your protection of my authentic being so that I may know and respect healthy boundaries for myself and for others. May all beings be guided by grace into healing, freedom and fulfilment. Through the highest wisdom for the greatest good, so be it.

You may like to do something that your inner child would enjoy. Dance, colour in, play a game, or curl up for a nap. Give to this part of yourself with generosity and love.

You have completed your healing process.

CHAPTER EIGHTEEN

SUPREME SPIRITUAL PROTECTION

STAR GUIDE: ALPHA CENTAURI

AS OUR SUN'S CLOSEST STAR SYSTEM, Alpha Centauri is just over four light-years away. It consists of a binary pair, Alpha Centauri A and Alpha Centauri B, and the smaller Proxima Centauri. Proxima Centauri is Earth's closest star after the Sun. Alpha Centauri A is a yellow star much like our sun, Alpha Centauri B is an orange star and Proxima Centauri is a red dwarf roughly seven times smaller than our Sun. All three stars are around 4.85 billion years old which makes them slightly older than our 4.6 billion-year-old Sun.

One of the star medicines Alpha Centauri offers is the ability to find like-minded people and other forms of spiritual support right under our noses. Sometimes what we need is much closer to home than we realise. Whilst I am a big believer in the positive effects of travel for the mind and the soul, and I love a good adventure, there are times when we don't need to go looking for an experience or an answer, as we have what we need within reach. Alpha Centauri reminds us that the spiritual resources we need will always be there for us and are in fact closer than we realise. When this star guide makes a connection with the soul, it means that help (or whatever is needed) is close at hand.

Alpha Centauri looks like a solitary star when viewed with the naked eye. It was only in 1689, after the invention of the telescope, that astronomers saw it was an orbiting pair. Proxima Centauri wasn't spotted until 1915. Alpha Centauri is in the southern part of the sky and is not visible all the time, to all people. Beyond 29 degrees north, including most of the USA, Alpha Centauri only rises a few degrees above the horizon. So, in much of the Northern Hemisphere it is difficult to see in any but the darkest skies. In the Southern Hemisphere, Alpha Centauri is circumpolar, so it can be viewed the whole year round. It is one of the pointer stars for the Southern Cross constellation.

Alpha Centauri teaches us that even when we cannot see it in the physical sense, sources of spiritual light are always shining upon us and having an effect in our world. We can go through times when we might feel ignored or rejected by Spirit or that we have lost contact in some way. This is an example of projecting our parental issues onto the Divine. The Universe never rejects us. Spirit never abandons us, and yet we all know there can be times when it feels that way. Alpha Centauri guides us to remember that even when the sun is covered by clouds, it is still shining and providing what is needed for life. Its light is not as clear from our perspective, but it is constant. There is also the guidance that when we go beneath the surface of things, we are more able to see the constant light of the Universe shining in our lives. Whether or not we see the workings of spiritual grace in our lives is a matter of our perspective, not a matter of whether it is there.

When this star connects with the soul, hidden connections will come to light. This can refer to spiritual connections or earthy relationships. This star teacher guides us to recognise that feeling alone and being alone are two different things. You may have become overly focused on the absence of certain people in your life, on loss or on grief. Whilst that is a legitimate element of a healing process, Alpha Centauri knows when it is time to gently encourage the soul to recognise the helping hands reaching out to it and that it is okay to acknowledge that and let people in.

According to Eratosthenes, who wrote of the constellations in the third century BCE, this star group depicts the mythological figure of Chiron. A fascinating figure, Chiron is a noble centaur and a skilful but wounded healer. He rose above the violent and basal nature of his fellow Centaurs. With divine parents, he was no ordinary centaur. His remarkable nature was loving, wise and gentle, the opposite of what one would expect from a typically aggressive centaur. Chiron demonstrates an ability to rise above the ways of one's own species. His divine parentage imbued him with finer traits. Our divine parentage is our spiritual nature. No matter what our ego might express at a base level, we can rise above it. This gives us hope for ourselves and for the human collective, especially in those moments where we may love humans but despair of humanity.

As a gifted oracle and revered teacher, Chiron also fulfilled the spiritual role of a saviour and gave his life to save that of another being. He is known as the wounded healer because even as a master of the healing arts, he could not heal the fatal wound that took his life. The story goes that he then joined the constellations as a bearer of light. The commonalities with the Christ story are striking. For example, at the time of his crucifixion, Jesus was jeered at because as the saviour he should be able to save himself. Chiron is an astrological emanation of the universal Christ Consciousness.

Chiron is present in the astrology chart of every human. His presence refers to the deep wounds of the soul that we all work through during our lifetime, in our own individual ways. Often these wounds are the source through which we develop skills. Having an absent father may open the way for someone to have a powerful spiritual relationship to the divine father, because no human man ever intercepted that role, for example. The wound of abandonment needs to be resolved, but at the same time, the skill for prayer or channelling spiritual guidance may be put to a higher use.

When Alpha Centauri connects with the soul it emanates Chironic wisdom to remind us that we don't have to be perfect to be able to help others. It guides us not to fall into the trap of denying our vulnerabilities. I sometimes see this tendency in healers who believe they shouldn't have needs of their own as their greater purpose is to serve others. They confuse service with self-abnegation. Eventually they become tired, sometimes with chronic health issues. They are like the wounded Chiron. They finally face the truth that a dry well cannot water the garden. Learning to embrace one's own needs helps us become full enough to nourish others. I have created a download on my website called *Healing the Healer* if you would like to explore these ideas further.

Chiron teaches us to have compassion, not to demand that we be other than we are and that we can be healers who have their own pains to deal with and still make offerings to the world. The unconscious Chiron tries to project their issues out onto the world and focuses on healing others when they would gain more and give more by working on themselves. The conscious Chiron learns from his or her wounds, grows in skilfulness through the process, and even with his or her vulnerabilities and frailties can make powerful offerings that help others in many ways. The unconscious Chiron martyrs themselves. The conscious Chiron devotes their lives to a higher and helpful calling while acknowledging that they are human beings with legitimate human needs. Chiron's wisdom is about rising above our lower nature of ego and aggression to align with the heart-infused soul that is within us. It is a journey that takes courage, is not always graceful, but benefits many, including ourselves.

Each one of us has an astrological transit known as the Chiron Return at around age 50. When Chiron returns to the point in its orbit where it was at the time of our birth, we can revisit our early wounding to either confront them for the first time (if we are beginning our inner work journey) or to experience them from a higher turn of the wisdom spiral. We can revisit those issues in a completely new way and potentially unlock their hidden blessings with more clarity and peace.

In its wisdom and compassion, Alpha Centauri helps us access the divine resources within us, find the divine blessings within our human journey and realise that nurturing ourselves can help us access the true depth and value of all we can share with the world.

THE CRYSTAL ANGEL OF RUTILATED QUARTZ

The first time I saw this stone, I held it up to the light and fell in love! The abundance of fine, golden, angel-hair threads within the smoky quartz felt like Mother Earth condensed a vitalising electrical circuit within the stone. This stone is electrically powerful and yet so incredibly harmonising and calming. I felt like I had a universal power tool in the palm of my hand! I also understood that the quietening effect of the stone manifests as it draws excess energies into its inner conductive network.

Rutilated quartz is available in clear or smoky quartz with fine, gold inclusions. This is a different stone to tourmalinated quartz which has much thicker black strands within clear quartz, although rutilated quartz can bring through a similarly protective, yet very refined energy. The rutile threads both soften and strengthen the natural frequencies of the quartz. Clear quartz is an amplifier and the grounding qualities of smoky quartz are healing and supportive for those who struggle with living in the head rather than the heart. Negative energies, depression or the *noise pollution* from various sources of technology and human minds can make it painful for sensitive types to live in their bodies. The fine rutile strands quicken the effects of quartz in the human energy field and nervous system, helping to balance the auric field and discharge excess energies. This can be so comforting for sensitive types.

Highly recommended for healers and all those working in environments where the energies are tough to handle, rutilated quartz can cleanse and protect the energy field. It thus strengthens the natural shield of the aura and empowers us to remain in a state of consciousness of our choosing, rather than being dragged into lower vibrational fields. It can strengthen our sense of centre, so we feel ourselves even when we are exposed to energies that are incompatible with our frequency. It helps to clear negative interference and offers spiritual protection at the soul level, so we can share ourselves, interact with others and keep a sense of authentic self.

On the physical level, it is supportive for healing the immune system, strengthening the nervous system and bringing a stronger sense of psychological and emotional boundaries. If someone is naturally open, psychically porous and tends to pick up energies, thoughts or even physical symptoms from others, this crystal can help them recognise, rather than unconsciously absorb, that material. This can reduce stress and help the person feel that they have more room to think and know how they feel. Rutilated quartz supports the creation of healthy boundaries without compromising the ability to perceive or feel subtle energies.

SPIRITUAL GUIDANCE: GENERATING A FIELD OF SPIRITUAL PROTECTION

Inner healing is an essential and effective contribution to remedying the apparently external sources of darkness in our lives and our world. However, I also recognise the value of creating a field of spiritual protection around ourselves every day. This is *not* in support of the idea that there is an outer evil that we must defend ourselves against. Such an idea can stimulate unnecessary anxiety and paranoia. It is an acknowledgement that there are negativities, whether they seem to be within us or around us, potential distractions and confusions, that can just make finding our path and sticking to it, more problematic than it needs to be.

With spiritual protection, life does not suddenly become devoid of challenge. We are on this planet to grow and evolve and sometimes obstacles are important stepping stones to discovering and expressing our authentic self. However, cultivating a field of spiritual protection makes a huge difference to our quality of life and the clarity with which we can discern the best way forward. Spiritual protection is like fertiliser for our soul. It increases our resourcefulness, inspiration, intuition and truth so that we can more readily find our way. We can work through a challenge, with greater understanding of what higher purpose it is serving and how we can manifest the greatest good even from a tricky situation.

A field of spiritual protection is something like having access to a coach in the game of life. Imagine you were given a ball and a bunch of people started running at you and you had no idea what was going on. You may feel rather concerned! If you knew you were meant to do your best to dodge the onslaught and get that ball to the end of the field for a touchdown, you'd have some perspective, drop the fear and go for it. You may even have fun. If you didn't quite make it, you could have a laugh, or be frustrated, or both, and learn. The next time the ball found its way to you, you'd have a clearer understanding and more developed skillset for the task at hand. If you never even knew you were in a game, you'd quite likely find the entire experience unnecessarily confusing and stressful.

Spiritual protection shows the way through challenges so that something good can come from any and all situations. It also creates a buffer zone that softens the potential impact from the emotionally and physically violent eruptions that sometimes come from within the human collective which sensitive and psychically open people oftentimes feel. Within a field of spiritual protection, we are still engaged with others and with life. We are still in the game, so to speak. We can absolutely be connected *and* protected. There is just more breathing space and room to sense what is taking place, what we can do about it, and how we can stay true to our path, keeping our light strong on this planet.

Spiritual protection is naturally built, strengthened and recognised as we do regular practices such as meditation, healing processes, prayer and invocations that align us with unconditional love. That field of protection becomes a saving grace, a boundary between the struggle that is necessary for our soul growth and the unnecessary pain which is so abundantly generated by ego. Connecting with a palpable field of spiritual protection can feel like waking up from a bad dream and realising that not only is it over, but we don't have to have such an experience again. That relief can become a huge motivator to continue with and commit to daily spiritual practice in the form of prayer, meditation, healing processes, oracle card readings or a combination of these things.

To be effective, spiritual practices do not necessarily need a lot of time, but they do need our complete attention. Five or ten minutes of focused attention is far better than hours of distracted practice where you are going through the motions, but not really bringing your mind and your presence into connection with what you are doing and why.

Building the capacity to be present during our spiritual practice takes time. Comfortably tolerating higher levels of spiritual energy and consciousness in your mind and body is rather like sunbathing. To adapt to the light, you expose yourself to the sun a little at a time, so that your body will adjust to the incoming energy. Your body knows how to receive benefits from such modulated exposure. Too much is not good for your health, nor is too little. Finding your natural resting point and learning to nudge slightly beyond that to trigger adaptation is how you work with sun exposure to heal rather than harm your body. The approach for adjusting to the higher levels of spiritual energy that the body and mind will attract through spiritual practices is the same.

The spiritual practices we commit to are our way of 'reaching' for Spirit. Our effort is needed to generate a field of spiritual protection around us. That is not because the Divine only gives energy if we beg for it! It is constantly streaming the most beautiful frequencies towards us in glorious abundance from multiple emanations of the one pure source — something I hope reading this book has reinforced in your mind.

Our effort creates the space to receive. It doesn't matter how many wonderful people are knocking at your door, wanting to love you, to talk with you, to bond and have a great laugh, if you never let them in … or if you do let them in but there's no space for them to stand or sit. We need to do our part in the relationship by learning to let the Divine in and creating some space, so it can take up the room we once reserved for ego. The Divine gives with such generosity but receiving is not passivity on our part. Like surrender, trust and faith, it is a spiritually active state that we summon with soul strength. Like most things, the more we practise the easier it gets.

The effort needed is our spiritual strength training. It helps us develop one of the most powerful self-healing and light-enhancing tools that we have at our disposal: our capacity for conscious choice. This can be choosing to place our hearts and minds in the spiritual sanctuary of divine presence, rather than in the painful realm of fear and doubt. That is quite simple to do, but as we discussed in Chapter Eight on astral gravity, habitual negativity can have a powerful pull on our minds, even when we know it's not good for us and there's a better option. That's why we practise. It is also why we gain so much from the increasingly potent field of spiritual protection that manifests around us as we continue to do our spiritual practices.

Learning how to bring ourselves into spiritual sanctuary by consciously evoking our spiritual connection does take time, but once you get the hang of it, you'll be able to do it more easily. It's a bit like learning a tricky yoga pose, a dance step or a new song. You can practise until your body has a memory of the steps, the way you feel as you do those steps, and what the correct alignment feels like, until it becomes second nature to you. As you continue with your practice, you will begin to feel that you are in that palpable field of spiritual protection most of the time. If something knocks you off your perch, such as a triggered wound that you need to work through, you will know the light is still there for you. Even if you cannot quite recognise it as easily as you usually do, you know that you'll be able to find your way back there again. That knowledge can make your heart rest easier when you are working through a challenging issue.

Healing processes, such as the ones in this book, are one way to grow your spiritual muscles, clean your soul, establish a stronger spiritual field around you and generally enhance your conscious connection to the Divine. Remember the analogy of sunbathing. More is not always better. Pace yourself. A little at a time on a regular basis is better than too much too soon.

To tune into what a field of spiritual protection may feel like—or if you already sense that you have that but are open to it becoming stronger—notice how you feel when you complete the healing processes in this book or do a meditation. I have created around twenty albums of guided meditations to support your journey. There is an abundance of techniques and teachings from many traditions that you can explore so seek out what suits you at this point on your path.

When you truly surrender into your practice, you leave behind your thoughts of daily life or whatever matter has been of concern to you. As you work through the steps of the healing process, for example, you will likely experience an altered awareness. If you are sensitive to energy that may be very noticeable for you. You may have feelings of bliss or sense a connection to an unconditionally loving consciousness awaken in your heart. You may sense that you are participating in a greater realm of spiritual play with more trust and that you are willingly engaged in the interaction of your human journey with a Divine presence that can and will be with you in such a way that everything can change for the better. You may sense that you are not as alone as you once felt, and perhaps begin to recognise a feeling of sacred interconnectedness and relationship with powerful and kind forces that permeate our Universe.

Even if you are not sensitive enough to energy to consciously perceive such effects, you can trust that they are taking place. During such experiences, a 'brick of light' is being added to your spiritually protective temple. This is an imperfect metaphor, as it is not a wall being built to keep experiences at bay — you are not here to avoid life. But it is a helpful visual, because it shows that there is a genuine solidity to the field of spiritual protection. It operates on the physical, emotional, psychological and spiritual levels.

Most of the time you won't recognise how this protective field works for you. Occasionally, however, you may realise that it is at work and what it has prevented from taking place — from a vehicle accident to derailing a situation that would have diverted you from your higher purpose. The intense crush that I described in Chapter Thirteen is an example of this. Although I really wanted to connect with that man at the time, the relationship didn't happen. Several factors didn't mesh well and eventually we simply parted ways. Sometime later I was looking back through wiser eyes and realised that the failure to get what I thought I wanted had been a form of spiritual protection. I began to see that man in a more realistic way and realised that he and my ex-boyfriend were mates because of how much they had in common — and that was more than my passing romantic interest! The issues he struggled with were like those my former partner was working through, too. I would have been leaving one relationship to dive headfirst into an even more intense version of it with someone else. That was hardly going to contribute to my growth or my greater happiness. They arise from soul healing, rather than the temporary nature of ego gratification. When it comes to the ego, the Dalai Lama's teaching that not getting what you want can be a wonderful thing is so apt!

So sometimes we can recognise our spiritual protection is working for us, even in a *no*. When we don't recognise the intricate workings of grace in our lives, we can still experience a more pronounced feeling of wellbeing and happiness, much like adopting a healthier lifestyle does for us on a physical level. We feel better within ourselves and are in a stronger position to deal with challenges when they do arise.

That we will no longer feel constantly plagued by challenges, as we can tend to be when our protective field is not quite as robust as we wish it to be, is a bonus. Even if we are going through a number of intense challenges simultaneously, (and there may be an important reason for that, such as you discovering your soul's strength and wisdom in a way that you have not yet accessed so you can become fearless and bold on your path), the field of spiritual protection will ensure that what will truly serve you gets through, and shield you from the rest of it.

Such protection is especially helpful for star seeds, for whom encounters with negative energy can be painfully puzzling. Many star seeds find it difficult to understand the darker side of human nature, why someone would behave with cruelty, for example, when that is such an anathema to them. Spiritual protection is beneficial for all, however those with pure hearts and a peace-loving nature who struggle to accept and process negativity may find that high levels of spiritual protection are required before they can settle into life with more ease. That was certainly the case for me.

As a young girl in kindergarten, I noticed one of my fellow classmates had stolen some puppets from the classroom toy box. She secretly returned them the next day — quite likely on the advice of her parents. After she stashed them back in the toybox, the teacher realised that they had been missing and were now returned. She questioned the girl about what had happened, to which the girl promptly replied that I had stolen them. The teacher believed her. I was too stunned to say anything! Her bold lie had shocked me to my core.

I didn't like getting into trouble for something I hadn't done as it offended my natural sense of justice, but I was more confused about why this little girl was behaving in such a way in the first place. I might have all sorts of explanations as an adult looking back at the situation, but what I recall most strongly was just how stunned I was at the behaviour of that child at the time. It gave rise to a fundamental confusion about less-than-noble human behaviours that took some years to unravel — and was likely one of the reasons I became drawn to the path of a healer. I really wanted to understand why someone would not demonstrate goodness, courage and grace. What would prompt someone to behave otherwise?

So began my initiation into the darker side of life. It was a reluctant exploration for me. My empathic nature, that tends to absorb what is going on around me, made exposure to such energies seem more intense for me than it did for most others. I was never going to be one of those people who could read about serial killers, for example, and just be fascinated rather than disturbed. When witnessing the darker side of human beings, I found it hard not to feel dragged down, disheartened and, at times, despairing.

To be clear, I knew I had my own dark side to contend with, too. I could generate considerable emotional drama when my brothers did something mean or annoying, such as kicking my favourite toy cat around like she was a football — admittedly she was extremely rotund. When she was rescued from their boyish antics, my mother laundered her, and hung on the clothesline to dry, pegged by one of her pert ears. I wasn't particularly happy about that either. My child's mind was sure that couldn't have been comfortable for her. Eventually she found her way back into my protective arms, away from my brothers' dirty shoes and my mother's well-meaning laundering. It took a little longer than that for me to forgive my brothers for their larrikin ways.

Even with some awareness of my dark side, I was still shocked by the negativities— cruelty, violence and sadism in particular—that I saw in the world. The first time my primary school friends watched a horror film, I had to remove myself from the room. The assault to my senses of such low frequency energy was too much for my youthful mind and body to receive. The others seemed to bond through their enjoyment of the experience, whilst I starkly realised that I was quite different in heart. I could find no joy or thrill, only deep sadness and confusion, in the face of such disturbed energies.

I personally believe that horror films are a depiction of unresolved trauma within the human collective, unconsciously expressed. When there is popularity and acceptance of a film (or television series, music clip or song lyric), it is because there is a resonance. At some deeper level there is engagement because it plays into collective fantasies and wounds. The level of violence often depicted in films is a representation of the unresolved trauma of violence in the minds and hearts of many members of the human collective. Many may mindlessly consume it as entertainment, but if you recognise it as an artform, and as such, an expression of what is happening in the culture that created it, one must take pause and realise that the true horror is not in the film, but in the wounds of a culture that accepts that content as normal and even entertaining.

Film can be a powerful medium for goodness and grace. I don't mean every movie we watch has to have a spiritual theme to it, but when it depicts authentic characters and stories, even if it takes one through a great tragedy, it fulfils a deep and longstanding cultural need to find meaning and instruction for life through storytelling. In the absence of tribes gathering around the fire and listening to the elders speak of things that the younger generations are yet to learn, we turn to film. It is such an important part of our cultural bonding.

Those who recognise that the creation of art such as horror films is driven by the cry of the soul that feels violated and torn apart by forces outside of our control, owe it to ourselves and our culture to acknowledge it. If we keep mindlessly consuming, we keep re-traumatising the soul. This is not necessary, wise or kind. To collapse under the weight of mass opinion and pretend that such things are acceptable is to lose integrity with one's own heart. If we want to do something constructive and creative to begin to heal a situation, we must first admit that there is a problem there and that not all people will have the awareness to see it as we do. If we stand firm in the truth of our heart's perceptions, a lack of general consensus won't dissuade us nor undermine our passion to do something about the sometimes-deranged state of human culture.

By acknowledging that something is 'off', even when we don't know what the answer or resolution to that situation could be, we open a divine channel for grace. We empower our field of spiritual protection and begin extending it for the benefit of others, which only further empowers our own field. This can happen when we simply say to the Universe, "I'd like something good to happen here, healing is needed, please show the way."

When the power of intention is used for the greater good, you set something in motion. The need for such generosity and goodwill is very strong. If we look at the state of the world and feel our hearts stir with compassion at the rate of self-harm, addiction, violence and abuse, then the Universe is asking us to do something about it. We don't need to feel overwhelmed by that.

Shifting our mindset away from denying or recoiling, and into active, spiritual, creative response, gives us a chance to feel empowered, and to break through the potentially immobilising, victimising effect of negative energy. Nature shows us that tiny creatures like termites can bring down massive structures. Wearing away at negativity through our small but consistent and positive actions can destabilise even powerful forces and create space for new voices of clarity and nobility to come forth.

One of the beautiful traits that many star seeds, lightworkers and priestesses share is a willingness to believe in the possibility of healing. No matter how much struggle or suffering they personally endure or see in the world around them, they believe that things can change in unforeseen and truly gracious ways. As our field of spiritual protection grows through our committed efforts, we become channels for that grace to find its way into our world. It is not limited to our own lives. It touches the lives of all that we connect with and any issue that we care to lend our heart to.

If you see something in this world and you know spiritual grace could be of benefit, you can ask for that grace to flow there. You don't direct it, you don't tell it what to do, you just ask that it be there, for the greatest good. The more your field of spiritual protection becomes real to you, the more you will recognise just how beautiful and important such actions are for all of us. And your heart will be buoyant in the goodness and generosity of what the Universe wishes to bestow for the benefit of all beings.

HEALING PROCESS

Take a few moments to place your hands at your heart. Notice the flow of your breath as it causes your lungs to expand and your chest and belly to rise and fall. Notice any tension in your body or mind. Imagine bringing a gentle, soothing energy in on the breath that begins to unlock and melt away that tension. There's no force in this process, just an invitation to let go and relax. When you are ready, say aloud:

> *I call upon star teacher Alpha Centauri, giving thanks for your wisdom, divine friendship, support and light. You teach me how to bring out the best in myself and others. I call upon the Crystal Angel of Rutilated Quartz, your golden angel hairs bring divine energy and healing swiftly through my body, mind and soul. I now honour myself with a field of spiritual protection and golden grace and open to receive goodness and blessings from the Universe. May all beings be gifted with the protection, grace and compassion they need. May the love within all beings be stronger and more conscious than anything else. May all beings be happy and free. Through the highest wisdom, for the greatest good, so be it.*

Imagine that you can now relax into a soft webbing of fine golden threads. Each thread is a golden hair of the Crystal Angel of Rutilated Quartz. The hairs spread out as if they are floating on an ocean of love, so you can rest upon them. Beautiful golden light emanates from these hairs and fill you from within. Eventually, you soften, relax and overflow with that golden light and realise it is shining gently upon our entire planet.

Imagine the golden light shining into the hearts of all beings open to receiving, and gently—without force—around those who are afraid to open. Just let it shine gracefully, kindly and lovingly for all beings. It demands nothing and offers everything. It is very safe and non-confronting to be a part of this energy.

Remain in it for as long as you wish. You may wish to close your visualisation by allowing that golden light to form a soft egg-shaped boundary around you, rising over your head and moving under your feet.

Finish with your hands in prayer and your head bowed to your hands.

You have completed your healing process.

AFTERWORD

What's next? Beloved, it has been an inspiration to take this journey with you. You may want to continue our journey together through the offerings I have created for you in the form of oracle decks, meditation recordings, music, films, books, online healer training and in-person events such as the powerful and special *The Kuan Yin Transmission*™ training workshop. It is my sincerest delight to contribute to your awakening through divine love.

You can visit me and find out more about the offerings I have available for you at **www.alanafairchild.com**

Trust your heart, trust your journey.
Namaste,
Alana

ABOUT ALANA FAIRCHILD

From my earliest memories, conscious connection with Spirit has been as natural as breathing to me. When something is natural for you, especially if it has been that way since childhood, you can assume it is natural for everyone. It took many years for me to realise my sensitivity, healing ability and innate awareness of the spiritual was unusual and that it could help people. I create beautiful sacred offerings in the form of books, oracles, music, meditations, and training programs to support the discovery and manifestation of the truth of your divine nature so that you can live with freedom, courage, happiness, and peace. If you would like to find out more, please visit me at my online home: **www.alanafairchild.com**

ABOUT THE ARTIST

Jane Marin is an accomplished artist, intuitive healer/coach, past life regressionist, author and Reiki/Seichim Master/Teacher.

She holds diplomas in Child Psychology, Hatha Yoga Teaching, Bach Flower Essences and Certificates in Past Life Regression, Journal Therapy, Angel Therapy™, Crystal Light Healing Practitioner Level III, and Motivational Kinesiology IV.

Her background in dance prompted her to explore the healing powers of music and dance leading her to the ancient art of bellydance. She has been teaching this form of dance since 2004.

Jane's spiritual art and photography can now be purchased in her online shop as can her beautiful coffee table books.

Jane is the author of *The Me Book – A Journey of Self-discovery*, published in 2011 by Balboa Press to compliment her popular "Me Book" workshops.

To find out more about Jane Marin and her work, please visit her website: **www.jaanemanart.com**

THEMATIC INDEX BY CHAPTER

1. CANOPUS (Self-nurture)
SHUNGITE (Purification and Psychic Protection)
EARTH SCHOOL

old souls
inner guidance
fame
manifestation
soul cleansing
assuming your place
tribal energies
alignment

2. VEGA (Spiritual and Physical Unity)
PREHNITE WITH EPIDOTE (Heart Healing)
SENSITIVE SOULS, PEACEFULNESS AND EXPERIENCES OF VIOLENCE

talent, art and music
sound healing
singing
mantra
discernment
amplification
sensitivity
compassion
inner work
psychic awakening

3. ALDEBARAN (Divine Vision)
PETALITE (Self-Realisation)
WHEN YOUR INNER WOLF WANTS TO HIJACK YOUR SPIRITUAL PRACTICE

vision
unrequited love
leadership
new horizons
feminine energy
receptivity
temporary identities
holographic reality
obsession
addiction
hunger

4. THE GALACTIC CENTRE (Divine Mother)
ZEBRA ROCK (Grounding)
CHANNELLING DIVINE ELECTRICITY WITHOUT NEEDING TO EAT AN ENTIRE PIZZA

galactic goddess
inner strength
capacity for growth
magnetism
higher purpose
changing beliefs
busy lifestyle
exhaustion
doctors and spiritual path
preparing for energy work

5. ANDROMEDA GALAXY (Embracing Greatness)
COVELLITE (Spiritual Knowledge)
THE HIDDEN HELPFULNESS OF BROKENNESS

expanding horizons
not playing small
wisdom of ageing
mix of old and new energies
spiritual maturity
late bloomers
pretty poisons
feeling our emotions
misleading images of spiritual perfection
social media

6. OMEGA CENTAURI (The Enduring Soul)
ELESTIAL QUARTZ (Unity)
STAR SEEDS

soul connections
difficult karmic relationships
eccentricity and uniqueness
advanced souls
it can be hard to be human
life-changing encounters
sacrifice to a greater purpose
light library
self-healing
star children

7. SPICA (Abundant Resources)
APOPHYLLITE (Higher Guidance)
PRAYING LIKE THE DIVINE BADASS YOU ARE

clairaudience
solitude
sacred feminine
symbolism of the egg
spiritual harvest
generosity
the path of surrender
balancing our path
talent as a healer
Mars and Venus
masculine and feminine
big purpose and small steps

8. POLARIS (Steering True)
BLUE HALITE (Supportive Healing)
CRISIS IS CONSCIOUSNESS ATTEMPTING TO BE BORN

following the light
Mother Mary
first ray of divine will
chaos and creative growth
finding peace during change
Shambhala
ascended masters
fifth dimension
clearing negativity
from crisis to consciousness
romantic relationship
Saturn and initiation

9. FOMALHAUT (Progress)
MOLDAVITE (Conscious Connection)
THE SECRET WISDOM OF ADDICTION

mass consciousness and the stars
Demeter
Christ
good fortune
not alone even if you think you are
trusting feelings over appearances
extra-terrestrial energy and higher
consciousness
synergy
addiction vs authenticity
hyper-independence and self-reliance
needing spirit and people
vagus nerve
gut instincts

10. ARCTURUS (Oneness)
STIBNITE (Attunement)
SWIMMING IN THE OCEAN OF CONSCIOUSNESS WITHOUT DROWNING IN IT

advanced spiritual civilisations
ascension and the fifth dimension
higher frequencies
unique soul paths
radical progress
self-attunement
crystals as cosmic mirrors
not being overcome by world suffering
terrorism
compassion fatigue
internal navigation system
optimism

11. ALCYONE (Synthesis)
MENALITE (Sacred Feminine Wisdom)
GAIA IS THE HIGH PRIESTESS FOR THE HUMAN SOUL

throat chakra
priestess energy
sacred geometry of the triangle
effective synthesis of modalities
managing complexity
goddess gnosis
modern life and connecting with
earth
from head to heart
from intellect to intuition
socially encouraged abuse of the
feminine
rage and self-healing
initiation in to the feminine

12. SKAT (Blessings)
GALAXITE (Reassurance)
TAPPING IN TO THE GENEROSITY OF THE UNIVERSE

wish fulfilment
good luck
white magic
manipulation
ancestral lines
spiritual lineage
psychic protection
galactic energy
prosperity
manifesting abundance
marketing with integrity
certainty in divine connection
you are here for a reason

13. SIRIUS (Activation)
CAVANSITE (Soul Voice)
LEARNING TO READ THE SIGNS

secret star
divine timing
sounds of the stars
creative manifestation
ancient Egypt and Goddess Sopdet
Goddess Isis
Goddess Tara
Kali Ma
Kuan Yin
overcoming too much noise
energetic language
misreading signs
healthy ways to channel anger
fresh starts after ending a relationship

14. SADALSUUD (Good Fortune)
BARITE (Inner Horizons)
THE UNIVERSE IS ALWAYS UP TO SOMETHING (GOOD)

ocean of consciousness
the New Age
finding the genuine light
emptiness and healing the heart
Yin energy
cosmic womb
destiny and timing
the Universe is actively helping you
inner-child healing
challenges in working with a therapist
karmic soul groups
breaking patterns of distrust
shooting stars
eagle wisdom

15. BETELGEUSE (Quickening)
NEBULA STONE (Lineage)
THE UNIVERSE IS ALWAYS LISTENING (SO WHAT ARE YOU SAYING?)

swift progress on the path
big spirits with far-reaching influence
support for future generations
positive contribution
working with light
absorbing higher energies
spiritual orphans
creating our own reality
not trying to convince others
past-life vows
not using spiritual teachings against yourself
healing collective wounds

16. REGULUS (Heart-Centred Leadership)
PHENACITE (Consciousness)
THE PHYSICAL REALITY OF THE SOUL

lion energy and the heart
rulership from the heart
going against mainstream conditioning
giving up opinion in favour of wisdom
king archetype
spiritual law
inner power to manifest your true path
physical effect of spiritual energy
encounters with higher beings
healing vs recovery
modern medicine and spiritual healing

17. ANTARES (Empowerment) SPHALERITE (Authentic Self) AUTHENTICITY TO FREE YOURSELF FROM CULTIC SYSTEMS

refusing to be dominated
self-sovereignty
astrological wisdom teachings of Scorpio
spiritual warrior
deflecting projections from other people
honouring authentic self
bullying
soul tribes and human needs
cultic groups
vampiric qualities of cults
obedience vs authenticity
withdrawing blessings is not possible
crossroads and insecurity
toxic patterns in spiritual communities
spiritual abuse and free will

18. ALPHA CENTAURI (What You Need is Now Given) RUTILATED QUARTZ (Auric Balance) GENERATING A FIELD OF SPIRITUAL PROTECTION

like-minded souls
feeling disconnected from Spirit
Chiron and our higher nature
Chiron and the wounded healer
clearing noise pollution and negative energies
not becoming paranoid about negativity
spiritual protection helps us grow not hide
building up your capacity for spiritual practice
less can be more
learning to reach for Spirit
film and its powerful influence
power of goodwill

INDEX

ALSO AVAILABLE IN THIS SERIES BY ALANA FAIRCHILD

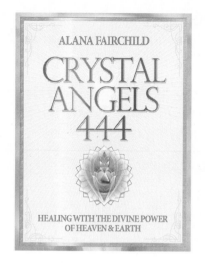

Crystal Angels 444
Healing with the Divine Power of Heaven & Earth

You have loving guides from the spiritual worlds of Crystals and Angels. They are ready to help you now.

In *Crystal Angels 444*, Alana Fairchild, author of the bestselling *Kuan Yin Oracle*, offers a truly unique approach to crystal healing, combining the natural healing properties of each crystal and its 'crystal angel' or 'spirit' with divine guidance channelled from heavenly angels such as Archangels Raphael, Gabriel, Metatron & Melchizedek. Together they help you bring your spirit and body together as one and live with more peace and prosperity, passion and purpose. Each chapter deals with a powerful precious stone and its heavenly angel and features a range of sacred rituals and processes to help you fully harness the healing potential of that stone, deepen your connection with yourself and the divine guidance supporting you and tap into the many gifts hidden within you.

You will delve deeply into a variety of topics including love, power and protection, eating and body image, self-esteem, addiction, feminine/masculine balance, wealth and prosperity, connecting with divinity, speaking your truth, dealing with your emotions, developing your spiritual talents and much more.

The book is enriched with many personal stories and spiritual experiences from the author which offer practical examples to bring the material to life.

You have important healing work to do on yourself and for the planet. *Crystal Angels 444* is written for you, to help you successfully complete your task, with greater happiness and fulfilment.

Featuring 18 full-colour Crystal Angel Mandalas by artist Jane Marin

Paperback book, 368 pages
ISBN: 978-1-922161-13-0

ALSO AVAILABLE IN THIS SERIES BY ALANA FAIRCHILD

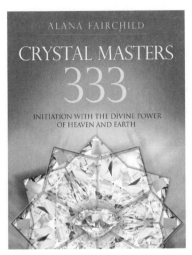

Crystal Masters 333
Initiation with the Divine Power of Heaven & Earth

You have wise spiritual guides from the spiritual worlds of Crystals and Ascended Masters. They are ready to help you on your path of spiritual growth now.

In *Crystal Masters 333*, Alana Fairchild, author of the bestselling *Kuan Yin Oracle*, continues the highly successful Crystal Spirituality Series, which began with *Crystal Angels 444*. She shares her unique approach to crystal healing, combining the natural healing properties of each crystal and its 'crystal angel' or 'spirit' with wisdom teachings from the loving Ascended Masters, such as Mother Mary, Kuan Yin, Jesus, the Buddha, Mary Magdalene and Merlin. Together they help you take the next steps on your path of spiritual growth, by preparing you with the teachings and tools you need to successfully navigate the demands of spiritual initiation.

Initiation is a path of advanced spiritual growth. When you are highly committed to your spiritual path and personal growth this lifetime, you will be on the path of initiation. This path can be very challenging but offers incredible rewards including the awakening of spiritual talents, assistance in bringing your divine light to the world and support in your own role as a healer and spiritual leader on the earth. Each chapter deals with a powerful precious stone and its heavenly angel and features spiritual teachings and stories from Alana's own life and work, as well as a healing process to help you fully harness the therapeutic potential of that stone and connect directly with the Ascended Masters, to receive their wisdom and blessings.

You will delve deeply into a variety of topics including aligning with divine will, healing the child within, planetary healing, spiritual communication, enlightenment and spiritual growth, the light body, the golden body, and much more.

You have important healing work to do on yourself and for the planet. *Crystal Masters 333* is written for you, to help you successfully complete your task, with greater happiness and fulfilment.

Featuring 18 full-colour Crystal Angel Mandalas by artist Jane Marin

Paperback book, 384 pages
ISBN: 978-1-922161-18-5

ALSO AVAILABLE IN THIS SERIES BY ALANA FAIRCHILD

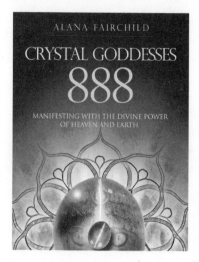

Crystal Goddesses 888
Manifesting with the Divine Power of Heaven and Earth

You have wise spiritual guides from the mystical worlds of Crystals and Goddesses. They are ready to help you now.

Manifesting from your soul feels good. It isn't about forcing the world to bend to your will, it is about co- creating with the power of life itself. When you manifest from your soul, you not only bring your visions to life, but you become more alive too. You are healing yourself through the process of creation whilst your world transforms along with you. This book is your guide to the many ways you can manifest from your soul. From exploring the power of sound and light, to embracing darkness and healing through joy, celebrating being different, honouring being a rebel and expressing your passion as well as your compassion, you will be offered many ways to heal and manifest your divine destiny.

Crystal Goddesses 888, the next volume in the highly successful Crystal Spirituality Series, will connect you to the power of heaven in the form of the wild and loving divine feminine (and her many faces as goddesses from different spiritual traditions), and the power of the earth in the form of crystals that support each goddess in bringing her gifts of healing to you. With real life stories from the author to make the material practical and accessible, this book guides you with humour and love to take the next step on your path, creating your own version of heaven on earth. Whether you are new to all this, or have been on your conscious path for years, you'll find a wealth of treasures in here. May you blossom wildly on your beautiful life journey, held in the grace of the wild feminine spirit that loves you unconditionally.

Featuring 18 full-colour Crystal Angel Mandalas by artist Jane Marin

Paperback book, 452 pages
ISBN: 978-1-922161-25-3

ALSO AVAILABLE IN THIS SERIES BY ALANA FAIRCHILD

Crystal Mandala Oracle
Channel the Power of Heaven & Earth

This unique oracle deck is encoded with crystal frequencies, and the high vibrational energy of angels, ascended masters and goddesses, to empower you to channel the divine healing power of Heaven and Earth.

In this stunning, stand-alone deck, you will work with the vibrant crystal mandalas by Jane Marin, as featured in Alana Fairchild's popular books *Crystal Angels 444*, *Crystal Masters 333* and *Crystal Goddesses 888*. Alana shares loving spiritual guidance from the angels, masters and goddesses to help you integrate the frequencies of the crystals and higher beings that are featured in each of the cards. The Crystal Angels will help you heal your body, mind and soul. The Crystal Masters will support your spiritual growth and help you successfully pass through spiritual tests and initiations. The Crystal Goddesses will empower you to embody your spirit and express your soul purpose in the world.

This powerful deck will enhance your connection to the sacred worlds of higher beings and crystal energy, opening your heart to divine beauty and empowering your soul with loving consciousness.

Artwork by Jane Marin

54 cards and 244-page guidebook, packaged in a hardcover box set.
ISBN: 978-1-922161-89-5

ALSO AVAILABLE BY ALANA FAIRCHILD

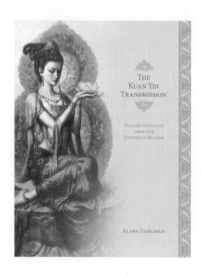

The Kuan Yin Transmission™
Healing Guidance from our Universal Mother

Be the light you were born to be.
The Universal Mother belongs to humanity and we belong to her. You are invited into the wisdom temple of her heart, a place of sanctuary, miraculous grace and healing. Through her compassion, a path is always shown, and all problems can be transformed into blessings. She wants you to realise that her light is your light. You are connected, heart to heart, and have the power to bring brilliance, strength and hope into your life and into the world.

Kuan Yin. Goddess Isis. Tara. Mother Mary. Kali.
Our Universal Mother manifests in unlimited forms to meet the needs of all beings. She is endlessly resourceful and willing to assist us. No matter how many mistakes we make or how far we stray, she never abandons, judges or betrays us. She is our constant guide and guardian, our most-faithful friend and our unconditionally loving protector. She is reaching for you, now. You, her precious child, can receive her infinite grace and manifest your authentic soul path.

Open your heart and take the journey...
Begin your experience of The Kuan Yin Transmission™ through the insight, wisdom and inspirational stories of best-selling author Alana Fairchild. Complete with stunning full-colour artwork, inspirational channelling and powerful healing processes to guide you into deeper conscious connection with the Universal Mother, this beautiful book unites Kuan Yin (Goddess of Compassion), Tara (Ancient Star Mother), Kali (fierce Black Madonna of India), Isis (winged Goddess of Magic and Soul Alchemy), Mother Mary (Madonna of Miracles), and more. Discover what it's really like to live as a channel of the sacred feminine. Embrace your magnificent divine destiny.

312 pages, full-colour, hardcover book.
ISBN: 978-1-925538-60-1

ALSO AVAILABLE BY ALANA FAIRCHILD

Earth Warriors Oracle
Rise of the Soul Tribe of Sacred Guardians
& Inspired Visionaries

A new world is being born. It is founded upon love and higher consciousness, instead of fear, hate and greed. This new world is gaining ground, becoming stronger, yet it also needs its protectors during this precious and important time of birth. Earth Warriors are the guardians, guides and way-showers for the new world, inspiring its people to prosper and thrive in harmony with the wisdom of life.

Defying convention and living from the heart, Earth Warriors urge the human race forward with enormous positive energy and a passionate desire for meaningful contribution and sacred purpose. Willing to shake things up for the right cause, the Earth Warriors bring truth out of darkness, when others who trade in fear would wish to keep it hidden.

Earth Warriors are the wise wild ones, cracking open mainstream consciousness with their loving awareness of freedom and grace. They are the bright lights, the holy hustlers, the creative visionaries and the sacred guardians of the soul.

Earth Warriors Oracle taps into universal tribal wisdom and pure spiritual guidance to empower your soul with courage and optimism to discover the Earth Warrior within and fulfil its sacred purpose.

Artwork by Isabel Bryna

44 cards and 216-page guidebook, packaged in a hardcover box set.
ISBN: 978-1-925538-29-8

Chapter One:
SPIRITUAL DIRECTION FOR OLD SOULS
Star Guide: Canopus
The Crystal Angel of Shungite
Spiritual Guidance: Earth School

Chapter Two:
RECALIBRATION INTO PRIMORDIAL SOUND
Star Guide: Vega
The Crystal Angel of Prehnite with Epidote
Spiritual Guidance: Sensitive Souls, Peacefulness and Experiences of Violence

Chapter Three:
TRUSTING YOUR SOUL PASSIONS AND HIGHER PURPOSE
Star Guide: Aldebaran
The Crystal Angel of Petalite
Spiritual Guidance: When Your Inner Wolf Wants to Hijack Your Spiritual Practice

Chapter Four:
GALACTIC CONSCIOUSNESS AND THE COSMIC CREATIX
Star Guide: The Galactic Centre
The Crystal Angel of Zebra Rock
Spiritual Guidance: Channelling Divine Electricity Without Needing to Eat an
Entire Pizza

Chapter Five:
AUTHENTICITY EXPANDS YOUR SPIRITUAL HORIZON
Star Guide: Andromeda Galaxy
The Crystal Angel of Covellite
Spiritual Guidance: The Hidden Helpfulness of Brokenness

Chapter Six:
SOUL CONNECTION, INDIVIDUAL ECCENTRICITY
AND SURRENDER TO A HIGHER PLAN
Star Guide: Omega Centauri
The Crystal Angel of Elestial Quartz
Spiritual Guidance: Star Seeds

Chapter Seven:
STRATEGIC SOLITUDE TO REINFORCE YOUR LIGHT
Star Guide: Spica
The Crystal Angel of Apophyllite
Spiritual Guidance: Praying like the Divine Badass You Are

Chapter Eight:
DARK INITIATIONS INTO FREEDOM AND LIGHT
Star Guide: Polaris
The Crystal Angel of Blue Halite
Spiritual Guidance: Crisis is Consciousness Attempting to be Born

Chapter Nine:
BODY WISDOM, ISOLATION, CONNECTION AND FREEDOM
Star Guide: Fomalhaut
The Crystal Angel of Moldavite
Spiritual Guidance: The Secret Wisdom of Addiction

Chapter Ten:
FROLICKING IN THE FIFTH DIMENSION
Star Guide: Arcturus
The Crystal Angel of Stibnite
Spiritual Guidance: Swimming in the Ocean of Consciousness
Without Drowning in it

Chapter Eleven:
THE COSMIC PRIESTESS
Star Guide: Alcyone
The Crystal Angel of Menalite
Spiritual Guidance: Gaia is the High Priestess for the Human Soul

Chapter Twelve:
THE UNIVERSE IS CONSPIRING FOR YOUR SUCCESS
Star Guide: Skat
The Crystal Angel of Galaxite
Spiritual Guidance: Tapping in to the Generosity of the Universe

Chapter Thirteen:
LIVING ACCORDING TO A HIGHER KNOWING, UNCONDITIONALLY
Star Guide: Sirius
The Crystal Angel of Cavansite
Spiritual Guidance: Learning to Read the Signs

Chapter Fourteen:
THE LUCKY COSMIC LOVE BOMB
Star Guide: Sadalsuud
The Crystal Angel of Barite
Spiritual Guidance: The Universe is Always Up to Something (Good)

Chapter Fifteen:
EXPANDING YOUR SPIRITUAL CONNECTIONS AND INFLUENCE
Star Guide: Betelgeuse
The Crystal Angel of Nebula Stone
Spiritual Guidance: The Universe is Always Listening (so what are you saying?)

Chapter Sixteen:
THE REORGANISING POWER OF YOUR HEART
Star Guide: Regulus
The Crystal Angel of Phenacite
Spiritual Guidance: The Physical Reality of the Soul

Chapter Seventeen:
SPIRITUAL FREEDOM TO OVERCOME TOXIC SYSTEMS OF POWER
Star Guide: Antares
The Crystal Angel of Sphalerite
Spiritual Guidance: Authenticity to Free Yourself from Cultic Systems

Chapter Eighteen:
SUPREME SPIRITUAL PROTECTION
Star Guide: Alpha Centauri
The Crystal Angel of Rutilated Quartz
Spiritual Guidance: Generating a Field Spiritual Protection

Shungite

Prehnite with Epidote

Petalite

Zebra Rock

Covellite

Elestial Quartz

Apophyllite

Blue Halite

Moldavite

Stibnite

Menalite

Galaxite

Cavansite

Green Barite

Nebula Stone

Phenacite

Sphalerite

Rutilated Quartz